P9-AGU-496

WITHDRAWN
CEDAR MILL LIBRARY

Agile Data Science 2.0
Building Full-Stack Data Analytics
Applications with Spark

Russell Jurney

Beijing · Boston · Farnham · Sebastopol · Tokyo

Agile Data Science 2.0

by Russell Jurney

Copyright © 2017 Data Syndrome LLC. All rights reserved.

Printed in the United States of America.

Published by O'Reilly Media, Inc., 1005 Gravenstein Highway North, Sebastopol, CA 95472.

O'Reilly books may be purchased for educational, business, or sales promotional use. Online editions are also available for most titles (*http://oreilly.com/safari*). For more information, contact our corporate/institutional sales department: 800-998-9938 or *corporate@oreilly.com*.

Editor: Shannon Cutt	**Indexer:** Lucie Haskins
Production Editor: Shiny Kalapurakkel	**Interior Designer:** David Futato
Copyeditor: Rachel Head	**Cover Designer:** Karen Montgomery
Proofreader: Kim Cofer	**Illustrator:** Rebecca Demarest

May 2017:   First Edition

Revision History for the First Edition

2017-05-26:   First Release

The O'Reilly logo is a registered trademark of O'Reilly Media, Inc. *Agile Data Science 2.0*, the cover image, and related trade dress are trademarks of O'Reilly Media, Inc.

While the publisher and the author have used good faith efforts to ensure that the information and instructions contained in this work are accurate, the publisher and the author disclaim all responsibility for errors or omissions, including without limitation responsibility for damages resulting from the use of or reliance on this work. Use of the information and instructions contained in this work is at your own risk. If any code samples or other technology this work contains or describes is subject to open source licenses or the intellectual property rights of others, it is your responsibility to ensure that your use thereof complies with such licenses and/or rights.

978-1-491-96011-0

[LSI]

Table of Contents

Part II. Climbing the Pyramid

Preface

I wrote the first edition of this book while disabled from a car accident after which I developed chronic pain and lost partial use of my hands. Unable to chop vegetables, I wrote it from bed and the couch on an iPad to get over a failed project that haunted me called Career Explorer. Having been injured weeks before the ship date, getting the product over the line, staying up for days and doing whatever it took, became a traumatic experience. During the project, we made many mistakes I knew not to make, and I was continuously frustrated. The product bombed. A sense of failure routinely bugged me while I was stuck, horizontal on my back most of the time with intractable chronic pain. Also suffering from a heart condition, missing a third of my heartbeats, I developed dementia. My mind sank to a dark place. I could not easily find a way out. I had to find a way to fix things, to grapple with failure. Strange to say that to fix myself, I wrote a book. I needed to write directions I could give to teammates to make my next project a success. I needed to get this story out of me. More than that, I thought I could bring meaning back to my life, most of which had been shed by disability, by helping others. By doing something for the greater good. I wanted to ensure that others did not repeat my mistakes. I thought that was worth doing. There was a problem this project illustrated that was bigger than me. Most research sits on a shelf and never gets into the hands of people it can benefit. This book is a prescription and methodology for doing applied research that makes it into the world in the form of a product.

This may sound quite dramatic, but I wanted to put the first edition in personal context before introducing the second. Although it was important to me, of course, the first edition of this book was only a small contribution to the emerging field of data science. But I'm proud of it. I found salvation in its pages, it made me feel right again, and in time I recovered from illness and found a sense of accomplishment that replaced the sting of failure. So that's the first edition.

In this second edition, I hope to do more. Put simply, I want to take a budding data scientist and accelerate her into an analytics application developer. In doing so, I draw from and reflect upon my experience building analytics applications at three Hadoop shops and one Spark shop. I hope this new edition will become the go-to guide for readers to rapidly learn how to build analytics applications on data of any size, using the lingua franca of data science, Python, and the platform of choice, Spark.

Spark has replaced Hadoop/MapReduce as the default way to process data at scale, so we adopt Spark for this new edition. In addition, the theory and process of the Agile Data Science methodology have been updated to reflect an increased understanding of working in teams. It is hoped that readers of the first edition will become readers of the second. It is also hoped that this book will serve Spark users better than the original served Hadoop users.

Agile Data Science has two goals: to provide a how-to guide for building analytics applications with data of any size using Python and Spark, and to help product teams collaborate on building analytics applications in an agile manner that will ensure success.

Agile Data Science Mailing List

You can learn the latest on Agile Data Science on *the mailing list* or on the web (*https://groups.google.com/d/forum/agile-data-science*).

I maintain a web page for this book (*http://datasyndrome.com/book*) that contains the latest updates and related material for readers of the book.

Data Syndrome, Product Analytics Consultancy

I have founded a consultancy called Data Syndrome (Figure P-1) to advance the adoption of the methodology and technology stack outlined in this book. If you need help implementing Agile Data Science within your company, if you need hands-on help building data products, or if you need "big data" training, you can contact me at *rjurney@datasyndrome.com* or via the website (*http://llc.datasyndrome.com*).

Data Syndrome offers a video course, Realtime Predictive Analytics with Kafka, PySpark, Spark MLlib and Spark Streaming (*http://datasyndrome.com/video*), that builds on the material from Chapters 7 and 8 to teach students how to build entire realtime predictive systems with Kafka and Spark Streaming and a web application frontend (see Figure P-2). For more information, visit *http://datasyndrome.com/video* or contact *rjurney@datasyndrome.com*.

Figure P-1. Data Syndrome

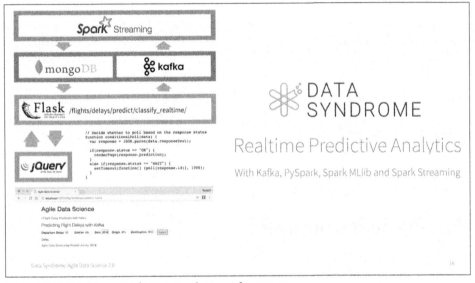

Figure P-2. Realtime Predictive Analytics video course

Live Training

Data Syndrome is developing a complete curriculum for live "big data" training for data science and data engineering teams. Current course offerings are customizable for your needs and include:

Agile Data Science
A three-day course covering the construction of full-stack analytics applications. Similar in content to this book, this course trains data scientists to be full-stack application developers.

Realtime Predictive Analytics
> A one-day, six-hour course covering the construction of entire realtime predictive systems using Kafka and Spark Streaming with a web application frontend.

Introduction to PySpark
> A one-day, three-hour course introducing students to basic data processing with Spark through the Python interface, PySpark. Culminates in the construction of a classifier model to predict flight delays using Spark MLlib.

For more information, visit *http://datasyndrome.com/training* or contact *rjurney@datasyndrome.com*.

Who This Book Is For

Agile Data Science is intended to help beginners and budding data scientists to become productive members of data science and analytics teams. It aims to help engineers, analysts, and data scientists work with big data in an agile way using Hadoop. It introduces an agile methodology well suited for big data.

This book is targeted at programmers with some exposure to developing software and working with data. Designers and product managers might particularly enjoy Chapters 1, 2, and 5, which will serve as an introduction to the agile process without focusing on running code.

Agile Data Science assumes you are working in a *nix environment. Examples for Windows users aren't available, but are possible via Cygwin.

How This Book Is Organized

This book is organized into two sections. Part I introduces the dataset and toolset we will use in the tutorial in Part II. Part I is intentionally brief, taking only enough time to introduce the tools. We go into their use in more depth in Part II, so don't worry if you're a little overwhelmed in Part I. The chapters that compose Part I are as follows:

Chapter 1, Theory
> Introduces the Agile Data Science methodology.

Chapter 2, Agile Tools
> Introduces our toolset, and helps you get it up and running on your own machine.

Chapter 3, Data
> Describes the dataset used in this book.

Part II is a tutorial in which we build an analytics application using Agile Data Science. It is a notebook-style guide to building an analytics application. We climb the data-value pyramid one level at a time, applying agile principles as we go. This part of the book demonstrates a way of building value step by step in small, agile iterations. Part II comprises the following chapters:

Chapter 4, Collecting and Displaying Records
Helps you download flight data and then connect or "plumb" flight records through to a web application.

Chapter 5, Visualizing Data with Charts and Tables
Steps you through how to navigate your data by preparing simple charts in a web application.

Chapter 6, Exploring Data with Reports
Teaches you how to extract entities from your data and parameterize and link between them to create interactive reports.

Chapter 7, Making Predictions
Takes what you've done so far and predicts whether your flight will be on time or late.

Chapter 8, Deploying Predictive Systems
Shows how to deploy predictions to ensure they impact real people and systems.

Chapter 9, Improving Predictions
Iteratively improves on the performance of our on-time flight prediction.

Appendix A, Manual Installation
Shows how to manually install our tools.

Conventions Used in This Book

The following typographical conventions are used in this book:

Italic
Indicates new terms, URLs, email addresses, filenames, and file extensions.

`Constant width`
Used for program listings, as well as within paragraphs to refer to program elements such as variable or function names, databases, data types, environment variables, statements, and keywords.

`Constant width bold`
Shows commands or other text that should be typed literally by the user.

`Constant width italic`
Shows text that should be replaced with user-supplied values or by values determined by context.

This icon signifies a tip, suggestion, or general note.

This icon indicates a warning or caution.

Using Code Examples

Supplemental material (code examples, exercises, etc.) is available for download at *https://github.com/rjurney/Agile_Data_Code_2*.

This book is here to help you get your job done. In general, if example code is offered with this book, you may use it in your programs and documentation. You do not need to contact us for permission unless you're reproducing a significant portion of the code. For example, writing a program that uses several chunks of code from this book does not require permission. Selling or distributing a CD-ROM of examples from O'Reilly books does require permission. Answering a question by citing this book and quoting example code does not require permission. Incorporating a significant amount of example code from this book into your product's documentation does require permission.

We appreciate, but do not require, attribution. An attribution usually includes the title, author, publisher, and ISBN. For example: "*Agile Data Science 2.0* by Russell Jurney (O'Reilly). Copyright 2017 Data Syndrome LLC, 978-1-491-96011-0."

If you feel your use of code examples falls outside fair use or the permission given above, feel free to contact us at *permissions@oreilly.com*.

O'Reilly Safari

 Safari (formerly Safari Books Online) is a membership-based training and reference platform for enterprise, government, educators, and individuals.

Members have access to thousands of books, training videos, Learning Paths, interactive tutorials, and curated playlists from over 250 publishers, including O'Reilly Media, Harvard Business Review, Prentice Hall Professional, Addison-Wesley Professional, Microsoft Press, Sams, Que, Peachpit Press, Adobe, Focal Press, Cisco Press, John Wiley & Sons, Syngress, Morgan Kaufmann, IBM Redbooks, Packt, Adobe

Press, FT Press, Apress, Manning, New Riders, McGraw-Hill, Jones & Bartlett, and Course Technology, among others.

For more information, please visit *http://oreilly.com/safari*.

How to Contact Us

Please address comments and questions concerning this book to the publisher:

O'Reilly Media, Inc.
1005 Gravenstein Highway North
Sebastopol, CA 95472
800-998-9938 (in the United States or Canada)
707-829-0515 (international or local)
707-829-0104 (fax)

To comment or ask technical questions about this book, send email to *bookquestions@oreilly.com*.

For more information about our books, courses, conferences, and news, see our website at *http://www.oreilly.com*.

Find us on Facebook: *http://facebook.com/oreilly*.

Follow us on Twitter: *http://twitter.com/oreillymedia*.

Watch us on YouTube: *http://www.youtube.com/oreillymedia*.

## PART I

Setup

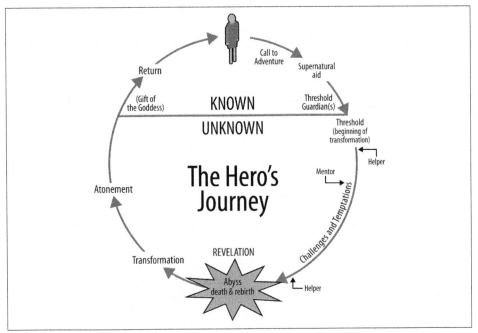

Figure I-1. The Hero's Journey, from Wikipedia (https://en.wikipedia.org/wiki/Hero %27s_journey)

## CHAPTER 1

Theory

We are uncovering better ways of developing software by doing it and helping others do it. Through this work we have come to value:

> **Individuals and interactions** over processes and tools
> **Working software** over comprehensive documentation
> **Customer collaboration** over contract negotiation
> **Responding to change** over following a plan

That is, while there is value in the items on the right, we value the items on the left more.

—The Agile Manifesto (*http://agilemanifesto.org*)

Introduction

Agile Data Science is an approach to data science centered around web application development. It asserts that the most effective output of the data science process suitable for effecting change in an organization is the web application. It asserts that application development is a fundamental skill of a data scientist. Therefore, doing data science becomes about building applications that describe the applied research process: rapid prototyping, exploratory data analysis, interactive visualization, and applied machine learning.

Agile software methods have become the de facto way software is delivered today. There are a range of fully developed methodologies, such as Scrum, that give a framework within which good software can be built in small increments. There have been some attempts to apply agile software methods to data science, but these have had unsatisfactory results. *There is a fundamental difference between delivering production software and actionable insights as artifacts of an agile process.* The need for insights to be actionable creates an element of uncertainty around the artifacts of data science—

they might be "complete" in a software sense, and yet lack any value because they don't yield real, actionable insights. As data scientist Daniel Tunkelang says, "The world of actionable insights is necessarily looser than the world of software engineering." Scrum and other agile software methodologies don't handle this uncertainty well. Simply put: agile software doesn't make Agile Data Science. This created the motivation for this book: to provide a new methodology suited to the uncertainty of data science along with a guide on how to apply it that would demonstrate the principles in real software.

The Agile Data Science "manifesto" is my attempt to create a rigorous method to apply agility to the practice of data science. *These principles apply beyond data scientists building data products in production.* The web application is the best format to share actionable insights both within and outside an organization.

Agile Data Science is not just about how to ship working software, but how to better align data science with the rest of the organization. There is a chronic misalignment between data science and engineering, where the engineering team often wonder what the data science team are doing as they perform exploratory data analysis and applied research. The engineering team are often uncertain what to do in the meanwhile, creating the "pull of the waterfall," where supposedly agile projects take on characteristics of the waterfall. Agile Data Science bridges this gap between the two teams, creating a more powerful alignment of their efforts.

This book is also about "big data." *Agile Data Science* is a development methodology that copes with the unpredictable realities of creating analytics applications from data at scale. It is a theoretical and technical guide for operating a Spark data refinery to harness the power of the "big data" in your organization. Warehouse-scale computing has given us enormous storage and compute resources to solve new kinds of problems involving storing and processing unprecedented amounts of data. There is great interest in bringing new tools to bear on formerly intractable problems, enabling us to derive entirely new products from raw data, to refine raw data into profitable insights, and to productize and productionize insights in new kinds of analytics applications. These tools are processor cores and disk spindles, paired with visualization, statistics, and machine learning. This is *data science*.

At the same time, during the last 20 years, the World Wide Web has emerged as the dominant medium for information exchange. During this time, software engineering has been transformed by the "agile" revolution in how applications are conceived, built, and maintained. These new processes bring in more projects and products on time and under budget, and enable small teams or single actors to develop entire applications spanning broad domains. This is *agile software development*.

But there's a problem. Working with real data in the wild, doing data science, and performing serious research takes time—longer than an agile cycle (on the order of months). It takes more time than is available in many organizations for a project sprint, meaning today's applied researcher is more than pressed for time. Data science is stuck in the old-school software schedule known as the *waterfall method*.

Our problem and our opportunity come at the intersection of these two trends: how can we incorporate data science, which is applied research and requires exhaustive effort on an unpredictable timeline, into the agile application? How can analytics applications do better than the waterfall method that we've long since left behind? How can we craft applications for unknown, evolving data models? How can we develop *new agile methods* to fit the data science process to create great products?

This book attempts to synthesize two fields, agile development and data science on large datasets; to meld research and engineering into a productive relationship. To achieve this, it presents a new agile methodology and examples of building products with a suitable software stack. The methodology is designed to maximize the creation of software features based on the most penetrating insights. The software stack is a lightweight toolset that can cope with the uncertain, shifting sea of raw data and delivers enough productivity to enable the agile process to succeed. The book goes on to show you how to iteratively build value using this stack, to get back to agility and mine data to turn it into dollars.

Agile Data Science aims to put you back in the driver's seat, ensuring that your applied research produces useful products that meet the needs of real users.

Definition

What is Agile Data Science (ADS)? In this chapter I outline a new methodology for analytics product development, something I hinted at in the first edition but did not express in detail. To begin, what is the goal of the ADS process?

Methodology as Tweet

The goal of the Agile Data Science process is to document, facilitate, and guide exploratory data analysis to discover and follow the *critical path* to a compelling analytics product (Figure 1-1. Agile Data Science "goes meta" and puts the lens on the exploratory data analysis process, to document insight as it occurs. This becomes the primary activity of product development. By "going meta," we make the process focus on something that is predictable, that can be managed, rather than the product output itself, which cannot.

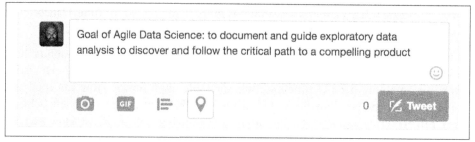

Figure 1-1. Methodology as tweet

A new agile manifesto for data science is needed.

Agile Data Science Manifesto

Agile Data Science is organized around the following principles:

- Iterate, iterate, iterate: tables, charts, reports, predictions.
- Ship intermediate output. Even failed experiments have output.
- Prototype experiments over implementing tasks.
- Integrate the tyrannical opinion of data in product management.
- Climb up and down the data-value pyramid as we work.
- Discover and pursue the critical path to a killer product.
- Get meta. Describe the process, not just the end state.

Let's explore each principle in detail.

Iterate, iterate, iterate

Insight comes from the twenty-fifth query in a chain of queries, not the first one. Data tables have to be parsed, formatted, sorted, aggregated, and summarized before they can be understood. Insightful charts typically come from the third or fourth attempt, not the first. Building accurate predictive models can take many iterations of feature engineering and hyperparameter tuning. In data science, iteration is the essential element to the extraction, visualization, and productization of insight. When we build, we iterate.

Ship intermediate output

Iteration is the essential act in crafting analytics applications, which means we're often left at the end of a sprint with things that aren't complete. If we didn't ship incomplete or intermediate output by the end of a sprint, we would often end up shipping nothing at all. And that isn't agile; I call it the "death loop," where endless time can be wasted perfecting things nobody wants.

Good systems are self-documenting, and in Agile Data Science we document and share the incomplete assets we create as we work. We commit all work to source control. We share this work with teammates and, as soon as possible, with end users. This principle isn't obvious to everyone. Many data scientists come from academic backgrounds, where years of intense research effort went into a single large paper called a thesis that resulted in an advanced degree.

Prototype experiments over implementing tasks

In software engineering, a product manager assigns a chart to a developer to implement during a sprint. The developer translates the assignment into a SQL GROUP BY and creates a web page for it. Mission accomplished? Wrong. Charts that are specified this way are unlikely to have value. Data science differs from software engineering in that it is part science, part engineering.

In any given task, we must iterate to achieve insight, and these iterations can best be summarized as experiments. Managing a data science team means overseeing multiple concurrent experiments more than it means handing out tasks. Good assets (tables, charts, reports, predictions) emerge as artifacts of exploratory data analysis, so we must think more in terms of experiments than tasks.

Integrate the tyrannical opinion of data

What is possible is as important as what is intended. What is easy and what is hard are as important things to know as what is desired. In software application development there are three perspectives to consider: those of the customers, the developers, and the business. In analytics application development there is another perspective: that of the data. Without understanding what the data "has to say" about any feature, the product owner can't do a good job. The data's opinion must always be included in product discussions, which means that they must be grounded in visualization through exploratory data analysis in the internal application that becomes the focus of our efforts.

Climb up and down the data-value pyramid

The data-value pyramid (Figure 1-2) is a five-level pyramid modeled after Maslow's hierarchy of needs. It expresses the increasing amount of value created when refining raw data into tables and charts, followed by reports, then predictions, all of which is intended to enable new actions or improve existing ones:

- The first level of the data-value pyramid (records) is about *plumbing*; making a dataset flow from where it is gathered to where it appears in an application.

- The *charts* and *tables* layer is the level where refinement and analysis begins.

- The *reports* layer enables immersive exploration of data, where we can really reason about it and get to know it.

- The *predictions* layer is where more value is created, but creating good predictions means feature engineering, which the lower levels encompass and facilitate.

- The final level, *actions*, is where the AI (artificial intelligence) craze is taking place. If your insight doesn't enable a new action or improve an existing one, it isn't very valuable.

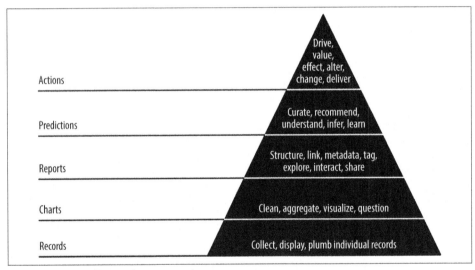

Figure 1-2. The data-value pyramid

The data-value pyramid gives structure to our work. The pyramid is something to keep in mind, not a rule to be followed. Sometimes you skip steps, sometimes you work backward. If you pull a new dataset directly into a predictive model as a feature, you incur technical debt if you don't make this dataset transparent and accessible by adding it to your application data model in the lower levels. You should keep this in mind, and pay off the debt as you are able.

Discover and pursue the critical path to a killer product

To maximize our odds of success, we should focus most of our time on that aspect of our application that is most essential to its success. But which aspect is that? This must be discovered through experimentation. Analytics product development is the search for and pursuit of a moving goal.

Once a goal is determined, for instance a prediction to be made, then we must find the critical path (*https://en.wikipedia.org/wiki/Critical_path_method*) to its implementation and, if it proves valuable, to its improvement. Data is refined step by step as it flows from task to task. Analytics products often require multiple stages of refinement, the employment of extensive ETL (extract, transform, load) processes, techniques from statistics, information access, machine learning, artificial intelligence, and graph analytics.

The interaction of these stages can form complex webs of dependencies. The team leader holds this web in his head. It is his job to ensure that the team discovers the critical path and then to organize the team around completing it. A product manager cannot manage this process from the top down; rather, a product scientist must discover it from the bottom up.

Get meta

If we can't easily ship good product assets on a schedule comparable to developing a normal application, what will we ship? If we don't ship, we aren't agile. To solve this problem, in Agile Data Science, we "get meta." The focus is on documenting the analytics process as opposed to the end state or product we are seeking. This lets us be agile and ship intermediate content as we iteratively climb the data-value pyramid to pursue the critical path to a killer product. So where does the product come from? From the *palette* we create by documenting our exploratory data analysis.

Synthesis

These seven principles work together to drive the Agile Data Science methodology. They serve to structure and document the process of exploratory data analysis and transform it into analytics applications. So that is the core of the method. But why? How did we get here? Let's take a look at a waterfall project to understand the problems these types of projects create.

 LinkedIn Career Explorer was an analytics application developed at LinkedIn in 2010 using the waterfall methodology, and its ultimate failure motivated the creation of this book. I was a newly hired Senior Data Scientist for Career Explorer. In this second edition, I use Career Explorer as a case study to briefly explore the problems discovered with the waterfall method during its eight-month development.

The Problem with the Waterfall

I should explain and get out of the way the fact that Career Explorer was the first recommender system or indeed predictive model that I had ever built. Much of its failure was due to my inexperience. My experience was in iterative and agile interactive visualization, which seemed a good fit for the goals of the project, but actually the recommendation task was more difficult than had been anticipated in the prototype —as it turned out, much more work was needed on the entity resolution of job titles than was foreseen.

At the same time, issues with the methodology employed on the product hid the actual state of the product from management, who were quite pleased with static mock-ups only days before launch. Last-minute integration revealed bugs in the interfaces between components that were exposed to the customer. A hard deadline created a crisis when the product proved unshippable with only days to go. In the end, I stayed up for the better part of a week resubmitting Hadoop jobs every five minutes to debug last-minute fixes and changes, and the product was just barely good enough to go out. This turned out not to matter much, as users weren't actually interested in the product concept. In the end, a lot of work was thrown away only months after launch.

The key issues with the project were to do with the waterfall methodology employed:

- The *application concept* was only tested in user focus groups and managerial reviews, and it failed to actually engage user interest.
- The *prediction presentation* was designed up front, with the actual model and its behavior being an afterthought. Things went something like this:

  "We made a great design! Your job is to predict the future for it."

  "What is taking so long to reliably predict the future?"

  "The users don't understand what 86% true means."

  Plane → Mountain.
- *Charts* were specified by product/design and failed to achieve real insights.
- A *hard deadline* was specified in a contract with a customer.
- *Integration* testing occurred at the end of development, which precipitated a deadline crisis.
- *Mock-ups* without real data were used throughout the project to present the application to focus groups and to management.

This is all fairly standard for a waterfall project. The result was that management thought the product was on track with only two weeks to go when integration finally revealed problems. Note that Scrum was used throughout the project, but the end product was never able to be tested with end users, thus negating the entire point of the agile methodology employed. To sum it up, the plane hit the mountain.

By contrast, there was another project at LinkedIn called InMaps (*https://tech crunch.com/2014/09/01/linkedin-is-quietly-retiring-network-visualization-tool-inmaps/*) that I led development on and product managed. It proceeded much more smoothly because we iteratively published the application using real data, exposing the "broken" state of the application to internal users and getting feedback across many release cycles. It was the contrast between these two projects that helped formalize Agile Data Science in my mind.

But if the methodology employed on Career Explorer was actually Scrum, why was it a waterfall project? It turns out that analytics products built by data science teams have a tendency to "pull" toward the waterfall. I would later discover the reason for this tendency.

Research Versus Application Development

It turns out that there is a basic conflict in shipping analytics products, and that is the conflict between the research and the application development timeline. This conflict tends to make every analytics product a waterfall project, even those that set out to use a software engineering methodology like Scrum.

Research, even applied research, is science. It involves iterative experiments, in which the learning from one experiment informs the next experiment. Science excels at discovery, but it differs from engineering in that there is no specified endpoint (see Figure 1-3).

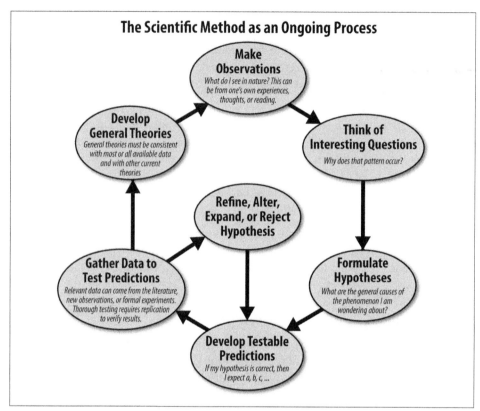

Figure 1-3. The scientific method, from Wikipedia (https://en.wikipedia.org/wiki/Scien tific_method)

Engineering employs known science and engineering techniques to build things on a linear schedule. Engineering looks like the Gantt chart in Figure 1-4. Tasks can be specified, monitored, and completed.

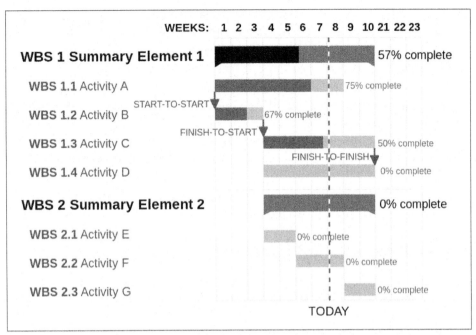

Figure 1-4. Gantt chart, from Wikipedia (https://en.wikipedia.org/wiki/Gantt_chart)

A better model of an engineering project looks like the PERT chart in Figure 1-5, which can model complex dependencies with nonlinear relationships. Note that even in this more advanced model, the points are known. The work is done during the lines.

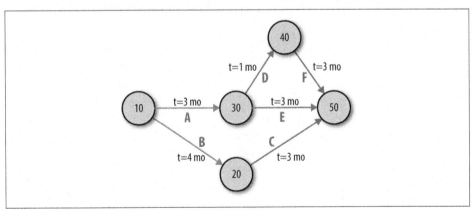

*Figure 1-5. PERT chart, from Wikipedia (https://en.wikipedia.org/wiki/Program_evalua
tion_and_review_technique)*

In other words: engineering is precise, and science is uncertain. Even relatively new fields such as software engineering, where estimates are often off by 100% or more, are more certain than the scientific process. This is the impedance mismatch that creates the problem.

In data science, the science portion usually takes much longer than the engineering portion, and to make things worse, the amount of time a given experiment will take is uncertain. Uncertainty in length of time to make working analytics assets—tables, charts, and predictions—tends to cause stand-ins to be used in place of the real thing. This results in feedback on a mock-up driving the development process, which aborts agility. This is a project killer.

The solution is to get agile... but how? How do agile software methodologies map to data science, and where do they fall short?

The Problem with Agile Software

Agile Software isn't Agile Data Science. In this section we'll look at the problems with mapping something like Scrum directly into the data science process.

Eventual Quality: Financing Technical Debt

Technical debt (*https://www.techopedia.com/definition/27913/technical-debt*) is defined by Techopedia as "a concept in programming that reflects the extra development work that arises when code that is easy to implement in the short run is used instead of applying the best overall solution." Understanding technical debt is essential when it comes to managing software application development, because deadline pressure can result in the creation of large amounts of technical debt. This technical debt can cripple the team's ability to hit future deadlines.

Technical debt is different in data science than in software engineering. In software engineering you retain all code, so quality is paramount. In data science you tend to discard most code, so this is less the case. In data science we must check in everything to source control but must tolerate a higher degree of ugliness until something has proved useful enough to retain and reuse. Otherwise, applying software engineering standards to data science code would reduce productivity a great deal. At the same time, a great deal of quality can be imparted to code by forcing some software engineering knowledge and habits onto academics, statisticians, researchers, and data scientists.

In data science, by contrast to software engineering, code shouldn't *always* be good; it should be *eventually good*. This means that some technical debt up front is acceptable, so long as it is not excessive. Code that becomes important should be able to be cleaned up with minimal effort. It doesn't have to be good at any moment, but as soon as it becomes important, it must become good. Technical debt forms part of the web of dependencies in managing an Agile Data Science project. This is a highly technical task, necessitating technical skills in the team leader or a process that surfaces technical debt from other members of the team.

Prototypes are financed on technical debt, which is paid off only if a prototype proves useful. Most prototypes will be discarded or minimally used, so the technical debt is never repaid. This enables much more experimentation for fewer resources. This also occurs in the form of Jupyter and Zeppelin notebooks, which place the emphasis on direct expression rather than code reuse or production deployment.

The Pull of the Waterfall

The stack of a modern "big data" application is much more complex than that of a normal application. Also, there is a very broad skillset required to build analytics applications at scale using these systems. This wide pipeline in terms of people and technology can result in a "pull" toward the waterfall even for teams determined to be agile.

Figure 1-6 shows that if tasks are completed in sprints, the thickness of the stack and team the combine to force a return to the waterfall model. In this instance a chart is desired, so a data scientist uses Spark to calculate the data for one and puts it into the database. Next, an API developer creates an API for this data, followed by a web developer creating a web page for the chart. A visualization engineer creates the actual chart, which a designer visually improves. Finally, the product manager sees the chart and another iteration is required. It takes an extended period to make one step forward. Progress is very slow, and the team is not agile.

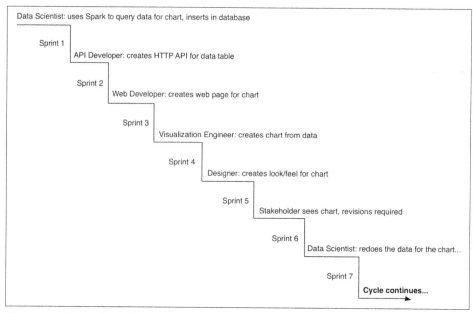

Data Scientist: uses Spark to query data for chart, inserts in database

Sprint 1

API Developer: creates HTTP API for data table

Sprint 2

Web Developer: creates web page for chart

Sprint 3

Visualization Engineer: creates chart from data

Sprint 4

Designer: creates look/feel for chart

Sprint 5

Stakeholder sees chart, revisions required

Sprint 6

Data Scientist: redoes the data for the chart...

Sprint 7

Cycle continues...

Figure 1-6. Sprint based cooperation becoming anything but agile

This illustrates a few things. The first is the need for generalists who can accomplish more than one related task. But more importantly, it shows that it is necessary to iterate within sprints as opposed to iterating in compartments between them. Otherwise, if you wait an entire sprint for one team member to implement the previous team member's work, the process tends to become a sort of stepped pyramid/waterfall.

The Data Science Process

Having introduced the methodology and described why it is needed, now we're going to dive into the mechanics of an Agile Data Science team. We begin with setting expectations, then look at the roles in a data science team, and finally describe how the process works in practice. While I hope this serves as an introduction for readers new to data science teams or new to Agile Data Science, this isn't an exhaustive description of how agile processes work in general. Readers new to agile and new to data science are encouraged to consult a book on Scrum before consuming this chapter.

Now let's talk about setting expectations of data science teams, and how they interact with the rest of the organization.

Setting Expectations

Before we look at how to compose data science teams and run them to produce actionable insights, we first need to discuss how a data science team fits into an organization. As the focus of data science shifts in Agile Data Science from a predetermined outcome to a description of the applied research process, so must the expectations for the team change. In addition, the way data science teams relate to other teams is impacted.

"When will we ship?" is the question management wants to know the answer to in order to set expectations with the customer and coordinate sales, marketing, recruiting, and other efforts. With an Agile Data Science team, you don't get a straight answer to that question. There is no specific date X when prediction Y will be shippable as a web product or API. That metric, the ship date of a predetermined artifact, is something you sacrifice when you adopt an Agile Data Science process. What you get in return is true visibility into the work of the team toward your business goals in the form of working software that describes in detail what the team is actually doing. With this information in hand, other business processes can be aligned with the actual reality of data science, as opposed to the fiction of a known shipping date for a predetermined artifact.

With a variable goal, another question becomes just as important: "What will we ship?" or, more likely, "What will we ship, when?" To answer these questions, any stakeholder can take a look at the application as it exists today as well as the plans for the next sprint and get a sense of where things are and where they are moving.

With these two questions addressed, the organization can work with a data science team as the artifacts of their work evolve into actionable insights. A data science team should be tasked with discovering value to address a set of business problems. The form the output of their work takes is discovered through exploratory research. The date when the "final" artifacts will be ready can be estimated by careful inspection of the current state of their work. With this information in hand, although it is more nuanced than a "ship date," managers positioned around a data science team can sync their work and schedules with the team.

In other words, we can't tell you exactly what we will ship, when. But in exchange for accepting this reality, you get a constant, shippable progress report, so that by participating in the reality of doing data science you can use this information to coordinate other efforts. That is the trade-off of Agile Data Science. Given that schedules with pre-specified artifacts and ship dates usually include the wrong artifacts and unrealistic dates, we feel this trade-off is a good one. In fact, it is the only one we can make if we face the reality of doing data science.

Data Science Team Roles

Products are built by teams of people, and agile methods focus on people over process. Data science is a broad discipline, spanning analysis, design, development, business, and research. The roles of Agile Data Science team members, defined in a spectrum from customer to operations, look something like Figure 1-7.

Figure 1-7. The roles in an Agile Data Science team

These roles can be defined as follows:

- *Customers* use your product, click your buttons and links, or ignore you completely. Your job is to create value for them repeatedly. Their interest determines the success of your product.

- *Business Development* signs early customers, either firsthand or through the creation of landing pages and promotion, and delivers traction in the market with the product.

- *Marketers* talk to customers to determine which markets to pursue. They determine the starting perspective from which an Agile Data Science product begins.

- *Product managers* take in the perspectives of each role, synthesizing them to build consensus about the vision and direction of the product.

- *User experience designers* are responsible for fitting the design around the data to match the perspective of the customer. This role is critical, as the output of statistical models can be difficult to interpret by "normal" users who have no concept of the semantics of the model's output (i.e., how can something be 75% true?).

- *Interaction designers* design interactions around data models so users find their value.

- *Web developers* create the web applications that deliver data to a web browser.

- *Engineers* build the systems that deliver data to applications.

- *Data scientists* explore and transform data in novel ways to create and publish new features and combine data from diverse sources to create new value. They make visualizations with researchers, engineers, web developers, and designers, exposing raw, intermediate, and refined data early and often.

- *Applied researchers* solve the heavy problems that data scientists uncover and that stand in the way of delivering value. These problems take intense focus and time and require novel methods from statistics and machine learning.

- *Platform or data engineers* solve problems in the distributed infrastructure that enable Agile Data Science at scale to proceed without undue pain. Platform engineers handle work tickets for immediate blocking bugs and implement long-term plans and projects to maintain and improve usability for researchers, data scientists, and engineers.

- *Quality assurance engineers* automate testing of predictive systems from end to end to ensure accurate and reliable predictions are made.

- *Operations/DevOps engineers* ensure smooth setup and operation of production data infrastructure. They automate deployment and take pages when things go wrong.

Recognizing the Opportunity and the Problem

The broad skillset needed to build data products presents both an opportunity and a problem. If these skills can be brought to bear by experts in each role working as a team on a rich dataset, problems can be decomposed into parts and directly attacked. Data science is then an efficient assembly line, as illustrated in Figure 1-8.

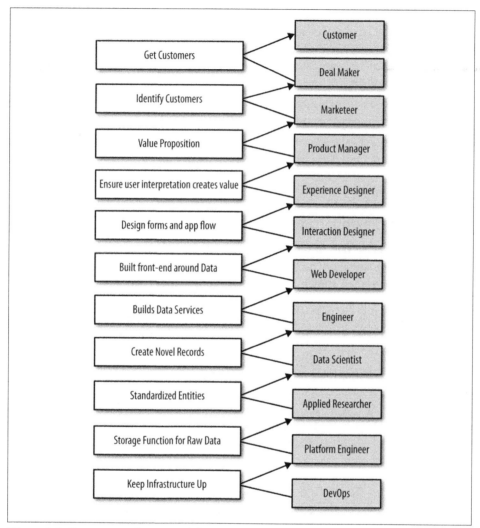

Figure 1-8. Expert contributor workflow

However, as team size increases to satisfy the need for expertise in these diverse areas, communication overhead quickly dominates. A researcher who is eight persons away from customers is unlikely to solve relevant problems and more likely to solve arcane problems. Likewise, team meetings of a dozen individuals are unlikely to be productive. We might split this team into multiple departments and establish contracts of delivery between them, but then we lose both agility and cohesion. Waiting on the output of research, we invent specifications, and soon we find ourselves back in the waterfall method.

And yet we know that agility and a cohesive vision and consensus about a product are essential to our success in building products. The worst product-development problem is one team working on more than one vision. How are we to reconcile the increased span of expertise and the disjoint timelines of applied research, data science, software development, and design?

Adapting to Change

To remain agile, we must embrace and adapt to these new conditions. We must adopt changes in line with lean methodologies to stay productive.

Several changes in particular make a return to agility possible:

- Choosing generalists over specialists
- Preferring small teams over large teams
- Using high-level tools and platforms: cloud computing, distributed systems, and platforms as a service (PaaS)
- Continuous and iterative sharing of intermediate work, even when that work may be incomplete

In Agile Data Science, a small team of generalists uses scalable, high-level tools and platforms to iteratively refine data into increasingly higher states of value. We embrace a software stack leveraging cloud computing, distributed systems, and platforms as a service. Then we use this stack to iteratively publish the intermediate results of even our most in-depth research to snowball value from simple records to predictions and actions that create value and let us capture some of it to turn data into dollars.

Let's examine each item in detail.

Harnessing the power of generalists

In Agile Data Science, we value generalists over specialists, as shown in Figure 1-9.

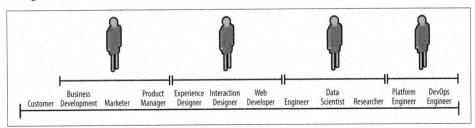

Figure 1-9. Broad roles in an Agile Data Science team

In other words, we measure the breadth of teammates' skills as much as the depth of their knowledge and their talent in any one area. Examples of good Agile Data Science team members include:

- Designers who deliver working CSS
- Web developers who build entire applications and understand the user interface and user experience
- Data scientists capable of both research and building web services and applications
- Researchers who check in working source code, explain results, and share intermediate data
- Product managers able to understand the nuances in all areas

Design in particular is a critical role in the Agile Data Science team. Design does not end with appearance or experience. Design encompasses all aspects of the product, from architecture, distribution, and user experience to work environment.

 In the documentary *The Lost Interview*, Steve Jobs said this about design: "Designing a product is keeping five thousand things in your brain and fitting them all together in new and different ways to get what you want. And every day you discover something new that is a new problem or a new opportunity to fit these things together a little differently. And it's that process that is the magic."

Leveraging agile platforms

In Agile Data Science, we use the easiest-to-use, most approachable distributed systems, along with cloud computing and platforms as a service, to minimize infrastructure costs and maximize productivity. The simplicity of our stack helps enable a return to agility. We use this stack to compose scalable systems in as few steps as possible. This lets us move fast and consume all the available data without running into scalability problems that cause us to discard data or remake our application in-flight. That is to say, *we only build it once*, and it adapts.

Sharing intermediate results

Finally, to address the very real differences in timelines between researchers and data scientists and the rest of the team, we adopt a sort of *data collage* as our mechanism of melding these disjointed scales. In other words, we piece our app together from the abundance of views, visualizations, and properties that form the "menu" for the application.

Researchers and data scientists, who work on longer timelines than agile sprints typically allow, generate data daily—albeit not in a "publishable" state. But in Agile Data Science, there is no unpublishable state. The rest of the team must see weekly, if not daily (or more often), updates to the state of the data. This kind of engagement with researchers is essential to unifying the team and enabling product management.

That means publishing intermediate results—incomplete data, the scraps of analysis. These "clues" keep the team united, and as these results become interactive, everyone becomes informed as to the true nature of the data, the progress of the research, and how to combine the clues into features of value. Development and design must proceed from this shared reality. The audience for these continuous releases can start small and grow as they become more presentable (as shown in Figure 1-10), but customers must be included quickly.

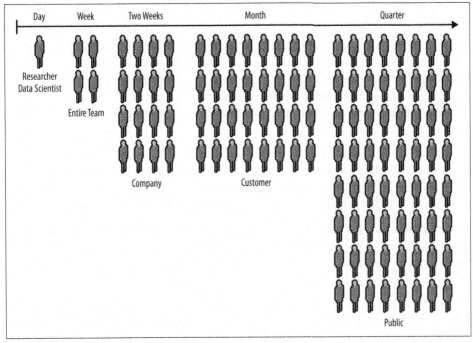

Figure 1-10. Growing audience from conception to launch

Notes on Process

The Agile Data Science process embraces the iterative nature of data science and the efficiency our tools enable to build and extract increasing levels of structure and value from our data.

Given the spectrum of skills within a data science team, the possibilities are endless. With the team spanning so many disciplines, building web products is inherently collaborative. To collaborate, teams need direction: every team member passionately and tenaciously pursuing a common goal. To get that direction, you require consensus.

Building and maintaining consensus while collaborating is the hardest part of building software. The principal risk in software product teams is building to different blueprints. Clashing visions result in incohesive holes that sink products.

Applications are sometimes *mocked* before they are built: product managers conduct market research, while designers iterate mocks with feedback from prospective users. These mocks serve as a common blueprint for the team.

Real-world requirements shift as we learn from our users and conditions change, even when the data is static. So our blueprints must change with time. Agile methods were created to facilitate implementation of evolving requirements, and to replace mock-ups with real working systems as soon as possible.

Typical web products—those driven by forms backed by predictable, constrained transaction data in relational databases—have fundamentally different properties than products featuring mined data. In CRUD (create, read, update, delete) applications, data is relatively consistent. The models are predictable SQL tables or documents, and changing them is a product decision. The data's "opinion" is irrelevant, and the product team is free to impose its will on the model to match the business logic of the application.

In interactive products driven by mined data, none of that holds. Real data is dirty. Mining always involves dirt. If the data wasn't dirty, it wouldn't be data mining. Even carefully extracted and refined mined information can be fuzzy and unpredictable. Presenting it on the consumer internet requires long labor and great care.

In data products, the data is ruthlessly opinionated. Whatever we wish the data to say, it is unconcerned with our own opinions. It says what it says. This means the waterfall model has no application. It also means that mocks are an insufficient blueprint to establish consensus in software teams.

Mocks of a data product are a specification of the application without its essential character, the true value of the information being presented. Mocks as blueprints make assumptions about complex data models they have no reasonable basis for making. When specifying lists of recommendations, mocks often mislead. When mocks specify full-blown interactions, they do more than that: they suppress reality and promote assumption. And yet we know that good design and user experience are about minimizing assumption. What are we to do?

The goal of agile product development is to identify the essential character of an application and to build that up first before adding other features. This imparts agility to the project, making it more likely to satisfy its real, essential requirements as they evolve. In data products, that essential character will surprise you. If it doesn't, either you are doing it wrong, or your data isn't very interesting. Information has context, and when that context is interactive, insight is not predictable.

Code Review and Pair Programming

To avoid systemic errors, data scientists must share their code with the rest of the team on a regular basis. This makes formal code review important.

It is easy to detect and fix errors in parsing. Systemic errors in algorithms are much harder to detect without a second, third, fourth pair of eyes. And they need not all be data scientists—if a data scientist presents her code with an explanation of what is happening, any programmer can catch inconsistencies and make helpful suggestions. What is more, having a formal code review process sets the standard for writing code that is understandable and can be shared and explained.

Without code review, a data scientist could end up sinking enormous efforts into improving a predictive model that is doing the wrong thing. Systemic errors are incredibly difficult to detect in your own code, as when reading your own code, your mind reads what you intended and not what you actually wrote.

Code review in every sprint is essential to maintaining standards of quality and readability; it is essential to avoid systemic errors in algorithmic work, and it fosters a sense of inclusion and sharing on the team. This cultural impact is perhaps the most important aspect of code review, because it creates cross-training among team members who become proficient at understanding and fixing components of the system they don't usually work on or maintain. You'll be glad you have a code review process in place when a critical data scientist or data engineer is out sick and you need someone else to find and fix a bug in production.

Agile Environments: Engineering Productivity

Rows of cubicles like cells of a hive. Overbooked conference rooms camped and decamped. Microsoft Outlook a modern punchcard. Monolithic insanity. A sea of cubes.

Deadlines interrupted by oscillating cacophonies of rumors shouted, spread like waves uninterrupted by naked desks. Headphone budgets. Not working, close together. Decibel induced telecommuting. The open plan.

Competing monstrosities seeking productivity but not finding it.

   —Poem by the author

Generalists require more uninterrupted concentration and quiet than do specialists. That is because the context of their work is broader, and therefore their immersion is deeper. Their environment must suit this need.

Invest in two to three times the space of a typical cube farm, or you are wasting your people. In this setup, some people don't need desks, which drives costs down.

We can do better. We should do better. It costs more, but it is inexpensive.

In Agile Data Science, we recognize team members as creative workers, not office workers. We therefore structure our environment more like a studio than an office. At the same time, we recognize that employing advanced mathematics on data to build products requires quiet contemplation and intense focus. So we incorporate elements of the library as well.

> Many enterprises limit their productivity enhancement of employees to the acquisition of skills. However, about 86% of productivity problems reside in the work environment of organizations. The work environment has effect on the performance of employees. The type of work environment in which employees operate determines the way in which such enterprises prosper.
>
> —Akinyele Samuel Taiwo

> It is much higher cost to employ people than it is to maintain and operate a building, hence spending money on improving the work environment is the most cost effective way of improving productivity because of small percentage increase in productivity of 0.1% to 2% can have dramatic effects on the profitability of the company.
>
> —Derek Clements-Croome and Li Baizhan

Creative workers need three kinds of space to collaborate and build together. From open to closed, they are: collaboration space, personal space, and private space.

Collaboration space

Collaboration space is where ideas are hatched. Situated along main thoroughfares and between departments, collaborative spaces are bright, open, comfortable, and inviting. They have no walls. They are flexible and reconfigurable. They are ever-changing, always being rearranged, and full of beanbag chairs, pillows, and comfortable chairs. Collaboration space is where you feel the energy of your company: laughter, big conversations, excited voices talking over one another. Invest in and showcase these areas. Real, not plastic, plants keep sound from carrying—and they make air!

Private space

Private space is where deadlines are met. Enclosed and soundproof, private spaces are libraries. There is no talking. Private space minimizes distractions: think dim light and white noise. There are beanbags, couches, and chairs, but ergonomics demand proper workstations too. These spaces might include separate sit/stand desks with docking stations behind (bead) curtains with 30-inch customized LCDs.

Personal space

Personal space is where people call home. In between collaboration and private space in its degree of openness, personal space should be personalized by each individual to suit his or her needs (e.g., shared office or open desks, half or whole cube). Personal space should come with a menu and a budget. Themes and plant life should be encouraged. This is where some people will spend most of their time. On the other hand, given adequate collaborative and private space, a notebook, and a mobile device, some people don't need personal space at all.

Above all, the goal of the agile environment is to create immersion in data through the physical environment: printouts, posters, books, whiteboards, and more, as shown in Figure 1-11.

Figure 1-11. Data immersion through collage

If you offer the team the three types of space, you will have a happy, productive team that can tackle data science challenges efficiently.

Realizing Ideas with Large-Format Printing

Easy access to large-format printing is a requirement for the agile environment. Visualization in material form encourages sharing, collage, expressiveness, and creativity.

Several companies make 24-inch-wide large-format printers that cost less than $1,000. Continuous ink delivery systems are available for less than $100 that bring the operational cost of large-format printing—for instance, 24×36-inch posters—to less than $1 per poster.

At this price point, there is no excuse not to give a data team easy access to several large-format printers for both plain-paper proofs and glossy prints. It is very easy to get people excited about data across departments when they can see concrete proof of the progress of the data science team.

## CHAPTER 2

Agile Tools

This chapter will briefly introduce our software stack. This stack is optimized for our process.

By the end of this chapter, you'll be collecting, storing, processing, publishing, and decorating data (Figure 2-1). Our stack enables one person to do all of this, to go "full stack."

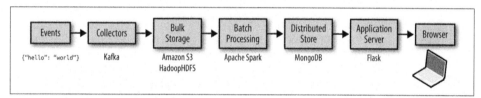

Figure 2-1. The software stack process

Full-stack skills are some of the most in demand for data scientists. We'll cover a lot here, and quickly, but don't worry: I will continue to demonstrate this software stack in Chapters 5 through 9. You need only understand the basics now; you will get more comfortable later.

We'll begin with instructions for running the stack in local mode on your own machine. In the next chapter, you'll learn how to scale this same stack in the cloud via Amazon Web Services. Let's get started!

Code examples for this chapter are available at *Agile_Data_Code_2/ch02* (*https:// github.com/rjurney/Agile_Data_Code_2/tree/master/ch02*). Clone the repository and follow along!

```
git clone https://github.com/rjurney/Agile_Data_Code_2.git
```

Scalability = Simplicity

As NoSQL tools like Spark, Hadoop, and MongoDB, data science, and big data have developed, much focus has been placed on the plumbing of analytics applications. However, this is not a book about infrastructure. This book teaches you to build applications that use such infrastructure. Once our stack has been introduced, we will take this plumbing for granted and build applications that depend on it. Thus, this book devotes only two chapters to infrastructure: one on introducing our development tools, and the other on scaling them up in the cloud to match your data's scale.

In choosing our tools, we seek linear, horizontal scalability, but above all, we seek simplicity. While the concurrent systems required to drive a modern analytics application at any kind of scale are complex, we still need to be able to focus on the task at hand: processing data to create value for the user. When our tools are too complex, when they require too much configuration and not enough convention, we start to focus on the tools themselves. We should be focusing on our data, our users, and new applications to help them. To achieve that, we need a simple stack. Such an effective stack enables collaboration by teams that include diverse sets of skills such as design and application development, statistics, and machine learning, but that don't require experts in distributed systems.

> The stack outlined in this book is not definitive. It has been selected as an example of the kind of end-to-end setup you should expect as a developer or should aim for as a platform engineer in order to rapidly and effectively build analytics applications. The takeaway should be an example stack you can use to jumpstart your application, and a standard to which you should hold other stacks.

Agile Data Science Data Processing

The first step in building analytics applications is to plumb (here I use plumb as in a verb that means to engage in plumbing!) your application from end to end: from collecting raw data to displaying something on the user's screen (see Figure 2-2). This is important because complexity can increase fast, and you need user feedback plugged into the process from the start, lest you start iterating without feedback (also known as the *death spiral*).

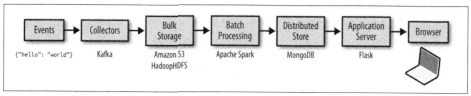

Figure 2-2. Flow of data processing in our stack

The components of our stack are as follows:

- *Events* are the things logs represent. An event is an occurrence that happens and is logged along with its features and timestamps.

  Events come in many forms—logs from servers, sensors, financial transactions, or actions our users take in our own application. To facilitate data exchange among different tools and languages, events are serialized in a common, agreed-upon format.

  In this book, we use JSON Lines (*http://jsonlines.org/*) to serialize data, which is a simple format with one JSON object per line of text, delimited by a carriage return. JSON Lines files use the *.jsonl* file ending. We will frequently employ gzip compression, where we will use the *.jsonl.gz* format.

  When performance calls for it, we use the columnar storage format Apache Parquet (*https://parquet.apache.org/*). Parquet is a cross-platform format easily accessed by many languages and tools. Loading a few columns from a Parquet file is much faster than loading compressed JSON.

- *Collectors* are event aggregators. They collect events from one or numerous sources and log them in aggregate to bulk storage, or queue them for action by real-time workers. Kafka has emerged as the leading solution for aggregating events to bulk storage.

- *Bulk storage* is a filesystem capable of high I/O (think many disks or SSDs) and parallel access by many concurrent processes. We'll be using S3 in place of the Hadoop Distributed File System (HDFS) for this purpose. HDFS set the standard for bulk storage, and without it, big data would not exist. There would be no cheap place to store vast amounts of data where it can be accessed with high I/O throughput for the kind of processing we do in Agile Data Science.

- *Distributed document stores* are multinode stores using document format. In Agile Data Science, we use them to publish data for consumption by web applications and other services. We'll be using MongoDB as our distributed document store. Many people dismiss MongoDB, because people using many of its features face scalability challenges, just as with any database. However, when used as a document store (to fetch documents, as opposed to aggregate or other queries), MongoDB scales as well as anything available. We simply don't tax it, or any other database.

- A minimalist web *application server* enables us to plumb our data as JSON through to the client for visualization, with minimal overhead. We use Python/Flask, because it means one less language for readers to know. Also, we can deploy machine learning services in Python using *sklearn* or *xgboost*. Other examples of simple web frameworks are Ruby/Sinatra or Node.js.

- A modern *browser* or mobile application enables us to present our data as an interactive experience for our users, who provide data through interaction and events describing those actions. In this book, we focus on web applications.

This list may look long and thus daunting, but in practice, these tools are easy to set up and match the crunch points in data science. Figure 2-3 shows the overall architecture. This setup scales easily and is optimized for analytic processing.

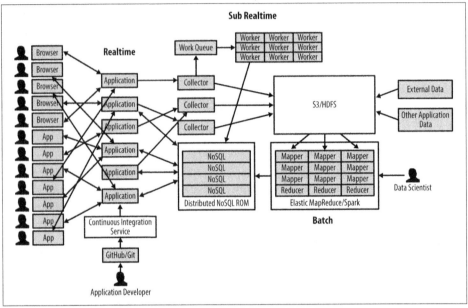

Figure 2-3. Overall architecture

Local Environment Setup

There are several ways for you to install the software that makes up the environment for the book. You can use a virtual machine, you can install the tools on your own computer, or you can use Amazon Web Services (AWS). **The recommended method to run the examples is to use the EC2 environment**.

In this section, we'll cover how to set up a virtual machine (VM) on your computer to run the examples. If you want to do a local install, you can use Appendix A and manually install the tools yourself. I recommend using Vagrant or AWS, as they are simple and easy, but your author runs all the tools locally on his MacBook Pro.

System Requirements

You will need 9 GB of RAM free for the Vagrant/VirtualBox VM to run the most memory-intensive examples (the model fitting in Chapters 7, 8, and 9). I suggest shutting down any unneeded programs and then restarting your machine before running the Vagrant VM. If your system can't meet these requirements, I suggest you use Amazon Web Services, as described in "EC2 Environment Setup" on page 34.

Setting Up Vagrant

Vagrant (*https://www.vagrantup.com/*) allows us to create and configure lightweight, reproducible, and portable development environments. The latest version of Vagrant as of the last update of this book is version 1.9.3. You'll find a link to the installation instructions on the download page (*https://www.vagrantup.com/downloads.html*).

To use Vagrant you will need VirtualBox (*https://www.virtualbox.org/*). Install directions are available in the VirtualBox User Manual (*https://www.virtualbox.org/manual/ch02.html*).

Note that if you already have VirtualBox installed, you may need to update it to the latest version for the Vagrant environment to work. Please do so now.

The book's Vagrantfile has setup instructions, which you can employ via:

```
vagrant up
```

This will take a few minutes. After this, you can connect to it via:

```
vagrant ssh
```

The example code is in the *Agile_Data_Code_2* directory. You will need to change directory (cd) to this directory for the code examples to run. If there aren't a dozen directories, including *hadoop*, *spark*, *kafka*, and *Agile_Data_Code_2*, in the Vagrant user's home directory, please wait a few minutes for the bootstrap script to finish processing.

Downloading the Data

You will need to run the script *download.sh* (*https://github.com/rjurney/Agile_Data_Code_2/blob/master/download.sh*) to download the example dataset for the book. It will store the data in the *Agile_Data_Code_2/data/* subdirectory. If you want to skip ahead to Chapter 8, you will need to run *ch08/download_data.sh* (*https://github.com/rjurney/Agile_Data_Code_2/blob/master/ch08/download_data.sh*).

EC2 Environment Setup

There is a script called *ec2.sh* (*https://github.com/rjurney/Agile_Data_Code_2/blob/master/ec2.sh*) that can be used to launch an EC2 instance with the project environment and code installed. To run this script, you will need the Amazon Web Services Command Line Interface (*https://aws.amazon.com/cli/*) (AWS CLI), which you can install via Python's `pip` command:

```
pip install awscli
```

Once you have installed the AWS CLI, check out *ec2.sh* (*https://github.com/rjurney/Agile_Data_Code_2/blob/master/ec2.sh*). It launches an `r3.xlarge` instance that uses *aws/ec2_bootstrap.sh* (*https://github.com/rjurney/Agile_Data_Code_2/blob/master/aws/ec2_bootstrap.sh*) to install the software requirements and check out the example code. At the time of writing, this instance costs $0.266/hr, so you may want to shut it down between practice sessions.

In order to use *ec2.sh*, you will need the utility `jq` (*https://stedolan.github.io/jq/*); this allows you to parse the JSON responses that the `aws` command produces. *ec2.sh* will attempt to install `jq` via your platform's package manager using the script *jq_install.sh* (*https://github.com/rjurney/Agile_Data_Code_2/blob/master/jq_install.sh*). If `jq` fails to install automatically, the script will point you to the installation page (*https://github.com/stedolan/jq/wiki/Installation*) so you can perform the install yourself. Once you have `jq` in your `PATH`, you can rerun the *ec2.sh* script; once it detects `jq`, it will continue to the next step.

ec2.sh creates a keypair called *agile_data_science*, which is stored in *agile_data_science.pem*. After that, it creates a security group called `agile_data_science`, which allows port 22 SSH access to your external IP address only. This means you won't be able to connect to this machine from computers other than your own. The script uses the keypair and security group it creates when it launches the `r3.xlarge` instance.

You will find the machine that the script boots in the Amazon EC2 Management Console (Figure 2-4). Make sure the region in the URL (for instance, *us-west-2*) matches the default region you configured via the `aws` command, or you won't see any instances. The machine will be named `agile_data_science_ec2`. If you aren't sure which region you configured the `aws` command to use, type `aws configure` and note the region that it prints.

Figure 2-4. Launch instance description in the EC2 Console

When it is done, the script will print out SSH instructions in red text and will instruct you to wait a few minutes before logging in, as the machine must initialize (Figure 2-5). After a few minutes have passed, run the script *ec2_create_tunnel.sh* (*https://github.com/rjurney/Agile_Data_Code_2/blob/master/ec2_create_tunnel.sh*) to create an SSH tunnels to forward ports 5000, 8080, and 8888 from the EC2 instance to your local ports 5000, 8080, and 8888 (Figure 2-6). This will allow you to run web applications on the EC2 instance and view them at *http://localhost:5000*, as well as Jupyter Notebooks at *http://localhost:8888* and the Apache Airflow interface at *http://localhost:8080*.

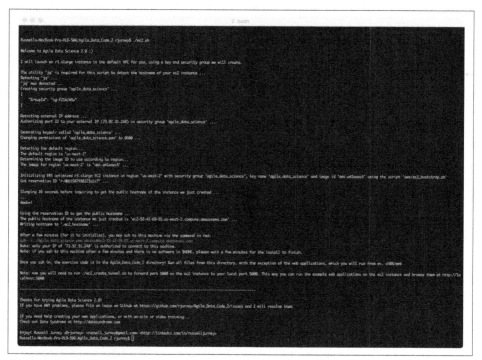

Figure 2-5. ec2.sh execution

 Once you are done with the EC2 instance, or if you want your ports back before then, you can get rid of these SSH tunnels with the *ec2_kill_tunnel.sh* (*https://github.com/rjurney/ Agile_Data_Code_2/blob/master/ec2_kill_tunnel.sh*) script. You can always re-create these port-forwarding tunnels by running the *ec2_create_tunnel.sh* (*https://github.com/rjurney/ Agile_Data_Code_2/blob/master/ec2_create_tunnel.sh*) script again.

Figure 2-6. ec2_create_tunnel.sh execution

Once you SSH into the machine, instructions will appear to direct you further (Figure 2-7). If they do not appear, the machine is not set up yet. Please disconnect and reconnect in a few minutes so that the boot script can finish; the instructions will appear then.

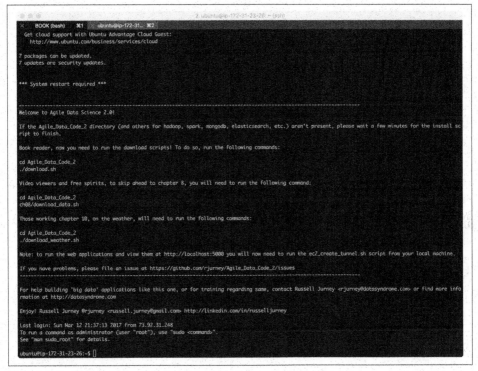

Figure 2-7. Instructions on using the agile_data_science_ec2 machine

Once you've logged in, begin by listing the contents of the home directory, where you will see all the software making up our environment, as well as the example code directory:

```
$ ls
Agile_Data_Code_2  agile_data_science.message  airflow  anaconda  elasticsearch
  elasticsearch-hadoop  hadoop  kafka  logs
  spark  zeppelin
```

Now change directory into the code examples directory, *Agile_Data_Code_2*, and list its contents:

```
$ cd Agile_Data_Code_2
$ ls

aws          ch05  ch09      download.sh       ec2.sh
jq_install.sh          manual_install.sh    spark-warehouse
bootstrap.sh  ch06  ch10      download_weather.sh  elastic_scripts
jupyter_notebook_config.py  models              Vagrantfile
ch02      ch07  data   ec2_create_tunnel.sh  images          lib
README.md   ch04       ch08  Dockerfile     ec2_kill_tunnel.sh
intro_download  .sh  LICENSE          requirements.txt
```

You're nearly ready to work with the examples. But first, you need to download the data!

Downloading the Data

Once you connect to the machine via SSH, you will need to run the script *download.sh* (*https://github.com/rjurney/Agile_Data_Code_2/blob/master/download.sh*) to download the example dataset for the book. It will store the data in the *Agile_Data_Code_2/data/* subdirectory. If you want to skip ahead to Chapter 8, you will need to run *ch08/download_data.sh* (*https://github.com/rjurney/ Agile_Data_Code_2/blob/master/ch08/download_data.sh*).

Getting and Running the Code

The code examples exist for you to actually run and play with, ultimately editing them to transform them into your own applications using your own datasets.

Getting the Code

In addition to the code on the EC2 or Vagrant images, you will also need a local copy of the code to read, edit, and play with. You can clone the code from GitHub and check the results via:

```
$ git clone https://github.com/rjurney/Agile_Data_Code_2
$ cd Agile_Data_Code_2
$ ls
```

Running the Code

The code examples are designed to run from the base *Agile_Data_Code_2* directory, and not from inside the individual chapter directories. The exception to this rule is the web application code, which should be run from within the chapter and web subdirectories (for instance, *ch08/web*).

Jupyter Notebooks

You will need to run Jupyter Notebooks from the root directory of the project, *Agile_Data_Code_2*. If you are using the Vagrant or EC2 setup, this has already been done for you in the boot script, and you can connect to Jupyter Notebooks at *http://localhost:8888*. We'll talk more about Jupyter Notebooks shortly.

Touring the Toolset

If you prefer to learn as you go, you can skim the rest of this chapter and move on to Chapter 3. In this section we're going to take a look at the tools we'll be using in the book, run a "Hello, World!" in each, and then see how they tie together to make a complete system. If you want more details on the installation of these tools, check out Appendix A.

Agile Stack Requirements

What is required of a technology stack in order to be agile while doing data science?

One thing we require is that every level of the stack must be horizontally scalable. Adding another machine to a cluster is greatly preferable to upgrading expensive, proprietary hardware. If you have to rewrite your predictive model's implementation in order to deploy it, you aren't being very agile. This is why we use Spark MLlib in preference to tools tailored for single machines.

We also require that transferring between layers of the stack, up and down, must be done in a single line of code. This is a tall order in today's configuration-intensive environment, but it is one we are able to satisfy through the careful selection of tools. Taken together, these requirements enable us to be productive at scale.

Python 3

In writing this book, I used Python 3, and I strongly recommend you do so as well. The Vagrant and EC2 images both have Python 3 installed already, so you don't need to do anything if you use those.

You *could* use Python 2.7 by changing the formatting of exceptions to match 2.7 syntax, whenever the code doesn't run. That is for the most part the only Python 3–specific syntax we use. The other use of Python 3–specific code is the use of bytes instead of strings in the Kafka API in Chapter 8. Python 2.7 users might find another bug or two, but it should be easy to resolve them with one-line changes. That being said, again, I strongly recommend using Python 3.

Note that Spark 2.1.0 doesn't work with Python 3.6, so we use Python 3.5 in this book. This will be resolved in Spark 2.1.1+, which will be out soon after the time of publication.

Anaconda and Miniconda

We use Anaconda Python 3.5 in this book, because Anaconda has emerged as the leading Python distribution for data science. Anaconda is a Python distribution by Continuum Analytics that includes over 400 of the most popular data science libraries. Compiling and installing libraries like numpy and scipy can be tough, so Anaconda gives you a jumpstart.

While I recommend full-blown Anaconda for your own computer, for the Vagrant and EC2 images I actually had to use Miniconda, Anaconda's little brother. This is because Anaconda is large and can take a long time (20 or 30 minutes) to download. Miniconda, on the other hand, downloads in a few minutes. Miniconda is like Anaconda, but has fewer packages installed. Fortunately, the conda and pip utilities can install those packages we require in no time, giving us a streamlined Python 3 distribution suited to our needs.

Jupyter notebooks

In Chapters 7 and 9 we use IPython/Jupyter notebooks (*http://jupyter.org/*) to work with Python interactively to visualize data and train and improve predictive models. Jupyter notebooks enable us to share our analyses on the web, complete with stored variables, charts, and data tables.

Why don't we try out Jupyter notebooks, just to get familiar with them? If you're using the Vagrant or EC2 images, a Jupyter notebook is already running in the project root directory, which you can visit at *http://localhost:8888*.

This will bring up a window listing files in the example code *Agile_Data_Code_2* directory. Select New→Python 3 (Figure 2-8).

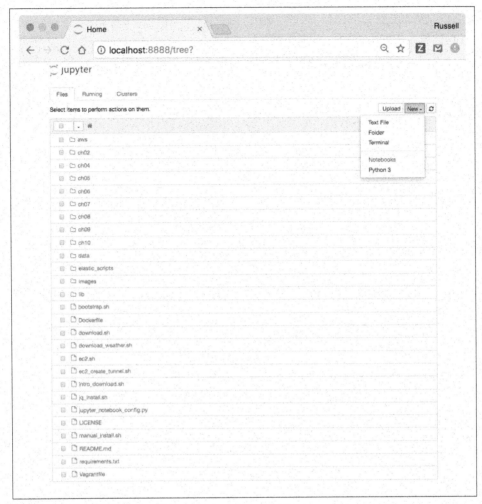

Figure 2-8. Jupyter home page

This will open a Jupyter notebook in a new tab of your browser (Figure 2-9). Type `print("Hello, World!")` and click the Play button. Python on the web—pretty cool, right?

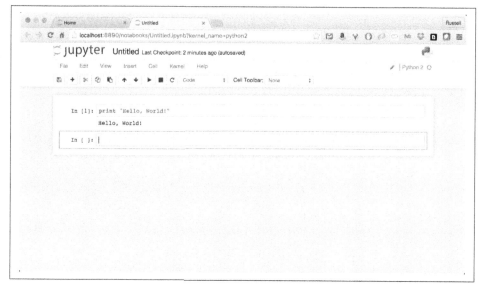

Figure 2-9. A Jupyter notebook

We'll stop here for now. Don't worry, we'll return to Jupyter notebooks in later chapters.

Serializing Events with JSON Lines and Parquet

In our stack, we use a serialization system called JSON Lines (*http://jsonlines.org/*) (see Figure 2-10). You may also hear this described as newline-delimited JSON, or NDJSON (*http://ndjson.org*), but technically JSON Lines does not support empty lines, whereas NDJSON does. JSON allows us to access our data in a common format across languages and tools.

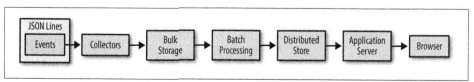

Figure 2-10. Serializing events

But JSON Lines isn't suitable for all use cases—in particular, when performance matters and data is tabular. In these instances, we'll use the Apache Parquet (*https://parquet.apache.org/*) format. Parquet is a cross-platform data format that stores data in such a way that pulling out a few columns is much more performant than loading entire lines. This will help keep our analysis realtime.

Abandoning Avro

The first edition of this book used Avro for serialization, but I have moved to carriage-return JSON (JSON Lines/NDJSON) for all data processing because while I have often regretted using Avro when I ran into a bug in one of the Avro libraries, I have never once, ever, regretted using JSON. Most programming languages support JSON natively. It is the best format available for building analytics applications.

Technically, there are many types of data that Avro can serialize more efficiently than doing so in JSON. For instance, it can be more efficient when encoding images, non-UTF-8 text, or binary blobs. However, key/value or blob stores are where images and blobs belong, and referring to them there from JSON is the best approach. Non-UTF-8 strings should be converted to UTF-8 before serialization, and Unicode in Avro can be painful (*https:// issues.apache.org/jira/browse/AVRO-565*). Avro has more features than JSON, but that is actually the problem I run into with it— Avro does things that are actually best handled elsewhere. Since we get to choose our architecture (many people don't), JSON is a better choice from the get-go. That doesn't mean Avro is a bad format; it isn't! Recall that we value simplicity, and JSON is far simpler than Avro. Sorry, Doug, we still love you though :)

JSON for Python

The `json` module is part of the Python 2.7 and 3.x standard library (*http://bit.ly/ 1upkGOV*). No installation is required. To read and write JSON Lines, a few lines of code are required. Follow along at *ch02/test_json.py* (*http://bit.ly/2oCtUxR*):

```
#
# How to read and write JSON and JSON Lines files using Python
#
import sys, os, re
import json
import codecs

ary_of_objects = [
  {'name': 'Russell Jurney', 'title': 'CEO'},
  {'name': 'Muhammad Imran', 'title': 'VP of Marketing'},
  {'name': 'Fe Mata', 'title': 'Chief Marketing Officer'},
]

path = "/tmp/test.jsonl"

#
# Write our objects to jsonl
#
f = codecs.open(path, 'w', 'utf-8')
```

```
    for row_object in ary_of_objects:
      # ensure_ascii=False is essential or errors/corruption will occur
      json_record = json.dumps(row_object, ensure_ascii=False)
      f.write(json_record + "\n")
    f.close()

    print("Wrote JSON Lines file /tmp/test.jsonl")

    #
    # Read this jsonl file back into objects
    #
    ary_of_objects = []
    f = codecs.open(path, "r", "utf-8")
    for line in f:
      record = json.loads(line.rstrip("\n|\r"))
      ary_of_objects.append(record)
    print(ary_of_objects)
    print("Read JSON Lines file /tmp/test.jsonl")
```

I've created some helpers that hide the details of these operations:

```
    import codecs, json

    def write_json_file(obj, path):
        '''Dump an object and write it out as JSON to a file.'''
        f = codecs.open(path, 'w', 'utf-8')
        f.write(json.dumps(obj, ensure_ascii=False))
        f.close()

    def write_json_lines_file(ary_of_objects, path):
        '''Dump a list of objects out as a JSON Lines file.'''
        f = codecs.open(path, 'w', 'utf-8')
        for row_object in ary_of_objects:
          json_record = json.dumps(row_object, ensure_ascii=False)
          f.write(json_record + "\n")
        f.close()

    def read_json_file(path):
        '''Turn a normal JSON file (no CRs per record) into an object.'''
        text = codecs.open(path, 'r', 'utf-8').read()
        return json.loads(text)

    def read_json_lines_file(path):
        '''Turn a JSON Lines file (CRs per record) into an array of objects.'''
        ary = []
        f = codecs.open(path, "r", "utf-8")
        for line in f:
          record = json.loads(line.rstrip("\n|\r"))
          ary.append(record)
        return ary
```

Verify that the records are present:

```
$ ls -lah /tmp/test.jsonl

-rw-r--r-- 1 rjurney wheel 154B Mar 17 17:19 /tmp/test.jsonl
```

And let's check that the contents of the file we wrote look right:

```
$ cat /tmp/test.jsonl

{"name": "Russell Jurney", "title": "CEO"}
{"name": "Muhammad Imran", "title": "VP of Marketing"}
{"name": "Fe Mata", "title": "Chief Marketing Officer"}
```

Everything looks okay! We'll make use of these helpers in the future, and you can find these and other utilities we use throughout the book at utils.py (*https://github.com/ rjurney/Agile_Data_Code_2/blob/master/lib/util.py*). That's it! Using JSON Lines in Python is nearly effortless.

Collecting Data

In addition to being used to perform work in real time, Kafka (Figure 2-11) has emerged as the preferred way to shuffle data wherever it is needed. For Agile Data Science to do its work, we need access to logs and other data on a distributed filesystem. For development purposes, however, it is easier to work locally. Accordingly, we'll be using our local filesystem for the examples in the book, and our data collection will mostly consist of downloading files to process locally. In production, we'd be more likely to collect events from Kafka or Amazon Kinesis and sync them to S3 for batch processing.

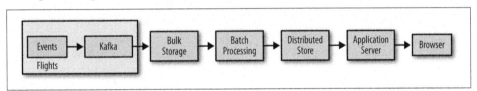

Figure 2-11. Collecting data with Kafka

Data Processing with Spark

Spark is the leading general-purpose distributed data processing platform. Spark works by breaking up data processing across networks of commodity PC machines, each acting on data on its own local disk and RAM. Spark's job is to coordinate these machines into a single computing platform. The fact that Spark is a distributed platform is essential to it scaling to data of any size, and Spark is great at this. It works well in "local mode" on one machine, and it works well on clusters of thousands of machines. This meets our requirement that our tools scale to data of any size. Spark is also excellent glue, with connectors to many different systems including Kafka and databases like MongoDB.

Spark is an iterative improvement on an older system called Hadoop, which we used in the first edition of this book. Spark has rapidly grown to replace Hadoop's Map-Reduce as the default way jobs are run on Hadoop clusters. Making use of the foundation created by the Hadoop Distributed File System (*http://bit.ly/2oL7OJQ*) (HDFS) and Apache Hadoop Common (*http://bit.ly/2oCuFa7*), Spark speeds things up by moving processing from on disk to in RAM. In this second edition, Spark replaces Hadoop outright (Figure 2-12). Spark is much faster, and is a comparative joy to work with!

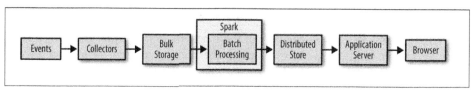

Figure 2-12. Processing data with Spark

Hadoop required

Spark is built on top of the Hadoop ecosystem, which is why its meteoric rise has been possible. Spark has now largely displaced Hadoop in the top shops, with the enterprise lagging somewhat. To use Spark, we need to take a quick detour and install Hadoop. This has been done for you on the Vagrant and EC2 images, but check Appendix A if you need to do a manual install.

Processing data with Spark

Figure 2-13 shows the Apache Spark ecosystem. Spark runs on top of HDFS or S3 and includes Spark SQL, Spark MLlib, and Spark Streaming.

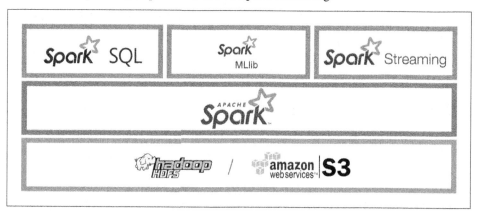

Figure 2-13. Apache Spark ecosystem

Spark local mode lets us run Spark on small data locally, for development. We'll be using Spark local mode throughout the book. The idea is that you can develop locally to learn, and then later on use a Spark cluster as your data grows—although we should note that, with EC2 instances available with 2 TB of RAM (*http://amzn.to/2oyyI5D*), "local mode" in Spark can still process pretty big datasets! The reason to use a cluster, then, is more around reliability through redundancy and satisfying the cost/benefit curve, where multiple cheaper machines are less expensive than one monster.

Once we've got Spark and its dependencies installed and our environment set up, we can get down to some dataflows in Spark. You can run PySpark anywhere via the pyspark command, but to run the examples in the book, make sure you're in the *Agile_Data_Code_2* root directory when you do so. If you're new to Spark, you should pull up the Spark Programming Guide (*https://spark.apache.org/docs/1.6.1/programming-guide.html*) and follow along.

You should see a prompt like the one in Figure 2-14.

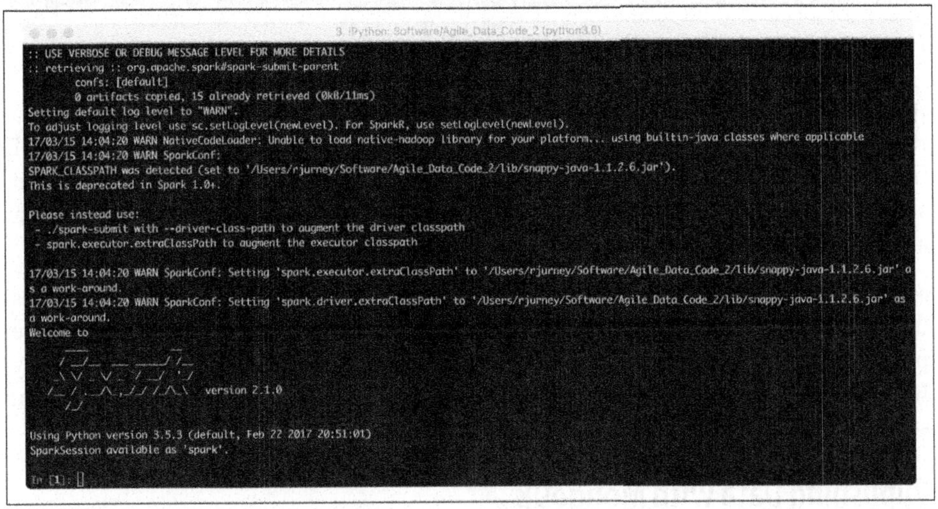

Figure 2-14. iPython PySpark console

Enter the following lines:

```
csv_lines = sc.textFile("data/example.csv")
data = csv_lines.map(lambda line: line.split(","))
data.collect()
```

This produces the output shown in Figure 2-15.

```
 3. IPython: Software/Agile_Data_Code_2 (python3.5)
 - ./spark-submit with --driver-class-path to augment the driver classpath
 - spark.executor.extraClassPath to augment the executor classpath

17/03/15 14:04:20 WARN SparkConf: Setting 'spark.executor.extraClassPath' to '/Users/rjurney/Software/Agile_Data_Code_2/lib/snappy-java-1.1.2.6.jar' a
s a work-around.
17/03/15 14:04:20 WARN SparkConf: Setting 'spark.driver.extraClassPath' to '/Users/rjurney/Software/Agile_Data_Code_2/lib/snappy-java-1.1.2.6.jar' as
a work-around.
Welcome to
      ____              __
     / __/__  ___ _____/ /__
    _\ \/ _ \/ _ `/ __/  '_/
   /__ / .__/\_,_/_/ /_/\_\   version 2.1.0
      /_/

Using Python version 3.5.3 (default, Feb 22 2017 20:51:01)
SparkSession available as 'spark'.

In [1]: csv_lines = sc.textFile("data/example.csv")
   ...: data = csv_lines.map(lambda line: line.split(","))
   ...: data.collect()
Out[1]:
[['Russell Jurney', 'Relato', 'CEO'],
 ['Florian Liebert', 'Mesosphere', 'CEO'],
 ['Don Brown', 'Rocana', 'CIO'],
 ['Steve Jobs', 'Apple', 'CEO'],
 ['Donald Trump', 'The Trump Organization', 'CEO'],
 ['Russell Jurney', 'Data Syndrome', 'Principal Consultant']]

In [2]:
```

Figure 2-15. Spark "Hello, World!"

As you work with PySpark, you will want to have the API documentation up in separate tabs in your browser for quick reference. There are two APIs to PySpark: RDD (*http://bit.ly/2p5IM9z*) and DataFrame (*http://bit.ly/2oewrvy*). (You will want to consult the RDD, DataFrame, and MLlib docs in separate tabs in your browser.) You may also want to consult the Spark ML docs (*http://bit.ly/2pDBt4X*).

So that is "Hello, World!" in Spark! We'll be using Spark any time we want to process data. Even if the size of the data doesn't require Spark right now, we are future-proofing our application against data growth or application scale by using Spark anyway. Our pattern is "aggregate, process, publish," so we won't be doing more than sorting our data in the database from which it is retrieved.

Publishing Data with MongoDB

Spark doesn't communicate directly with web application servers. To feed our data to a web application, we need to publish it in some kind of database. While many choices are appropriate, we'll use MongoDB for its ease of use, document orientation, and excellent Spark integration (Figure 2-16). With MongoDB and PySpark, we can define any arbitrary schema in PySpark, and save it to a corresponding relation with that schema in MongoDB. There is no overhead in managing schemas as we derive new relations—we simply manipulate our data into publishable form in PySpark. That's agile! This satisfies the requirement that transferring between layers of the stack should take a single command, or one line of code.

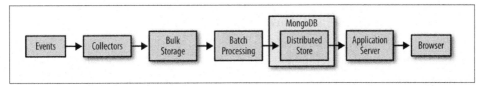

Figure 2-16. Publishing data to MongoDB

Booting Mongo

To get started with MongoDB, all you have to do is invoke the Mongo client and supply it with a database name:

```
mongo agile_data_science
```

This will bring up the Mongo console, which uses JavaScript. It gives you the `db` object with which to interact with the database. Instead of tables, Mongo has collections. You can insert a document in a collection like so:

```
> db.my_collection.insert({"name": "Russell Jurney"});
```

And you can retrieve one like so:

```
> db.my_collection.find({"name": "Russell Jurney"});
{ "_id" : ObjectId("58cb6959271b8bc38063eb01"), "name" : "Russell Jurney" }
```

That is about all we will demand of our database for now, so that is where we will leave it. We do our data processing in Spark, and only publish data in Mongo. The most complex data processing we will perform in Mongo is to list and sort records.

Pushing data to MongoDB from PySpark

Pushing data to MongoDB from PySpark is easy.

Note that we have already configured PySpark to connect to MongoDB via the `mongo-hadoop` (*https://github.com/mongodb/mongo-hadoop*) project, so we can run PySpark as normal. Check out *ch02/pyspark_mongodb.py* (*http://bit.ly/2oelwSG*), where we use the `pymongo_spark` (*http://bit.ly/2oepp9Z*) module to store the documents to MongoDB that we loaded earlier. Note that we must both import and activate the `pymongo_spark` package in order for it to add the `saveToMongoDB` method to the RDD interface:

```
import pymongo_spark
# Important: activate pymongo_spark
pymongo_spark.activate()

csv_lines = sc.textFile("data/example.csv")
data = csv_lines.map(lambda line: line.split(","))
schema_data = data.map(
  lambda x: {'name': x[0], 'company': x[1], 'title': x[2]}
)
```

```
schema_data.saveToMongoDB(
  'mongodb://localhost:27017/agile_data_science.executives'
)
```

Now we'll query our data in Mongo:

```
$ mongo agile_data_science
```

```
$ > db.executives.find()
```

```
{ "_id" : ObjectId("56f3231cd6ee8112ccbba785"),
  "name" : "Don Brown", "company" : "Rocana",
  "title" : "CIO" }
{ "_id" : ObjectId("56f3231cd6ee8112ccbba783"),
  "name" : "Russell Jurney", "company" : "Relato",
  "title" : "CEO" }
{ "_id" : ObjectId("56f3231cd6ee8112ccbba784"),
  "name" : "Florian Liebert", "company" :
  "Mesosphere", "title" : "CEO" }
```

Congratulations, you've published data from Spark to a NoSQL database! Note how easy that was: once we had our data prepared, it is a one-liner to publish it with Mongo. There is no schema overhead, which is what we need for how we work. We don't know the schema until we're ready to store, and when we do, there is little use in specifying it externally to our PySpark code. This is but one part of the stack, but this property helps us work rapidly and enables agility.

Searching Data with Elasticsearch

Elasticsearch (*http://www.elasticsearch.org/*) has become the "Hadoop for search," in that it provides a robust, easy-to-use search solution that lowers the barrier of entry to individuals wanting to search their data, large or small. Elasticsearch has a simple RESTful JSON interface, so we can use it from the command line or from any language. We'll be using Elasticsearch to search our data, to make it easy to find the records we'll be working so hard to create.

Elasticsearch should be running in the Vagrant or EC2 image you are running, but if it is not you can start it with:

```
elasticsearch -d
```

Querying Elasticsearch is a simple matter with the `curl` (*https://curl.haxx.se/*) command, which is preinstalled on the Vagrant and EC2 images, but which you should also install locally on your machine if it is not already installed.

To create an `agile_data_science` index on Elasticsearch, you can use `curl`. Check out the Elasticsearch docs on index creation (*http://bit.ly/2oCsFyP*), which feature a "copy as curl" button that gives the `curl` command for each example operation. Note that our local/cloud Elasticsearch daemon should be on port 9200.

We'll create an index with one shard and one replica, which is suitable for development. For production you would want to split the index across shards and also replicate it more than once, for redundancy and performance. You'll want to run this command from the Vagrant/EC2 image:

```
curl -XPUT 'localhost:9200/agile_data_science?pretty' \
  -H 'Content-Type: application/json' -d'
{
    "settings" : {
        "index" : {
            "number_of_shards" : 1,
            "number_of_replicas" : 1
        }
    }
}
'
```

Which should return a JSON message of success:

```
{
  "acknowledged" : true,
  "shards_acknowledged" : true
}
```

Now let's try inserting a document into the test index and then searching for it. Check out the docs on index insertion (*http://bit.ly/2nPJY0o*). The insert command uses an HTTP PUT:

```
curl -XPUT 'localhost:9200/agile_data_science/test/1?pretty' \
  -H 'Content-Type: application/json' -d'
{
    "name" : "Russell Jurney",
    "message" : "trying out Elasticsearch"
}
'
```

Which returns another message indicating success:

```
{
  "_index" : "agile_data_science",
  "_type" : "test",
  "_id" : "1",
  "_version" : 1,
  "result" : "created",
  "_shards" : {
    "total" : 2,
    "successful" : 1,
    "failed" : 0
  },
  "created" : true
}
```

Check out the docs on searching indexes (*http://bit.ly/2pZp7Y2*). The search command uses an HTTP GET:

```
curl -XGET 'localhost:9200/agile_data_science/_search?q=name:Russell&pretty'
```

We get the record and a description of the query process and the index it was in:

```
{
  "took" : 3,
  "timed_out" : false,
  "_shards" : {
    "total" : 1,
    "successful" : 1,
    "failed" : 0
  },
  "hits" : {
    "total" : 1,
    "max_score" : 0.25811607,
    "hits" : [
      {
        "_index" : "agile_data_science",
        "_type" : "test",
        "_id" : "1",
        "_score" : 0.25811607,
        "_source" : {
          "name" : "Russell Jurney",
          "message" : "trying out Elasticsearch"
        }
      }
    ]
  }
}
```

That's enough Elasticsearch for now. Now let's try writing to Elasticsearch from PySpark!

Elasticsearch and PySpark

To write data from PySpark to Elasticsearch (or read data from Elasticsearch), we'll need to use Elasticsearch for Hadoop (*https://www.elastic.co/products/hadoop*). On the prepared images, we have already preconfigured PySpark to use this project, so you won't need to do anything special to load this library. If you're using a manual install, this should be similarly configured by the install script (see Appendix A).

Making PySpark data searchable. We save from PySpark to Elasticsearch in *ch02/pyspark_elasticsearch.py (https://github.com/rjurney/Agile_Data_Code_2/blob/master/ch02/pyspark_elasticsearch.py)*:

```
csv_lines = sc.textFile("data/example.csv")
data = csv_lines.map(lambda line: line.split(","))
schema_data = data.map(
```

```
    lambda x: ('ignored_key', {'name': x[0], 'company': x[1], 'title': x[2]})
)
schema_data.saveAsNewAPIHadoopFile(
  path='-',
  outputFormatClass="org.elasticsearch.hadoop.mr.EsOutputFormat",
  keyClass="org.apache.hadoop.io.NullWritable",
  valueClass="org.elasticsearch.hadoop.mr.LinkedMapWritable",
  conf={ "es.resource" : "agile_data_science/executives" })
```

Searching our data. Now, searching our data is easy, using `curl`:

```
curl \
  'localhost:9200/agile_data_science/executives/_search?q=name:Russell*&pretty'
```

Which results in:

```
{
  "took" : 19,
  "timed_out" : false,
  "_shards" : {
    "total" : 1,
    "successful" : 1,
    "failed" : 0
  },
  "hits" : {
    "total" : 2,
    "max_score" : 1.0,
    "hits" : [
      {
        "_index" : "agile_data_science",
        "_type" : "executives",
        "_id" : "AVrfrAbdfdS5Z0IiIt78",
        "_score" : 1.0,
        "_source" : {
          "company" : "Relato",
          "name" : "Russell Jurney",
          "title" : "CEO"
        }
      },
      {
        "_index" : "agile_data_science",
        "_type" : "executives",
        "_id" : "AVrfrAbdfdS5Z0IiIt79",
        "_score" : 1.0,
        "_source" : {
          "company" : "Data Syndrome",
          "name" : "Russell Jurney",
          "title" : "Principal Consultant"
        }
      }
    ]
  }
}
```

Elasticsearch has generated an _id for us. This is a good time to point out that Elasticsearch is a great key/value or document store! It could easily replace MongoDB in our stack, and doing so could simplify and enhance scalability by reducing components. Remember, simplicity is key to scalability. That being said, Mongo has features we'll be thankful for later, so don't write it off.

Python and Elasticsearch with pyelasticsearch

pyelasticsearch (*http://pyelasticsearch.readthedocs.org/en/latest/*) is a good choice for accessing data in Elasticsearch from Python.

Using pyelasticsearch is easy—run *ch02/test_elasticsearch.py* (*http://bit.ly/2oewEPo*):

```
from pyelasticsearch import ElasticSearch
es = ElasticSearch('http://localhost:9200/')
es.search('name:Russell', index='agile_data_science')
```

Which results in:

```
{'_shards': {'failed': 0, 'successful': 1, 'total': 1},
 'hits': {'hits': [{'_id': '1',
    '_index': 'agile_data_science',
    '_score': 0.7417181,
    '_source': {'message': 'trying out Elasticsearch',
     'name': 'Russell Jurney'},
    '_type': 'test'},
   {'_id': 'AVrfrAbdfdS5Z0IiIt78',
    '_index': 'agile_data_science',
    '_score': 0.7417181,
    '_source': {'company': 'Relato', 'name': 'Russell Jurney', 'title': 'CEO'},
    '_type': 'executives'},
   {'_id': 'AVrfrAbdfdS5Z0IiIt79',
    '_index': 'agile_data_science',
    '_score': 0.7417181,
    '_source': {'company': 'Data Syndrome',
     'name': 'Russell Jurney',
     'title': 'Principal Consultant'},
    '_type': 'executives'}],
  'max_score': 0.7417181,
  'total': 3},
 'timed_out': False,
 'took': 3}
```

Searching with pyelasticsearch is as easy as with curl.

Distributed Streams with Apache Kafka

According to its website (*https://kafka.apache.org/*), "Kafka™ is used for building real-time data pipelines and streaming apps. It is horizontally scalable, fault-tolerant, wicked fast, and runs in production in thousands of companies." We'll be using Kafka streams to make predictions in "sub real time," using Spark Streaming. Kafka can also be used to collect data and aggregate it to bulk storage like HDFS or Amazon S3.

Starting up Kafka

In the prepared images, ZooKeeper and Kafka are already running. If you are not using these, you will need to start Apache Zookeeper (*https://zookeeper.apache.org/*) before you can start Kafka. Zookeeper helps to orchestrate Kafka. Start up a new console for Zookeeper, and run:

```
kafka/bin/zookeeper-server-start.sh kafka/config/zookeeper.properties
```

Now, in another new console, run the Kafka server:

```
kafka/bin/kafka-server-start.sh kafka/config/server.properties
```

Topics, console producer, and console consumer

Kafka messages are grouped into topics, so we need to create one before we can send messages through Kafka:

```
$ kafka/bin/kafka-topics.sh --create --zookeeper localhost:2181 \
  --replication-factor 1 --partitions 1 --topic test

Created topic "test".
```

We can see the topic we created with the list topics command:

```
$ kafka/bin/kafka-topics.sh --list --zookeeper localhost:2181

test
```

Now we can use the "console producer" to type some messages in manually, and send them to the test topic. Enter this command:

```
kafka/bin/kafka-console-producer.sh --broker-list localhost:9092 --topic test
```

Then type in a simple JSON message and press Return (there will be no output, so hit Ctrl-C to exit once you're done):

```
{"message": "Hello, World!"}
```

Now we can play back the test topic from the beginning, and see our message. Once again, hit Ctrl-C to exit:

```
$ kafka/bin/kafka-console-consumer.sh --bootstrap-server localhost:9092 \
  --topic test --from-beginning

{"message": "Hello, World!"}
^CProcessed a total of 1 messages
```

Realtime versus batch computing with Spark

Using Kafka is straightforward, but we'll see later how this simple framework can create complex dataflows in a way that is simple to operate. The global queue abstraction Kafka provides is extremely powerful. We'll only be using Kafka to deploy predictions using Spark Streaming, but it can do much more.

Despite Kafka's power, we'll spend most of our time in this book doing batch processing. The rule is, "If you can do it in batch, you should do it in batch." Operating a Spark cluster is much simpler than operating a pool of realtime workers using Kafka. While you can replay Kafka's history to do the equivalent of batch operations, batch computing is optimized for the process of applied research that constitutes data science work.

If you do decide to move from batch computing to realtime streams, though, PySpark has you covered! You can use the same code with PySpark Streaming to process messages in Kafka that you used to process them in batch mode using PySpark. It is quite natural to prototype streaming applications in batch and then convert them to streams later.

Kafka in Python with kafka-python

kafka-python (*https://github.com/dpkp/kafka-python*) provides a simple way to interact with Kafka from Python. To try it out, let's open the `Python console` and write a simple program to read from the `test` topic we just created. You can follow along at *ch02/python_kafka.py* (*http://bit.ly/2oitHfJ*), and by reading the `KafkaConsumer` documentation (*http://bit.ly/2nPvu0x*). Creating a consumer takes one line of code, but to seek to the beginning of a topic we need to assign our consumer to partition 0. Then we can `seek_to_beginning` (*http://bit.ly/2oCsuna*) and start looping through our consumer to read individual messages.

Note that our message value is in bytes, so we must `bytes.decode` (*https://docs.python.org/3/library/stdtypes.html#bytes.decode*) it before parsing the JSON (if you're using Python 2, this doesn't apply):—

```
import sys, os, re
import json

from kafka import KafkaConsumer, TopicPartition
consumer = KafkaConsumer()
consumer.assign([TopicPartition('test', 0)])
consumer.seek_to_beginning()

for message in consumer:
  message_bytes = message.value
  message_string = message_bytes.decode()
  message_object = json.loads(message_string)
  print(message_object)
```

This prints:

```
{'message': 'Hello, World!'}
```

Even after this one message prints, the loop will keep going. This how things would normally operate, so you'll need to hit Ctrl-C to exit the loop.

That's Kafka! We'll be using `kafka-python` in Chapter 8 to emit prediction events from our Flask web application, in order to have them carried out in PySpark Streaming. We'll be using PySpark Streaming to process messages from Kafka streams at scale.

Go ahead and leave the consoles running Zookeeper and Kafka up for a little while longer, as we will use them in the next section.

Processing Streams with PySpark Streaming

Starting up PySpark Streaming with Kafka is a little more complex than vanilla Spark. To begin, start a console producer in another SSH console, and leave it sitting idle for a moment:

```
kafka/bin/kafka-console-producer.sh --broker-list localhost:9092 --topic test
```

Next, change directory into the *Agile_Data_Code_2* directory. To run PySpark Streaming, you'll need to add the `spark-streaming-kafka` (*http://bit.ly/2oCSzT1*) Maven package to the command line:

```
pyspark --packages org.apache.spark:spark-streaming-kafka-0-8_2.11:2.1.0
```

Now, in iPython, the following code will initialize a PySpark `StreamingContext` (*http://bit.ly/2oitER4*). You can follow along in *ch02/pyspark_streaming.py* (*http://bit.ly/2p5RDrx*). Note that the `PERIOD` defines how often Spark Streaming will process mini-batches (*http://bit.ly/2oCCdK9*)—in this case, every 10 seconds:

```
import sys, os, re
import json

from pyspark import SparkContext, SparkConf
from pyspark.streaming import StreamingContext
from pyspark.streaming.kafka import KafkaUtils, OffsetRange, TopicAndPartition

# Process data every 10 seconds
PERIOD=10
BROKERS='localhost:9092'
TOPIC='test'

conf = SparkConf().set("spark.default.parallelism", 1)
sc = SparkContext(
  appName = "Agile Data Science: PySpark Streaming 'Hello, World!'", conf=conf
)
ssc = StreamingContext(sc, PERIOD)
```

With our `StreamingContext` ready, we can create a Kafka stream:

```
stream = KafkaUtils.createDirectStream(
  ssc,
  [TOPIC],
  {
    "metadata.broker.list": BROKERS,
    "group.id": "0",
  }
)
```

And finally, we can read the JSON messages and print them to the console:

```
object_stream = stream.map(lambda x: json.loads(x[1]))
object_stream.pprint()
```

To start the `StreamingContext` and begin processing Kafka messages, simply run:

```
ssc.start()
```

Now, in the Kafka console producer you set up a moment ago, type a simple JSON message and hit Return:

```
{"message": "Testing PySpark Streaming!"}
```

Switching back to our iPython console, within 10 seconds we will see something like this:

```
-------------------------------------------
Time: 2016-11-19 19:54:50
-------------------------------------------
{'message': 'Testing PySpark Streaming'}
```

And that is how to process Kafka streams with PySpark Streaming! We'll return to Spark Streaming in Chapter 8, to deploy a Spark MLlib classifier in real time. For now, you can close the consoles for Zookeeper, Kafka, and the console producer.

Machine Learning with scikit-learn and Spark MLlib

We will be building predictive models using `scikit-learn` (sklearn for short) and with Spark MLlib. We'll be creating a regression in `sklearn` and a classification in Spark MLlib.

Why scikit-learn as well as Spark MLlib?

While Spark has machine learning capabilities through Spark MLlib (*http://spark.apache.org/mllib/*), `scikit-learn` contains many useful utilities around dataflow and process that MLlib lacks. `sklearn` also lets us classify or regress new examples in real time without using Kafka and Spark Streaming, which is much simpler.

The main reason we're including `scikit-learn` in a book that otherwise uses "big data" tools is that it is still incredibly useful in practice. Spark MLlib is designed to scale, but big data often reduces into small data when summarized to extract features. This means `sklearn` is sometimes a better option than Spark MLlib. If you need a simple machine learning algorithm in the middle of a dataflow, then by all means employ MLlib. But if you need to make predictions in real time and your data fits in RAM, think hard about `sklearn`. We'll cover both in Chapter 7, and move on to only working with Spark MLlib in Chapters 8 and 9.

Scheduling with Apache Airflow (Incubating)

Apache Airflow (incubating) (*https://airflow.incubator.apache.org/*) is a scheduler for directed acyclic graphs (DAGs), which are graphs that flow in one direction without loops. DAGs are very handy for describing data pipelines like the ones we'll be creating in PySpark. Airflow lets us break long data pipelines into multiple scripts that are joined logically. We'll use Airflow to deploy the data pipelines (or "dataflows") that make up the predictive application we'll be building in this book. Airflow will enable us to schedule our application to run periodically: daily, hourly, etc.

Airflow is emerging as the leading open source scheduler for data pipelines because it is controlled using Python code as opposed to configuration files. This turns out to be a much "cleaner" way to configure a scheduler.

Airflow is a tool for batch computing. It is worth noting that if you can deploy an application in batch, you probably should deploy an application in batch. If you can wrangle your application code to run daily, hourly, or even every 10 minutes, it will be simpler to deploy, operate, and maintain. The operation of a scheduler that runs a task periodically is simpler than that of a system that operates continuously in real time (although as Kafka matures this is less the case).

The code for Airflow is available on GitHub (*https://github.com/apache/incubator-airflow*). Airbnb created Airflow, and has an excellent page on Airflow (*http://nerds.airbnb.com/airflow/*) with screenshots, videos, and other documentation. Note that we'll configure Airflow for development. For production use, you will need to verify that Airflow works against a real Spark cluster.

Use Caution with Oozie

Whether an application is easier to deploy in batch or realtime mode depends heavily on one's choice of scheduler. Systems that employ convention as opposed to ruthlessly specific and voluminous configuration are easier to operate.

While Apache Oozie is the standard scheduler in the leading Hadoop distributions, **projects with deadlines should regard it with extreme caution**. At a startup I worked at, we planned to allocate one entire headcount to operate Apache Oozie for a single application. The reader is cautioned to investigate convention-based schedulers like Azkaban and Apache Airflow before using Oozie simply because it is included with the Hadoop or Spark distribution you are using.

Oozie can easily require multiple pages of XML code to achieve simple tasks. Turing-complete XML languages are a nightmare for the programmer compared to real programming languages. Oozie is optimized for the most complex applications at the most complex enterprises. If that doesn't describe your company and project, steer clear if you can. You will give thanks for having done so. This is by no means a personal attack on Oozie's developers, who built it to satisfy the most demanding enterprise scheduling requirements at Yahoo! and large enterprises, at the expense of usability for common tasks.

Alternatives to Oozie include Azkaban (*https://azkaban.github.io/*), Luigi (*https://github.com/spotify/luigi*), and Apache Airflow (*https://airflow.incubator.apache.org/*). Evaluate these before adopting Oozie.

Installing Airflow

Airflow is installed through `pip`, and is already installed on the prepared Vagrant/EC2 images. You can follow along using the Airflow installation guide (*http://bit.ly/2nPQ94A*) and Airflow configuration guide (*http://bit.ly/2p5PLiA*). Airflow is just a `pip` module, so installing it anywhere is easy. There are many options to install extra Airflow packages; for instance, if you need MySQL or Postgres support, check out the Extra Packages section of the installation guide (*http://bit.ly/2pDJx63*).

We interact with Airflow using the `airflow` command, which we'll use to control the Airflow scheduler and web application. The default path for the Airflow database, configuration file, and DAGs is ~/airflow/:

```
$ ls ~/airflow
dags  logs  plugins
```

Now visit the Airflow web interface at *http://localhost:8080/admin/*. You should see something like Figure 2-17.

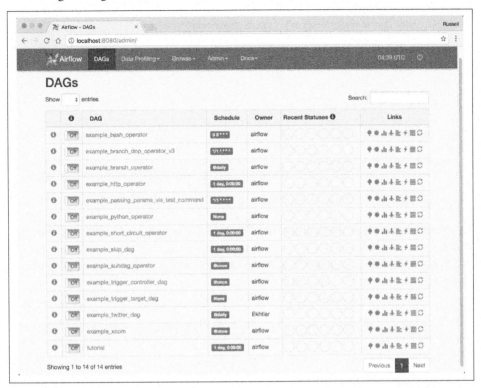

Figure 2-17. Airflow web interface

Preparing a script for use with Airflow

Although it is not in the documentation, certain things are required to create a PySpark script that can run both locally and in production with Airflow and a Spark cluster. First, we must conditionally set up the PySpark environment. Next, we must parameterize our script so that it can be called from bash at the command line with the date and relative path to the data. Together, these things let us use a script in the PySpark console during development and with Airflow in production.

Conditionally initializing PySpark. There is a simple way to write Spark scripts in such a way that they can be used interactively in the PySpark console or submitted via spark-submit with Airflow. We use the Python package findspark (*https://github.com/minrk/findspark*) to conditionally create the Spark context and session used in PySpark scripts (including those in this book), but only if they are not already existent because the PySpark console has created them. In this way, scripts can run both in the PySpark console and via spark-submit.

Check out the snippet I've created at *lib/setup_spark.py* (*http://bit.ly/2oCEODT*):

```
APP_NAME = "my_script.py"

# If there is no SparkSession, create the environment
try:
  sc and spark
except (NameError, UnboundLocalError) as e:

  import findspark
  findspark.init()
  import pyspark
  import pyspark.sql

  sc = pyspark.SparkContext()
  spark = pyspark.sql.SparkSession(sc).builder.appName(APP_NAME).getOrCreate()

# continue...
```

Parameterizing scripts on the command line. To make a script work with Airflow's date functions, you need to write a script that accepts the date/time as a command-line argument. To write a script so that it works both locally and on a Spark cluster, you must also pass in the base path to reach the data.

Let's look at how this works. We need to wrap our script in a main function and call it with command-line arguments using sys.argv. The first argument is the iso_date, which directs the script to the data for that day. The second argument is the base_path, which directs Spark to the data overall:

```
# Pass date and base path to main() from Airflow
def main(iso_date, base_path):
  APP_NAME = "pyspark_task_one.py"

  ...

  # Get today's date
  today_dt = iso8601.parse_date(iso_date)
  rounded_today = today_dt.date()

  # Load today's data
  today_input_path = "{}/ch02/data/example_name_titles_daily.json/{}".format(
    base_path,
    rounded_today.isoformat()
  )

...

if __name__ == "__main__":
  main(sys.argv[1], sys.argv[2])
```

The script can then be run from the command line:

```
python ch02/pyspark_task_one.py 2016-12-01 .
```

Creating an Airflow DAG in Python

Let's try running a simple task using Airflow. Remember, do not name a file *airflow.py* or it will mess up the Airflow Python system imports!

The first thing we need to do is initialize the Airflow database, if it hasn't already been initialized:

```
airflow initdb
```

Next, we need to link our Airflow DAG setup script, *airflow_test.py (http://bit.ly/2oCwLHe)*, into our Airflow DAGs directory, *~/airflow/dags*. It will not work outside of *~/airflow/dags*. Check out *ch02/setup_airflow_test.sh (http://bit.ly/2oCAnZN)*:

```
#!/usr/bin/env bash

ln -s $PROJECT_HOME/ch02/airflow_setup.py ~/airflow/dags/
```

Our Airflow setup script, *airflow_test.py (http://bit.ly/2oCwLHe)*, is fairly simple. First we define a configuration object, and use it to create a DAG *(http://bit.ly/2oCwW5f)*:

```
import sys, os, re

from airflow import DAG
from airflow.operators.bash_operator import BashOperator

from datetime import datetime, timedelta
import iso8601

project_home = os.environ["PROJECT_HOME"]

default_args = {
  'owner': 'airflow',
  'depends_on_past': False,
  'start_date': iso8601.parse_date("2016-12-01"),
  'email': ['russell.jurney@gmail.com'],
  'email_on_failure': True,
  'email_on_retry': True,
  'retries': 3,
  'retry_delay': timedelta(minutes=5),
}

# timedelta 1 is 'run daily'
dag = DAG(
  'agile_data_science_airflow_test',
  default_args=default_args,
  schedule_interval=timedelta(1)
)
```

Next, we create a BashOperator (*https://airflow.incubator.apache.org/code.html#airflow.operators.BashOperator*) for each script in our dataflow. We define the command that runs our script from bash with variables for its parameters and path, and use built-in and user-supplied parameters to fill out this command. The ds variable is a built-in variable that contains the date the Airflow uses to run that command. Then we feed in the filename of our script along with the base_path:

```
# Run a simple PySpark script
pyspark_local_task_one = BashOperator(
    task_id = "pyspark_local_task_one",
    bash_command = """spark-submit \
    --master {{ params.master }}
    {{ params.base_path }}/{{ params.filename }} {{ ds }} {{ params.base_path }}
    """,
    params = {
        "master": "local[8]",
        "filename": "ch02/pyspark_task_one.py",
        "base_path": "{}/".format(project_home)
    },
    dag=dag
)

# Run another simple PySpark script that depends on the previous one
pyspark_local_task_two = BashOperator(
    task_id = "pyspark_local_task_two",
    bash_command = """spark-submit \
    --master {{ params.master }}
    {{ params.base_path }}/{{ params.filename }} {{ ds }} {{ params.base_path }}
    """,
    params = {
        "master": "local[8]",
        "filename": "ch02/pyspark_task_two.py",
        "base_path": "{}/".format(project_home)
    },
    dag=dag
)
```

Finally, we set a dependency between the first and second scripts:

```
# Add the dependency from the second to the first task
pyspark_local_task_two.set_upstream(pyspark_local_task_one)
```

Now we just run the script we linked into *~/airflow/dags*, and it will be available to the Airflow system. Note that the script must be linked or copied to *~/airflow/dags*, or running it will not have any effect. Note also that the date and timestamp in the output here and later in the text have been removed because of page width constraints:

```
$ python ~/airflow/dags/airflow_test.py

[... 15:04:37,875] {__init__.py:36} INFO - Using executor SequentialExecutor
```

That's it! The script has created a DAG within Airflow that we can run, schedule, and backfill. Let's take a look at the complete scripts we're using in this example as part of the Airflow DAG we just created.

Complete scripts for Airflow

We have created two scripts to go along with our Airflow DAG, *ch02/pyspark_task_one.py* (*http://bit.ly/2nPByGm*) and *ch02/pyspark_task_two.py* (*http://bit.ly/2oii9cI*). The two scripts are short and simple. Combined, they take a list of names and titles and compute a master title for each name, before storing the result in MongoDB. Along with the Airflow DAG, the scripts are set up to run daily, operating on one day's input data and writing out one day's output data.

Check out *ch02/pyspark_task_one.py* (*http://bit.ly/2nPByGm*), which reads today's input path, creates a master title for each name, and stores the result in today's output path. Note that this script must have +x permissions to be executable by Airflow:

```
#!/usr/bin/env python

import sys, os, re
import json
import datetime, iso8601

# Pass date and base path to main() from Airflow
def main(iso_date, base_path):
  APP_NAME = "pyspark_task_one.py"

  # If there is no SparkSession, create the environment
  try:
    sc and spark
  except NameError as e:
    import findspark
    findspark.init()
    import pyspark
    import pyspark.sql

    sc = pyspark.SparkContext()
    spark = pyspark.sql.SparkSession(sc).builder.appName(APP_NAME).getOrCreate()

  # Get today's date
  today_dt = iso8601.parse_date(iso_date)
  rounded_today = today_dt.date()

  # Load today's data
  today_input_path = "{}/ch02/data/example_name_titles_daily.json/{}".format(
    base_path,
    rounded_today.isoformat()
  )

  # Otherwise load the data and proceed...
```

```
people_titles = spark.read.json(today_input_path)
people_titles.show()

# Group by as an RDD
titles_by_name = people_titles.rdd.groupBy(lambda x: x["name"])

# Accept the group key/grouped data and concatenate the various titles
# into a master title
def concatenate_titles(people_titles):
  name = people_titles[0]
  title_records = people_titles[1]
  master_title = ""
  for title_record in sorted(title_records):
    title = title_record["title"]
    master_title += "{}, ".format(title)
  master_title = master_title[:-2]
  record = {"name": name, "master_title": master_title}
  return record

people_with_contactenated_titles = titles_by_name.map(concatenate_titles)
people_output_json = people_with_contactenated_titles.map(json.dumps)

# Get today's output path
today_output_path = "{}/ch02/data/example_master_titles_daily.json/{}".format(
  base_path,
  rounded_today.isoformat()
)

# Write/replace today's output path
os.system("rm -rf {}".format(today_output_path))
people_output_json.saveAsTextFile(today_output_path)

if __name__ == "__main__":
  main(sys.argv[1], sys.argv[2])
```

We can test the script at the command line like so:

```
python ch02/pyspark_task_one.py 2016-12-01 .
```

Which has the debug output:

```
+-------------+-------------+
|         name|        title|
+-------------+-------------+
|Russell Jurney|Data Scientist|
|Russell Jurney|       Author|
|Russell Jurney|    Dog Lover|
|    Bob Jones|          CEO|
|    Susan Shu|     Attorney|
+-------------+-------------+
```

The second script, *ch02/pyspark_task_two.py* (*http://bit.ly/2oii9cI*), is similar, reading the output from the first script and storing it to MongoDB (again, this script must have +x permissions to be executable by Airflow):

```python
#!/usr/bin/env python

import sys, os, re
import json
import datetime, iso8601

# Pass date and base path to main() from Airflow
def main(iso_date, base_path):
  APP_NAME = "pyspark_task_two.py"

  # If there is no SparkSession, create the environment
  try:
    sc and spark
  except NameError as e:
    import findspark
    findspark.init()
    import pyspark
    import pyspark.sql

    sc = pyspark.SparkContext()
    spark = pyspark.sql.SparkSession(sc).builder.appName(APP_NAME).getOrCreate()

  import pymongo
  import pymongo_spark
  # Important: activate pymongo_spark.
  pymongo_spark.activate()

  # Get today's date
  today_dt = iso8601.parse_date(iso_date)
  rounded_today = today_dt.date()

  # Load today's data
  today_input_path = "{}/ch02/data/example_master_titles_daily.json/{}".format(
    base_path,
    rounded_today.isoformat()
  )

  # Otherwise load the data and proceed
  people_master_titles_raw = sc.textFile(today_input_path)
  people_master_titles = people_master_titles_raw.map(json.loads)
  print(people_master_titles.first())

  people_master_titles.saveToMongoDB(
    'mongodb://localhost:27017/agile_data_science.people_master_titles'
  )

if __name__ == "__main__":
  main(sys.argv[1], sys.argv[2])
```

We can test this script at the command line like so:

```
python ch02/pyspark_task_two.py 2016-12-01 .
```

Which, along with Spark's output, will print the debug output:

```
{'master_title': 'Author, Data Scientist, Dog Lover', 'name': 'Russell Jurney'}
```

Note that the scripts are logically linked in the DAG, and this will make operating them much easier than if we'd scheduled them with something like `cron`.

Testing a task in Airflow

Now that we have an Airflow DAG and its corresponding tasks, we need to test the tasks though Airflow. Before we get started, let's inspect Airflow's list of commands:

```
$ airflow

[...,293] {__init__.py:36} INFO - Using executor SequentialExecutor
usage: airflow [-h]
                {variables,worker,upgradedb,task_state,trigger_dag,clear,
                scheduler,resetdb,pause,serve_logs,render,backfill,
                flower,webserver,kerberos,version,list_tasks,
                initdb,list_dags,test,run,unpause}
                ...
airflow: error: the following arguments are required: subcommand
```

Let's start by listing the available DAGs to see if ours is available:

```
$ airflow list_dags

agile_data_science_airflow_test
example_bash_operator
example_branch_dop_operator_v3
example_branch_operator
...
```

Next up, let's list the available tasks for our DAG:

```
$ airflow list_tasks agile_data_science_airflow_test

pyspark_local_task_one
pyspark_local_task_two
```

Now let's run `pyspark_local_task_one`:

```
airflow test agile_data_science_airflow_test pyspark_local_task_one 2016-12-01
```

We should see the same output as from our command-line test of the *pyspark_task_one.py (http://bit.ly/2ooqfBZ)* script, albeit piped through Airflow's `BashOperator`:

```
[...,508] {bash_operator.py:77} INFO - +--------------+--------------+
[...,508] {bash_operator.py:77} INFO - |          name|         title|
[...,508] {bash_operator.py:77} INFO - +--------------+--------------+
[...,508] {bash_operator.py:77} INFO - |Russell Jurney|Data Scientist|
[...,508] {bash_operator.py:77} INFO - |Russell Jurney|        Author|
[...,508] {bash_operator.py:77} INFO - |Russell Jurney|     Dog Lover|
[...,508] {bash_operator.py:77} INFO - |     Bob Jones|           CEO|
[...,508] {bash_operator.py:77} INFO - |     Susan Shu|      Attorney|
[...,508] {bash_operator.py:77} INFO - +--------------+--------------+
[...,508] {bash_operator.py:77} INFO -
[...,953] {bash_operator.py:80} INFO - Command exited with return code 0
```

Now let's test pyspark_local_task_two:

```
airflow test agile_data_science_airflow_test pyspark_local_task_two 2016-12-01
```

Again, we should see the expected debug output, piped through BashOperator:

```
[...,046] {bash_operator.py:77} INFO - {'name': 'Russell Jurney', 'master_title':
    'Author, Data Scientist, Dog Lover'}
[...,476] {bash_operator.py:80} INFO - Command exited with return code 0
```

Running a DAG in Airflow

Now that we've tested out the tasks individually, we need to run them in such a way
that their execution is logged to the database so this period's run won't be repeated.
The run command is just like the test command:

```
airflow run agile_data_science_airflow_test pyspark_local_task_one 2016-12-01
```

You can see the logs of this run in *~/airflow/logs*:

```
$ cat ~/airflow/logs/agile_data_science_airflow_test/pyspark_local_task_one \
    /2016-12-01T00\:00\:00

...

[...,723] {sequential_executor.py:26} INFO - Executing command:
airflow run agile_data_science_airflow_test pyspark_local_task_one
...T00:00:00 --local -sd DAGS_FOLDER/airflow_test.py
[... 15:40:13,815] {models.py:154} INFO - Filling up the DagBag
from /Users/rjurney/airflow/dags/airflow_test.py
[... 15:40:14,951] {models.py:154} INFO - Filling up the DagBag
from /Users/rjurney/airflow/dags/airflow_test.py
[... 15:40:14,997] {models.py:1150} INFO - Task <TaskInstance:
agile_data_science_airflow_test.pyspark_local_task_one 2016-12-01
00:00:00 [success]> previously succeeded on 2016-12-04 15:36:47
.869543
```

To clear the record of this run, use the clear command:

```
airflow clear -s 2016-12-01 -e 2016-12-01 agile_data_science_airflow_test
```

Backfilling data in Airflow

It is great to be able to schedule operations, but what about redoing yesterday's work? For instance, what if we create a new kind of prediction, and in addition to scheduling it to run every night from now on, we also need to go back and fill in the data for the last two weeks? The `backfill` command handles this type of operation.

It's a one-liner to backfill just one day of data (the only day we have):

```
airflow backfill -s 2016-12-01 -e 2016-12-01 agile_data_science_airflow_test
```

Pretty cool! This is a very powerful feature. For instance, if a server went down, this command could easily regenerate its content in short order. Airflow saves us from building our own system to handle this inevitable situation.

The power of Airflow

I hope this section has demonstrated the power of Airflow and shown why we went to so much trouble wrangling our scripts into command-line form so that they could work with Airflow date handling and `spark-submit` relative paths. You'll follow a similar path when moving any batch PySpark script to production, so keep this section in mind as you do so. The documentation doesn't spell out what is required to make Airflow work with PySpark, so this should be a handy reference.

We'll talk more about Airflow in Chapter 8, when we deploy PySpark data pipelines in batch mode using Airflow.

Reflecting on Our Workflow

Compared to querying MySQL or MongoDB directly, this workflow might seem hard. Notice, however, that our stack has been optimized for time-consuming and thoughtful data processing, with occasional publishing. Also, this way we won't hit a wall when our realtime queries don't scale anymore as they become increasingly complex.

Once our application is plumbed efficiently, the team can work together efficiently—but not before. The stack is the foundation of our agility.

Lightweight Web Applications

The next step is turning our published data into an interactive application. As shown in Figure 2-18, we'll use lightweight web frameworks to do that.

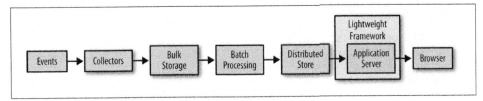

Figure 2-18. To the web with Python and Flask

We choose lightweight web frameworks because they are simple and fast to work with. Unlike with CRUD applications, mined data is the star of the show here. We use read-only databases and simple application frameworks because that fits with the applications we build and how we offer value.

Given the following examples in Python/Flask, you can easily implement a solution in Sinatra, Rails, Django, Node.js, or your favorite language and web framework.

Python and Flask

According to the Bottle documentation (*http://bottlepy.org/docs/dev/*), "Flask is a fast, simple, and lightweight WSGI micro web framework for Python."

Excellent instructions for using Flask are available on the website (*http://flask.pocoo.org/*).

Flask echo microservice. Run our echo Flask app, *ch02/web/test_flask.py* (*http://bit.ly/2nPMZxV*):

```
from flask import Flask
app = Flask(__name__)

@app.route("/<input>")
def hello(input):
  return input

if __name__ == "__main__": app.run(debug=True)
```

And verify it works with `curl`:

```
$ curl http://localhost:5000/hello%20world!
```

```
hello world!
```

Python and Mongo with pymongo. `pymongo` presents a simple interface for MongoDB in Python. To test it out, run *ch02/test_pymongo.py* (*http://bit.ly/2pkiYWL*):

```
from pymongo import MongoClient
client = MongoClient()
db = client.agile_data_science
list(db.executives.find({"name": "Russell Jurney"}))
```

The output is like so:

```
[{u'_id': ObjectId('56f32e65d6ee81199682dcce'),
  u'company': u'Relato',
  u'name': u'Russell Jurney',
  u'title': u'CEO'}]
```

Displaying executives in Flask. Now we use pymongo with Flask to display the sent_counts we stored in Mongo using Pig and MongoStorage. Run *ch02/web/ flask_pymongo.py (http://bit.ly/2oLplC2)*:

```python
from flask import Flask
from pymongo import MongoClient
import bson.json_util

# Set up Flask
app = Flask(__name__)

# Set up Mongo
client = MongoClient() # defaults to localhost
db = client.agile_data_science

# Fetch from/to totals, given a pair of email addresses
@app.route("/executive/<name>")
def executive(name):
  executive = db.executives.find({"name": name})
  return bson.json_util.dumps(list(executive))

if __name__ == "__main__": app.run(debug=True)
```

Now we can visit the URL in a browser or curl this web service and see our data:

```
[{"company": "Relato",
  "_id": {"$oid": "56f32e65d6ee81199682dcce"},
  "name": "Russell Jurney", "title": "CEO"
}]
```

And we're done! (See Figure 2-19.)

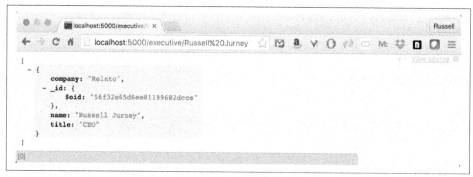

Figure 2-19. Undecorated data on the web

Congratulations! You've published data on the web. Now let's make it presentable.

Presenting Our Data

Design and presentation impact the value of your work. In fact, one way to think of Agile Data Science is as iterative data design. The output of our data models matches our views, and in that sense design and data processing are not distinct. Instead, they are part of the same collaborative activity: data design. With that in mind, it is best that we start out with a solid, clean design for our data and work from there (see Figure 2-20).

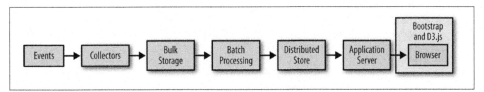

Figure 2-20. Presenting our data with Bootstrap and d3.js

Booting Bootstrap

Let's try wrapping our previous example in a table, styled with Bootstrap.

In *ch02/web/test_flask_bootstrap.py (https://github.com/rjurney/Agile_Data_Code_2/ blob/master/ch02/web/test_flask_bootstrap.py)*:

```
from flask import Flask, render_template
from pymongo import MongoClient
import bson.json_util

# Set up Flask
app = Flask(__name__)

# Set up Mongo
client = MongoClient() # defaults to localhost
db = client.agile_data_science

# Fetch from/to totals, given a pair of email addresses
@app.route("/executive/<name>")
def executive(name):
  executives = db.executives.find({"name": name})
  return render_template('table.html', executives=list(executives))

if __name__ == "__main__": app.run(debug=True)
```

Tables, Oh My!

That's right: tables for tabular data! Bootstrap lets us use them without shame. Now we'll update our controller to stash our data, and create a simple template to print a table.

And in our template, *ch02/web/templates/table.html* *(https://github.com/rjurney/Agile_Data_Code_2/blob/master/ch02/web/templates/table.html)*:

```html
<div class="container">
  <div class="page-header">
    <h1>Agile Data Science</h1>
  </div>
  <p class="lead">Executives</p>
  <table class="table">
    <thead>
      <th>Name</th>
      <th>Company</th>
      <th>Title</th>
    </thead>
    <tbody>
      {% for executive in executives -%}
      <tr>
        <td>{{executive.name}}</td>
        <td>{{executive.company}}</td>
        <td>{{executive.title}}</td>
      </tr>
      {% endfor -%}
    </tbody>
  </table>
</div>
```

The result, shown in Figure 2-21, is human-readable data with very little trouble!

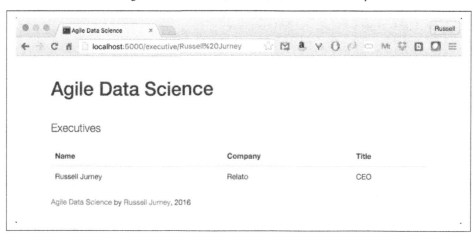

Figure 2-21. Simple data in a Bootstrap-styled table

Visualizing data with D3.js

D3.js *(http://d3js.org/)* enables data-driven documents. According to its creator, Mike Bostock:

d3 is not a traditional visualization framework. Rather than provide a monolithic system with all the features anyone may ever need, d3 solves only the crux of the problem: efficient manipulation of documents based on data. This gives d3 extraordinary flexibility, exposing the full capabilities of underlying technologies such as CSS3, HTML5, and SVG.

We'll be using D3.js to create charts in our application. Like Bootstrap, it is already installed in */static*. We'll be making charts with D3.js later on. For now, take a look at the examples gallery (*https://github.com/mbostock/d3/wiki/Gallery*) to see what is possible with D3.js.

Conclusion

We've toured our environment and have executed "Hello, World!" in each tool. Together, these tools form a data pipeline of distributed systems capable of collecting, processing, publishing, and decorating data of any size. This pipeline is easy to modify at every stage with one line of code. This pipeline will scale without our worrying about optimization at each step—optimization will be one concern, but not our main concern.

As we'll see in the next chapter, because we've created an arbitrarily scalable pipeline where every stage is easily modifiable, it is possible to return to agility. We won't quickly hit a wall as soon as we need to switch from a relational database to something else that "scales better," and we aren't subjecting ourselves to the limitations imposed by tools designed for other tasks, like online transaction processing.

We now have total freedom to use best-of-breed tools within this framework to solve hard problems and produce value. We can choose any language, any framework, and any library and glue it together to get things built.

## CHAPTER 3

Data

This chapter introduces the dataset we will work with in the rest of the book. It will also cover the kinds of tools we'll be using, and our reasoning for doing so. Finally, it will outline multiple perspectives we'll use in analyzing data for you to think about moving forward.

Air Travel Data

Air travel is an essential part of modern life. It is a fundamental part of globalized culture, linking major cities across the planet into a global urban economy. Thanks to regulation, there is a lot of aviation data out there that is freely available. In the course of the book, we'll use many aviation datasets. The core or atomic logs we'll be using are on-time records for each flight. We will supplement this with data on airlines, weather, routes, and more.

Flight on-time records aren't quite big data, but they do add up to several gigabytes per year, uncompressed. We will immediately face a "big" (or actually, a "medium") data problem—processing the data on your local machine will be just barely feasible. Working with data too large to fit in RAM requires that we use scalable tools, which is helpful as a learning device. Air travel is a familiar experience to all of us, and we'll use it to give you a sense for how to analyze and query flight data and to help you see which techniques are effective. This is cultivating *data intuition*, a major theme in Agile Data Science.

In this book, we use the same tools that you would use at petabyte scale, but in local mode on your own machine. This is more than an efficient way to process data; our choice of tools ensures that we only have to build it once, and that our application will scale up. This imparts simplicity in everything that we do, and simplicity is the heart of agility.

Flight On-Time Performance Data

Records of 90–95% of flights that originate in the US are available from the Bureau of Transportation Statistics (*http://www.transtats.bts.gov/DL_SelectFields.asp?Table_ID=236&DB_Short_Name=On-Time*). You can download these monthly, but we have already collected them for the year 2015 for you here in a single large gzipped CSV file (*http://bit.ly/2nNmsNu*).

The fields of this data are many:

```
"Year","Quarter","Month",
 "DayofMonth","DayOfWeek","FlightDate","UniqueCarrier",
 "AirlineID","Carrier","TailNum","FlightNum",
"OriginAirportID","OriginAirportSeqID","OriginCityMarketID",
"Origin","OriginCityName","OriginState","OriginStateFips",
"OriginStateName","OriginWac","DestAirportID","DestAirportSeqID",
"DestCityMarketID","Dest","DestCityName","DestState",
"DestStateFips","DestStateName","DestWac","CRSDepTime","DepTime",
"DepDelay","DepDelayMinutes","DepDel15","DepartureDelayGroups",
"DepTimeBlk","TaxiOut","WheelsOff","WheelsOn","TaxiIn",
"CRSArrTime","ArrTime","ArrDelay","ArrDelayMinutes",
"ArrDel15","ArrivalDelayGroups","ArrTimeBlk","Cancelled",
"CancellationCode","Diverted","CRSElapsedTime",
"ActualElapsedTime","AirTime","Flights","Distance",
"DistanceGroup","CarrierDelay","WeatherDelay","NASDelay","Security
Delay","LateAircraftDelay","FirstDepTime","TotalAddGTime",
"LongestAddGTime","DivAirportLandings","DivReachedDest",
"DivActualElapsedTime","DivArrDelay","DivDistance","Div1Airport",
"Div1AirportID","Div1AirportSeqID","Div1WheelsOn",
"Div1TotalGTime","Div1LongestGTime","Div1WheelsOff",
"Div1TailNum","Div2Airport","Div2AirportID",
"Div2AirportSeqID","Div2WheelsOn","Div2TotalGTime",
"Div2LongestGTime","Div2WheelsOff","Div2TailNum","Div3Airport",
"Div3AirportID","Div3AirportSeqID","Div3WheelsOn",
"Div3TotalGTime","Div3LongestGTime","Div3WheelsOff","Div3TailNum",
"Div4Airport","Div4AirportID","Div4AirportSeqID",
"Div4WheelsOn","Div4TotalGTime","Div4LongestGTime",
"Div4WheelsOff","Div4TailNum","Div5Airport","Div5AirportID",
"Div5AirportSeqID","Div5WheelsOn","Div5TotalGTime",
"Div5LongestGTime","Div5WheelsOff","Div5TailNum"
```

And a few truncated rows (formatted to fit the page) look like this:

```
2015,1,1,1,4,2015-01-01,"AA",19805,"AA","N787AA","1",12478,1247802,...,"JFK", ...
2015,1,1,2,5,2015-01-02,"AA",19805,"AA","N795AA","1",12478,...,31703,"JFK", ...
2015,1,1,3,6,2015-01-03,"AA",19805,"AA","N788AA","1",12478,...,31703,"JFK", ...
```

A description of the fields (*http://bit.ly/2plXWqS*) is available from the BTS; an excerpt is shown in Figure 3-1 We'll use to this reference to understand these numerous fields throughout the book.

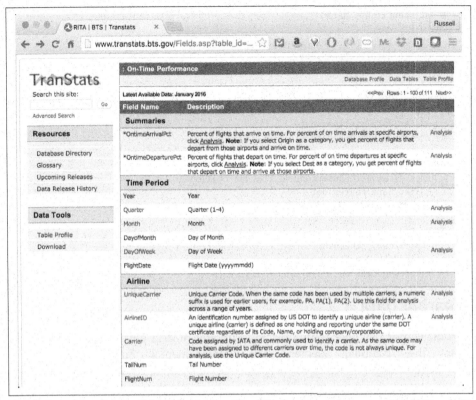

Figure 3-1. Description of fields in the On-Time Performance dataset on the BTS website

This is one fully denormalized table, and while it is inefficient when compared to normalized data, it is our preferred form of data. This is called *semistructured data*.

OpenFlights Database

OpenFlights.org publishes a database (*http://openflights.org/data.html*) of information on airports, airlines, and routes. We'll be using this database to characterize airports in our analysis. It costs money to gather this data, but the database is free to download (though a donation is suggested—please, if you make use of this data in a real application, consider donating to support the collection of this invaluable dataset).

Check out *download.sh* (*http://bit.ly/2pFwyjX*), where we fetch the OpenFlights database:

```
# Get openflights data
wget -P /tmp/ \
  https://raw.githubusercontent.com/jpatokal/openflights/ \
    master/data/airports.dat
mv /tmp/airports.dat data/airports.csv

wget -P /tmp/ \
  https://raw.githubusercontent.com/jpatokal/openflights/ \
    master/data/airlines.dat
mv /tmp/airlines.dat data/airlines.csv

wget -P /tmp/ \
  https://raw.githubusercontent.com/jpatokal/openflights/ \
    master/data/routes.dat
mv /tmp/routes.dat data/routes.csv

wget -P /tmp/ \
  https://raw.githubusercontent.com/jpatokal/openflights/ \
    master/data/countries.dat
mv /tmp/countries.dat data/countries.csv
```

Weather Data

Fortunately for us, there is an enormous amount of data on the weather available from the National Centers for Environmental Information (*https:// www.ncdc.noaa.gov/*) (NCEI), formerly the National Climatic Data Center (NCDC).

Check out *download_weather.sh* (*http://bit.ly/2nRYGjB*), where we download the WBAN Master List. This list comes with geographical coordinates, latitudes and longitudes, which we'll use to associate stations with airports to enhance the prediction of flight delays. This script can take a while, so you may want to run it in the background now and come back to it:

```
cd data

# Get the station master list as pipe-separated values
curl -Lko /tmp/wbanmasterlist.psv.zip \
  http://www.ncdc.noaa.gov/homr/file/wbanmasterlist.psv.zip
unzip -o /tmp/wbanmasterlist.psv.zip
```

We'll also download quality-controlled hourly and daily summaries of the weather for all WBAN stations for the year 2015:

```
# Get monthly files of daily summaries for all stations
# curl -Lko /tmp/ \
  http://www.ncdc.noaa.gov/orders/qclcd/ \
    QCLCD201501.zip
for i in $(seq -w 1 12)
do
  curl -Lko /tmp/QCLCD2015${i}.zip http://www.ncdc.noaa.gov/orders/qclcd/ \
    QCLCD2015${i}.zip
```

```
    unzip -o /tmp/QCLCD2015${i}.zip
  done
```

Data Processing in Agile Data Science

Data Processing in Agile Data Science is done using semistructured data, with both SQL queries and *NoSQL* dataflow programming. We use evolving schemas that are defined on the fly, and we serialize data as JSON. Taken together, these methods enable us to be productive as we refine data into new forms.

Structured Versus Semistructured Data

Wikipedia (*http://bit.ly/2p3LbRm*) defines semistructured data as:

> A form of structured data that does not conform with the formal structure of data models associated with relational databases or other forms of data tables, but nonetheless contains tags or other markers to separate semantic elements and enforce hierarchies of records and fields within the data.

This is in contrast to relational, structured data, which means data described by rigorous external schemas and broken up into multiple tables that refer to one another to avoid data duplication. This is done before analytics begin for more efficient querying thereafter. Relational databases handling Online Transaction Processing (OLTP) (*http://bit.ly/2oDfD46*) tasks use highly normalized schemas to simplify the encoding of business rules about data.

Relational databases were the primary way data was processed and stored from the 1970s through the 2000s. SQL became the primary way people interacted directly with structured data. Before Hadoop ignited the NoSQL movement, data processing was so dominated by the relational database that it became oppressive. Data processing outside academia was locked inside relational systems. The frustration and anger that resulted is what put the "no" in NoSQL.

While Hadoop was developed to handle volumes of data too large for existent relational databases to handle, it brought about a model of data processing that was liberated from the relational schema. More importantly, Hadoop connected the tools of statistical inference and learning from academia with business data and processes. In this way, the big data trend has made new kinds of applications—analytics applications—possible.

Concurrently, other NoSQL systems for OLTP processing have replaced the relational database for many common applications. MongoDB (*https://github.com/mongodb/mongo*), which we use in the book for publishing (as opposed to processing) data, has become the go-to option for web applications.

A structured, relational view of flight data is demonstrated in the flight database of the book *Learning MySQL* (*http://oreil.ly/2pq1o0F*), by Seyed M.M. Tahaghoghi and Hugh E. Williams:, also from O'Reilly (see Figure 3-2).

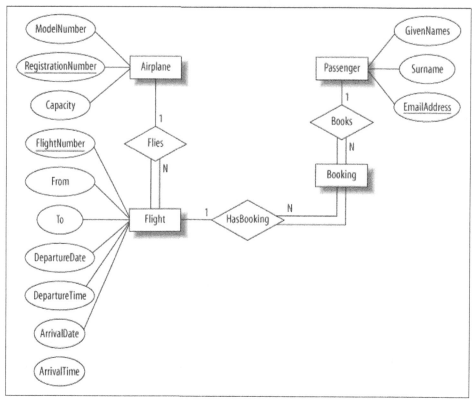

Figure 3-2. Fully structured flight database from Learning MySQL

SQL Versus NoSQL

The NoSQL movement freed us from the bonds of SQL. What does this mean? It means that NoSQL gave us options other than SQL inside relational databases to process our data. The problem with the SQL paradigm wasn't the SQL language; it was the lack of options, so that it seemed people were stuck with SQL for all data processing regardless of whether it fit or not.

In the first edition of this book, like many in the NoSQL community, we avoided SQL completely except to show that it was unsuited to our domain: building analytics applications. In this edition, we take a broader view. New tools have emerged, Spark specifically, that unify SQL and NoSQL. People have come to realize that so long as there are many options for how to process data, having SQL around is quite useful. Both SQL and NoSQL have their role in Agile Data Science, as we'll soon see.

SQL

What is the role of SQL in building analytics applications? To query a relational, structured schema, we typically use *declarative* programming languages like SQL. In SQL, we specify what we want, rather than what to do. This is different than *imperative* programming in languages like Java, Scala, or Python. In SQL, we specify the desired output rather than a set of operations on our data.

SQL is very efficient at expressing simple ad hoc queries such as this one, which uses the schema in Figure 3-2 to ask how many flights flew between pairs of cities on January 1, 2015:

```
SELECT From, To, COUNT(*)
    FROM Flight
      WHERE DepartureDate == '2015-01-01'
        GROUP BY From, To;
```

This kind of declarative programming is ideally suited to consuming and querying structured data in aggregate to produce simple charts and figures. When we know what we want, we can efficiently tell the SQL engine what that is, and it will compute the relations for us. We don't have to worry about the details of the query's execution.

SQL has two limits. The first is that we have to rely on the database to figure out how to execute our query, and it may be good or bad at this task depending on the query. With big data, this can be problematic. If the query planner screws up, we may wait literally forever for a query to return. That is to say that with large amounts of data, sometimes you must be involved in specifying the optimal query plan, and can't rely on a query planner to do it for you. With PySpark, we get to specify the *how* of any operation through dataflow programming—if we want. If not, the SQL abstraction is there to figure it out for us. We get the best of both worlds.

The other problem is complexity. Once a query becomes too complex, SQL is highly obscure. Queries become subqueries that in turn have subqueries, and this means code becomes impenetrable. For complex operations, humans are better at reading and understanding imperative code than declarative. While it was still possible to break large queries into stages with relational systems, they were not optimized to do so.

When SQL was our only option, these limits made many people miserable. In any case, now that we have other options, SQL is everyone's friend again. For simple queries, it is powerful, concise, and easy to learn.

NoSQL and Dataflow Programming

In contrast to SQL, when building analytics applications we often don't know the query we want to run, so we can't specify it. Much experimentation and iteration is required to arrive at the solution to any given problem. Data is often unavailable in a relational format. Data in the wild is not normalized; it is denormalized, fuzzy, and dirty. Extracting structure is a lengthy process that we perform iteratively as we process data to extract different features. Specifying schemas up front is not possible.

For these reasons, in Agile Data Science we often employ imperative languages against distributed systems. Imperative languages like Python and PySpark describe steps to manipulate data in pipelines. Rather than precomputing indexes against structure we don't yet have, we use many processing cores in parallel to read individual records through brute force. Spark (and Hadoop before it) makes this possible.

In addition to mapping well to technologies like Hadoop and Spark, which enable us to easily scale our data processing, imperative languages put the focus of our tools where most of the work in building analytics applications is: in iteratively and incrementally crafting one or two hard-won, key steps where we do clever things that deliver much of the value of our application. Discovering these steps is an inherently imperative process.

Compared to writing SQL queries, arriving at these clever operations is a lengthy and often exhaustive process, as we employ techniques from statistics, machine learning, and social science. Imperative programming fits the task.

Spark: SQL + NoSQL

So, SQL is optimized for querying data, whereas dataflow-oriented tools are optimized for refining it. We need to both query data—to ask questions of it—and process data—to compute new things from one or more sources of data. Fortunately for us, *Spark supports both programming paradigms!* This is the most innovative part of Spark's interface. This feature enables us to switch back and forth between declarative SQL and imperative Python, as we see fit. This is a big benefit of Spark, and it is a great leap forward compared with Hadoop, where Pig (dataflow programming) and Hive (SQL) were separate tools with, unfortunately, somewhat hostile communities.

Schemas in NoSQL

When schemas are rigorous, and SQL is our lone tool, our perspective comes to be dominated by tools optimized for consuming, rather than mining, data. Specifying tables with rigorously defined schemas gets in the way of getting things done. Our ability to connect intuitively with the data is inhibited. Working with semistructured data, on the other hand, enables us to focus on the data directly, manipulating it iteratively to extract value and to transform it into a product.

We use dataflow languages to define the form of our data in code, and then query it with SQL, or we publish it directly to a document store—all without ever formally specifying a schema! The schema is carried with the data; it is inherent rather than extrinsic. This is optimized for our process: doing data science, where we're deriving new information from multiple sources of existing data. There is no benefit to externally specifying schemas in this context—it is pure overhead. After all, we don't know what we'll wind up with until it's ready! Data science will always surprise.

Data Serialization

Although we can work with semistructured data as pure text, it is helpful to impose some kind of structure on the raw records using a format that includes a schema. Serialization systems give us this functionality. Available serialization systems include the following:

- Thrift (*http://thrift.apache.org*)
- Protobuf (*http://code.google.com/p/protobuf/*)
- Avro (*http://avro.apache.org*)

In the first edition of this book, we chose Avro. Avro allows complex data structures, it includes a schema with each file, and it has support in many tools and languages. However, we often came across bugs in the Avro implementations for different languages, and this hurt our productivity. Over and over. As a result, in this second edition, we are moving from Avro to JSON Lines (*http://jsonlines.org/*). JSON Lines, also called newline-delimited JSON (NDJSON) (*http://ndjson.org/*), is simple: one JSON record per line of text.

Extracting and Exposing Features in Evolving Schemas

As Pete Warden notes in his talk "Embracing the Chaos of Data" (*http://bit.ly/171ulz7*), most freely available data is crude and unstructured. It is the availability of huge volumes of such ugly data, and not carefully cleaned and normalized tables, that makes it "big data." Therein lies the opportunity in mining crude data into refined information, and using that information to drive new kinds of actions.

Extracted features from unstructured data get cleaned only in the harsh light of day, as users consume them and complain; if you can't ship your features as you extract them, you're in a state of free fall. The hardest part of building data products is pegging entity and feature extraction to products smaller than your ultimate vision. This is why schemas must start as blobs of unstructured text and evolve into structured data only as features are extracted.

Features must be exposed in some product form as they are created, or they will never achieve a product-ready state. Derived data that lives in the basement of your product is unlikely to shape up. It is better to create entity pages to bring entities up to a "consumer-grade" form, to incrementally improve these entities, and to progressively combine them than to try to expose myriad derived data in a grand vision from the get-go.

While mining data into well-structured information, using that information to expose new facts and make predictions that enable actions offers enormous potential for value creation. Data is brutal and unforgiving, and failing to mind its true nature will dash the dreams of the most ambitious product manager.

As we'll see throughout the book, schemas evolve and improve, and so do features that expose them. When they evolve concurrently, we are truly agile.

Conclusion

That wraps our description of the data we'll be working with. We'll introduce each additional dataset as we employ it. In the next chapter, we'll start climbing the data-value pyramid!

Climbing the Pyramid

If you can see your path laid out in front of you step by step, you know it's not your path.
Your own path you make with every step you take. That's why it's your path.

—Joseph Campbell

Part II introduces the schema for the rest of the book: the data-value pyramid. Throughout the rest of our lessons, we will use the data-value pyramid to iteratively build value from very simple records up to interactive predictions. We begin with theory, then dive into practice using the framework I previously introduced.

Building Agile Data Science products means staging an environment where reproducible insights occur, are reinforced, and are extended up the value stack. It starts simply with displaying records. It ends with driving actions that create value and capture some of it. Along the way is a voyage of discovery.

The structure of this voyage, shown in Figure II-1, is called the data-value pyramid.

The data-value stack mirrors Maslow's hierarchy of needs in the sense that lower levels must precede higher levels. The higher levels (like predictions) depend on the lower levels (like reports), so we can't skip steps. If we do so, we will lack sufficient structure and understanding of our data to easily build features and value at the higher levels.

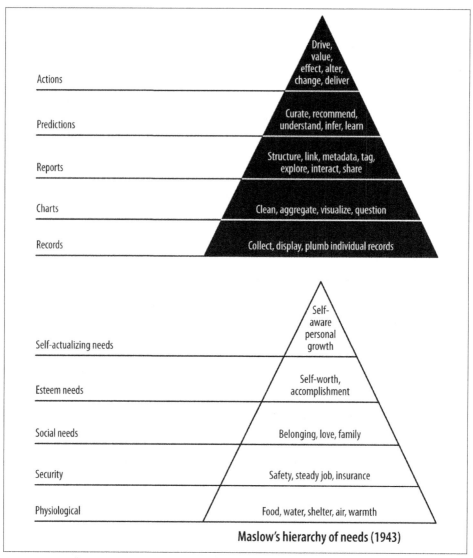

Figure II-1. The Jurney–Warden data-value pyramid of 2011

The data-value stack begins with the simple display of records, where the focus is on connecting or "plumbing" our data pipeline all the way through from the raw data to the user's screen. We then move on to charts, where we extract enough structure from our data to display its properties in aggregate and start to familiarize ourselves with those properties. Next comes identifying relationships and exploring data through interactive reports. This enables statistical inference to generate predictions. Finally, we use these predictions to drive user behavior in order to create and capture value.

## CHAPTER 4

Collecting and Displaying Records

In this chapter, our first agile sprint, we climb level 1 of the data-value pyramid (Figure 4-1). We will connect, or plumb, the parts of our data pipeline all the way through from raw data to a web application on a user's screen. This will enable a single developer to publish raw data records on the web. In doing so, we will activate our stack against our real data, thereby connecting our application to the reality of our data and our users.

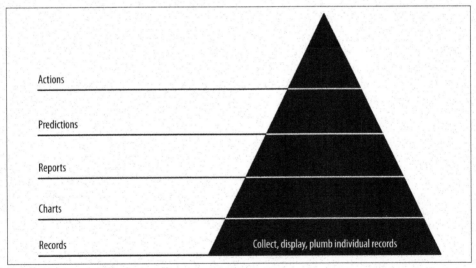

Figure 4-1. Level 1: displaying base records

If you already have a popular application, this step may seem confusing in that you already have the individual (or atomic) records displaying in your application. The point of this step, then, is to pipe these records through your analytical pipeline to bulk storage and then on to a browser. Bulk storage provides access for further processing via ETL (extract, transform, load) or some other means.

This first stage of the data-value pyramid can proceed relatively quickly, so we can get on to higher levels of value. Note that we will return to this step frequently as we enrich our analysis with additional datasets. We'll make each new dataset explorable as we go. We'll be doing this throughout the book as we work through the higher-level steps. The data-value pyramid is something you step up and down in as you do your analysis and get feedback from users. This setup and these browsable records set the stage for further advances up the data-value pyramid as our complexity and value snowball.

If your atomic records are petabytes, you may not want to publish them all to a document store. Moreover, security constraints may make this impossible. In that case, a sample will do. Prepare a sample and publish it, and then constrain the rest of your application as you create it.

Code examples for this chapter are available at *Agile_Data_Code_2/ch04* (*http://bit.ly/2qrIc6w*). Clone the repository and follow along!

```
git clone https://github.com/rjurney/Agile_Data_Code_2.git
```

Putting It All Together

Setting up our stack was a bit of work. The good news is, with this stack, we don't have to repeat this work as soon as we start to see load from users on our system increase and our stack needs to scale. Instead, we'll be free to continue to iterate and improve our product from now on.

Now, let's work with some atomic records—on-time records for each flight originating in the US in 2015—to see how the stack works for us.

An atomic record is a base record, the most granular of the events you will be analyzing. We might aggregate, count, slice, and dice atomic records, but they are indivisible. As such, they represent ground truth to us, and working with atomic records is essential to plugging into the reality of our data and our application. The point of big data is to be able to analyze the most granular data using NoSQL tools to reach a deeper level of understanding than was previously possible.

Collecting and Serializing Flight Data

You can see the process of serializing events in Figure 4-2. In this case, we're going to download the core data that we'll use for the remainder of the book using a script, *download.sh* (*http://bit.ly/2pFwyjX*):

```
# Get on-time records for all flights in 2015 - 273MB
wget -P data/ \
 http://s3.amazonaws.com/agile_data_science/ \
  On_Time_On_Time_Performance_2015.csv.bz2

# Get openflights data
wget -P /tmp/ \
 https://raw.githubusercontent.com/jpatokal/openflights/ \
  master/data/airports.dat
mv /tmp/airports.dat data/airports.csv

wget -P /tmp/ \
 https://raw.githubusercontent.com/jpatokal/openflights/ \
  master/data/airlines.dat
mv /tmp/airlines.dat data/airlines.csv

wget -P /tmp/ \
 https://raw.githubusercontent.com/jpatokal/openflights/ \
  master/data/routes.dat
mv /tmp/routes.dat data/routes.csv

wget -P /tmp/ \
 https://raw.githubusercontent.com/jpatokal/openflights/ \
  master/data/countries.dat
mv /tmp/countries.dat data/countries.csv

# Get FAA data
wget -P data/ http://av-info.faa.gov/data/ACRef/tab/aircraft.txt
wget -P data/ http://av-info.faa.gov/data/ACRef/tab/ata.txt
wget -P data/ http://av-info.faa.gov/data/ACRef/tab/compt.txt
wget -P data/ http://av-info.faa.gov/data/ACRef/tab/engine.txt
wget -P data/ http://av-info.faa.gov/data/ACRef/tab/prop.txt
```

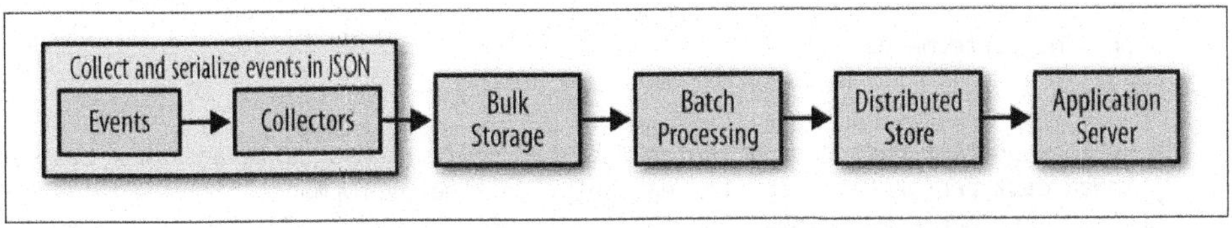

Figure 4-2. Serializing events

To get started, we'll trim the unneeded fields from our on-time flight records and convert them to Parquet format. This will improve performance when loading this data, something we'll be doing throughout the book. In practice, you would want to retain all the values that might be of interest in the future. Note that there is a bug in the `inferSchema` option of `spark-csv`, so we'll have to cast the numeric fields manually before saving our converted data.

If you want to make sense of the following query, take a look at the Bureau of Transportation Statistics description of the data (*http://www.transtats.bts.gov/Fields.asp? Table_ID=236*), On-Time Performance records (this data was introduced in Chapter 3).

Run the following code to trim the data to just the fields we will need:

```
# Loads CSV with header parsing and type inference, in one line!
on_time_dataframe = spark.read.format('com.databricks.spark.csv')\
  .options(
    header='true',
    treatEmptyValuesAsNulls='true',
  )\
  .load('data/On_Time_On_Time_Performance_2015.csv.bz2')
on_time_dataframe.registerTempTable("on_time_performance")

trimmed_cast_performance = spark.sql("""
SELECT
  Year, Quarter, Month, DayofMonth, DayOfWeek, FlightDate,
  Carrier, TailNum, FlightNum,
  Origin, OriginCityName, OriginState,
  Dest, DestCityName, DestState,
  DepTime, cast(DepDelay as float), cast(DepDelayMinutes as int),
  cast(TaxiOut as float), cast(TaxiIn as float),
  WheelsOff, WheelsOn,
  ArrTime, cast(ArrDelay as float), cast(ArrDelayMinutes as float),
  cast(Cancelled as int), cast(Diverted as int),
  cast(ActualElapsedTime as float), cast(AirTime as float),
  cast(Flights as int), cast(Distance as float),
  cast(CarrierDelay as float), cast(WeatherDelay as float),
  cast(NASDelay as float),
  cast(SecurityDelay as float),
  cast(LateAircraftDelay as float),
  CRSDepTime, CRSArrTime
FROM
  on_time_performance
""")

# Replace on_time_performance table# with our new, trimmed table and show its contents
trimmed_cast_performance.registerTempTable("on_time_performance")
trimmed_cast_performance.show()
```

Which shows a much simplified format (here abbreviated):

Year	Quarter	Month	DayofMonth	DayOfWeek	FlightDate	Carrier	TailNum	FlightNum	Origin
2015	1	1	1	4	2015-01-01	AA	N001AA	1519	DFW
2015	1	1	1	4	2015-01-01	AA	N001AA	1519	MEM
2015	1	1	1	4	2015-01-01	AA	N002AA	2349	ORD
2015	1	1	1	4	2015-01-01	AA	N003AA	1298	DFW
2015	1	1	1	4	2015-01-01	AA	N003AA	1422	DFW

Let's make sure our numeric fields work as desired:

```
# Verify we can sum numeric columns
spark.sql("""SELECT
  SUM(WeatherDelay), SUM(CarrierDelay), SUM(NASDelay),
  SUM(SecurityDelay), SUM(LateAircraftDelay)
FROM on_time_performance
""").show()
```

This results in the following output (formatted to fit the page):

sum(WeatherDelay)	sum(CarrierDelay)	sum(NASDelay)	sum(SecurityDelay)	sum(LateAircraftDelay)
3100233.0	2.0172956E7	1.4335762E7	80985.0	2.4961931E7

Having trimmed and cast our fields and made sure the numeric columns work, we can now save our data as JSON Lines and Parquet. Note that we also load the data back, to verify that it loads correctly. Make sure this code runs without error, as the entire rest of the book uses these files:

```
# Save records as gzipped JSON Lines
trimmed_cast_performance.toJSON()\
  .saveAsTextFile(
    'data/on_time_performance.jsonl.gz',
    'org.apache.hadoop.io.compress.GzipCodec'
  )

# View records on filesystem
# gunzip -c data/On_Time_On_Time_Performance_2015.jsonl.gz/part-00000.gz | head

# Save records using Parquet
trimmed_cast_performance.write.parquet("data/on_time_performance.parquet")

# Load JSON records back
on_time_dataframe = spark.read.json('data/on_time_performance.jsonl.gz')
on_time_dataframe.show()

# Load the Parquet file back
on_time_dataframe = spark.read.parquet('data/trimmed_cast_performance.parquet')
on_time_dataframe.show()
```

Note that the Parquet file is only 248 MB, compared with 315 MB for the original gzip-compressed CSV and 259 MB for the gzip-compressed JSON. In practice the Parquet will be much more performant, as it will only load the individual columns we actually use in our PySpark scripts.

We can view the gzipped JSON with `gunzip -c` and `head`:

```
gunzip -c data/On_Time_On_Time_Performance_2015.jsonl.gz/part-00000.gz | head
```

We can now view the on-time records directly, and understand them more easily than before:

```
{
  "Year":2015,
  "Quarter":1,
  "Month":1,
  "DayofMonth":1,
  "DayOfWeek":4,
  "FlightDate":"2015-01-01",
  "UniqueCarrier":"AA",
  "AirlineID":19805,
  "Carrier":"AA",
  "TailNum":"N787AA",
  "FlightNum":1,
  ...
}
```

Loading the gzipped JSON Lines data in PySpark is easy, using a `SparkSession` (*http://bit.ly/2nRGlqX*) called `spark`:

```
# Load JSON records back on_time_dataframe = spark.read.json(
  'data/On_Time_On_Time_Performance_2015.jsonl.gz'
)
on_time_dataframe.show()
```

Loading the Parquet data is similarly easy:

```
# Load the Parquet file
on_time_dataframe = spark.read.parquet('data/on_time_performance.parquet')
on_time_dataframe.first()
```

Processing and Publishing Flight Records

Having collected our flight data, let's process it (Figure 4-3). In the interest of plumbing our stack all the way through with real data to give us a base state to build from, let's publish the on-time flight records right away to MongoDB and Elasticsearch, so we can access them from the web with Mongo, Elasticsearch, and Flask.

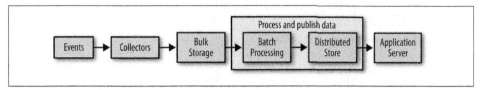

Figure 4-3. Processing and publishing data

Publishing Flight Records to MongoDB

MongoDB's Spark integration makes this easy. We simply need to import and activate pymongo_spark, convert our DataFrame to an RDD, and call saveToMongoDB. We do this in *ch04/pyspark_to_mongo.py* (*http://bit.ly/2nRIX8d*):

```
import pymongo
import pymongo_spark
# Important: activate pymongo_spark
pymongo_spark.activate()

on_time_dataframe = spark.read.parquet('data/on_time_performance.parquet')

# Note we have to convert the row to a dict
# to avoid https://jira.mongodb.org/browse/HADOOP-276
as_dict = on_time_dataframe.rdd.map(lambda row: row.asDict())
as_dict.saveToMongoDB
  ('mongodb://localhost:27017/agile_data_science.on_time_performance')
```

If something goes wrong, you can always drop the collection and try again:

```
$ mongo agile_data_science

> db.on_time_performance.drop()

true
```

The beauty of our infrastructure is that everything is reproducible from the original data, so there is little worrying to be done about our database becoming corrupted or crashing (although we do employ a fault-tolerant cluster). In addition, because we're using our database as a document store, where we simply fetch documents by some ID or field, we don't have to worry much about performance, either.

Finally, let's verify that our flight records are in MongoDB:

```
> db.on_time_performance.findOne()

{
        "_id" : ObjectId("56f9ed67b0504718f584d03f"),
        "Origin" : "JFK",
        "Quarter" : 1,
        "FlightNum" : 1,
        "Div4TailNum" : "",
        "Div5TailNum" : "",
        "Div2TailNum" : "",
        "Div3TailNum" : "",
        "ArrDel15" : 0,
        "AirTime" : 378,
        "Div5WheelsOff" : "",
        "DepTimeBlk" : "0900-0959",
        ...
}
```

Now let's fetch one flight record, using its minimum unique identifiers—the airline carrier, the flight date, and the flight number:

```
> db.on_time_performance.findOne(
  {Carrier: 'DL', FlightDate: '2015-01-01', FlightNum: 478})
```

You might notice that this query does not return quickly. Mongo lets us query our data by any combination of its fields, but there is a cost to this feature. We have to think about and maintain indexes for our queries. In this case, the access pattern is static, so the index is easy to define:

```
> db.on_time_performance.ensureIndex({Carrier: 1, FlightDate: 1, FlightNum: 1})
```

This may take a few moments to run, but our queries will be fast thereafter. This is a small price to pay for the features Mongo gives us. In general, the more features of a database we use, the more we have to pay in terms of operational overhead. So, always try to use database features sparingly, unless you enjoy tuning databases in production.

Presenting Flight Records in a Browser

Now that we've published on-time flight records to a document store and queried them, we're ready to present our data in a browser via a simple web application (Figure 4-4).

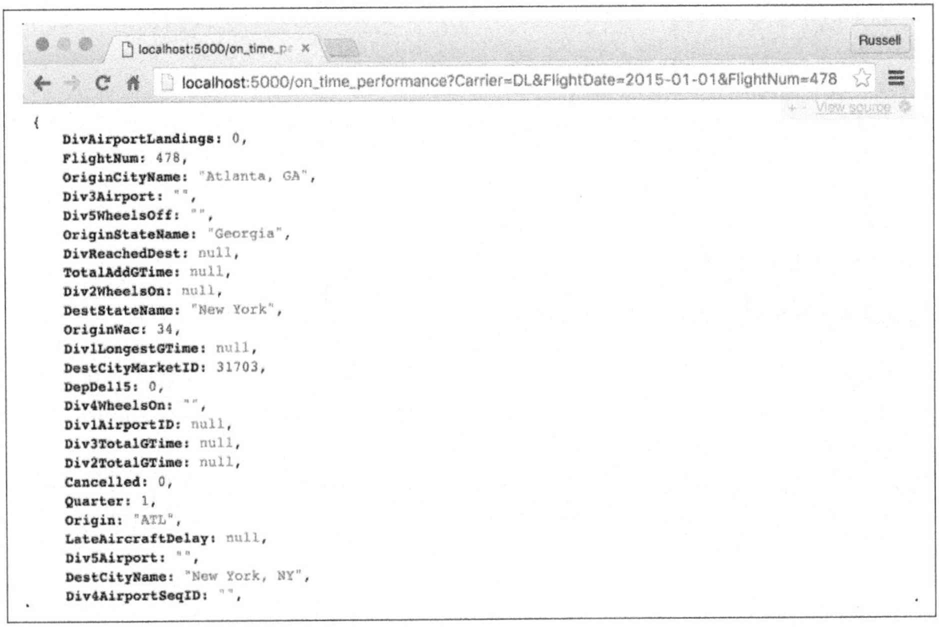

```
localhost:5000/on_time_p   ×                                          Russell

←  →  C  ⌂   localhost:5000/on_time_performance?Carrier=DL&FlightDate=2015-01-01&FlightNum=478   ☆   ≡
                                                                        + - View source

{
    DivAirportLandings: 0,
    FlightNum: 478,
    OriginCityName: "Atlanta, GA",
    Div3Airport: "",
    Div5WheelsOff: "",
    OriginStateName: "Georgia",
    DivReachedDest: null,
    TotalAddGTime: null,
    Div2WheelsOn: null,
    DestStateName: "New York",
    OriginWac: 34,
    Div1LongestGTime: null,
    DestCityMarketID: 31703,
    DepDel15: 0,
    Div4WheelsOn: "",
    Div1AirportID: null,
    Div3TotalGTime: null,
    Div2TotalGTime: null,
    Cancelled: 0,
    Quarter: 1,
    Origin: "ATL",
    LateAircraftDelay: null,
    Div5Airport: "",
    DestCityName: "New York, NY",
    Div4AirportSeqID: "",
```

Figure 4-4. Displaying a raw flight record

Serving Flights with Flask and pymongo

Flask and pymongo make querying and returning flights easy. *ch04/web/on_time_flask.py* (*http://bit.ly/2ojYLvV*) returns JSON about a flight on the web. This code might serve as an API, and we'll create and use JSON APIs later in the book. Note that we can't use json.dumps(), because we are JSON-izing pymongo records, which json doesn't know how to serialize. Instead we must use bson.json_util.dumps():

```python
from flask import Flask, render_template, request
from pymongo import MongoClient
from bson import json_util

# Set up Flask and Mongo
app = Flask(__name__)
client = MongoClient()

# Controller: Fetch a flight and display it
@app.route("/on_time_performance")
def on_time_performance():

  carrier = request.args.get('Carrier')
  flight_date = request.args.get('FlightDate')
  flight_num = request.args.get('FlightNum')
```

```
    flight = client.agile_data_science.on_time_performance.find_one({
      'Carrier': carrier,
      'FlightDate': flight_date,
      'FlightNum': flight_num
    })

    return json_util.dumps(flight)

if __name__ == "__main__":
    app.run(debug=True)
```

Rendering HTML5 with Jinja2

As we did in Chapter 3, let's turn this raw JSON into a web page with a Jinja2 template. Check out *ch04/web/on_time_flask_template.py* (*http://bit.ly/2nRRk3E*). Jinja2 makes it easy to transform raw flight records into web pages:

```
from flask import Flask, render_template, request
from pymongo import MongoClient
from bson import json_util

# Set up Flask and Mongo
app = Flask(__name__)
client = MongoClient()

# Controller: Fetch a flight and display it
@app.route("/on_time_performance")
def on_time_performance():

  carrier = request.args.get('Carrier')
  flight_date = request.args.get('FlightDate')
  flight_num = request.args.get('FlightNum')

  flight = client.agile_data_science.on_time_performance.find_one({
    'Carrier': carrier,
    'FlightDate': flight_date,
    'FlightNum': int(flight_num)
  })

  return render_template('flight.html', flight=flight)

if __name__ == "__main__":
    app.run(debug=True)
```

Note that render_template in our example points at the file *ch04/web/templates/ flight.html* (*http://bit.ly/2pmtE7p*). This is a partial template that fills in the dynamic content area of our layout page. The layout page that it subclasses, *ch04/web/ templates/layout.html* (*http://bit.ly/2pmnioF*), imports Bootstrap and handles the global design for each page, such as the header, overall styling, and footer. This saves us from repeating ourselves in each page to create a consistent layout for the application.

The layout template contains an empty content block, {% block content %}{% end block %}, into which our partial template containing our application data is rendered:

```html
<!DOCTYPE html>
<html lang="en">
  <head>
    <meta charset="utf-8">
    <title>Agile Data Science</title>
    <meta name="viewport" content="width=device-width, initial-scale=1.0">
    <meta name="description"
            content="Chapter 5 example in Agile Data Science, 2.0">
    <meta name="author" content="Russell Jurney">
    <link href="/static/bootstrap.min.css" rel="stylesheet">
    <link href="/static/bootstrap-theme.min.css" rel="stylesheet">
  </head>

  <body>
    <div id="wrap">

      <!-- Begin page content -->
      <div class="container">
        <div class="page-header">
          <h1>Agile Data Science</h1>
        </div>
        {% block body %}{% endblock %}
      </div>

      <div id="push"></div>
    </div>

    <div id="footer">
      <div class="container">
        <p class="muted credit">
         <a href="http://shop.oreilly.com/product/ \
            0636920025054.do"> \
            Agile Data Science</a> by \
            <a href="http://www.linkedin.com/in/ \
            russelljurney">Russell Jurney</a>, 2016
      </div>
    </div>
    <script src="/static/bootstrap.min.js"></script>
  </body>
</html>
```

Our flight-specific partial template works by subclassing the layout template. Jinja2 templates perform control flow in {% %} tags to loop through tuples and arrays and apply conditionals. We display variables by putting bound data or arbitrary Python code inside the {{ }} tags. For example, our flight template looks like this:

```
{% extends "layout.html" %}
{% block body %}
  <div>
    <p class="lead">Flight {{flight.FlightNum}}</p>
    <table class="table">
      <thead>
        <th>Airline</th>
        <th>Origin</th>
        <th>Destination</th>
        <th>Tail Number</th>
        <th>Date</th>
        <th>Air Time</th>
        <th>Distance</th>
      </thead>
      <tbody>
        <tr>
          <td>{{flight.Carrier}}</td>
          <td>{{flight.Origin}}</td>
          <td>{{flight.Dest}}</td>
          <td>{{flight.TailNum}}</td>
          <td>{{flight.FlightDate}}</td>
          <td>{{flight.AirTime}}</td>
          <td>{{flight.Distance}}</td>
        </tr>
      </tbody>
    </table>
  </div>
{% endblock %}
```

Our body content block is what renders the page content for our data. We start with a raw template, plug in values from our data (via the flight variable we bound to the template), and get the page displaying a record.

We can see the flight in our web page with a Carrier, FlightDate, and FlightNum. To test things out, grab a flight record directly from MongoDB:

```
$ mongo agile_data_science

> db.on_time_performance.findOne()

{
  "_id" : ObjectId("56fd7391b05047327f19241f"),
  "Origin" : "IAH",
  "FlightNum" : 1044,
  "Carrier" : "AA",
  "FlightDate" : "2015-07-03",
  "DivActualElapsedTime" : null,
  "AirTime" : 122,
  "Div5WheelsOff" : "",
  "DestCityMarketID" : 32467,
  "Div3AirportID" : null,
  "Div3TotalGTime" : null,
  "Month" : 7,
```

```
    "CRSElapsedTime" : 151,
    "DestStateName" : "Florida",
    "DestAirportID" : 13303,
    "Distance" : 964,
    ...
}
```

We can now fetch a single flight via */ch04/web/templates/layout.html* (*http://bit.ly/2pmnioF*), as shown in Figure 4-5.

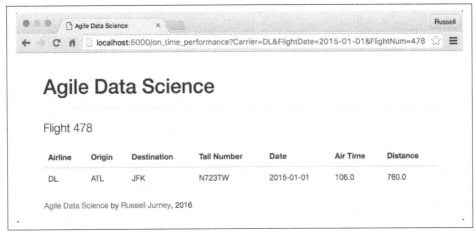

Figure 4-5. Presenting a single flight

Our Flask console shows the resources being accessed (dates and timestamps removed because of page width constraints):

```
127.0.0.1 - - [...]
   "GET /on_time_performance?Carrier=DL& \
      FlightDate=2015-01-01&FlightNum=478 HTTP/1.1" 200 -
127.0.0.1 - - [...] "GET /static/bootstrap.min.css HTTP/1.1" 200 -
127.0.0.1 - - [...] "GET /static/bootstrap-theme.min.css HTTP/1.1" 200 -
127.0.0.1 - - [...] "GET /static/bootstrap.min.js HTTP/1.1" 200 -
127.0.0.1 - - [...] "GET /favicon.ico HTTP/1.1" 404 -
```

Great! We made a web page from raw data! But ... so what? What have we achieved?

We've completed the base of the pyramid, level 1—displaying atomic records—in our standard data pipeline. This is a foundation. Whatever advanced analytics we offer, in the end, the user will often want to see the signal itself—that is, the raw data backing our inferences. There is no skipping steps here: if we can't correctly "visualize" a single atomic record, then our platform and strategy have no base. They are weak.

Agile Checkpoint

Since we now have working software, it is time to let users in to start getting their feedback. "Wait, really? This thing is embarrassing!" Get over yourself!

We all want to be Steve Jobs; we all want to have a devastating product launch, and to make a huge splash with a top-secret invention. But with analytics applications, when you hesitate to ship, you let your fragile ego undermine your ability to become Steve Jobs by worrying about not looking like him in your first draft. If you don't ship crap as step 1, you're unlikely to get to a brilliant step 26. I strongly advise you to learn customer development (*http://steveblank.com/category/customer-development/*) and apply it to your projects. If you're in a startup, the *Startup Owner's Manual* (*http://amzn.to/1pOhPmt*) by Steve Blank (K&S Ranch) is a great place to start.

You will notice immediately when you ship this (maybe to close friends or insiders who clone the source from GitHub at this point) that users can't find which flights to retrieve by their Carrier, FlightDate, and FlightNum. To get real utility from this data, we need list and search capabilities.

You may well have anticipated this. Why ship something obviously broken or incomplete? Because although step 2 is obvious, *step 13 is not*. We must involve users at this step because their participation is a fundamental part of completing step 1 of the data-value pyramid. Users provide validation of our underlying assumptions, which at this stage might be stated in the form of two questions: "Does anyone care about flights?" and "What do they want to know about a given flight?" We think we have answers to these questions: "Yes" and "Airline, origin, destination, tail number, date, air time, and distance flown." But without validation, we don't really know anything for certain. Without user interaction and learning, we are building in the dark. Success that way is unlikely, just as a pyramid without a strong foundation will soon crumble.

The other reason to ship something now is that the act of publishing, presenting, and sharing your work will highlight a number of problems in your platform setup that would likely otherwise go undiscovered until the moment you launch your product. In Agile Data Science, you *always ship* after a sprint. As a team member, you don't control whether to ship or not. You control what to ship and how broad an audience to release it to. This release might be appropriate for five friends and family members, and you might have to hound them to get it running or to click the link. But in sharing your budding application, you will optimize your packaging and resolve dependencies. You'll have to make it presentable. Without such work, without a clear deliverable to guide your efforts, technical issues you are blinded to by familiarity will be transparent to you.

Now, let's add listing flights and extend that to enable search, so we can start generating real clicks from real users.

Listing Flights

Flights are usually presented as a price-sorted list, filtered by the origin and destination, with the cheapest flight first. We lack price data, so instead we'll list all flights on a given day between two destinations, sorted by departure time as a primary key, and arrival time as a secondary key. A list helps group individual flights with other similar flights. Lists are the next step in building this layer of the data-value pyramid, after displaying individual records.

Listing Flights with MongoDB

Before we search our flights, we need the capacity to list them in order to display our search results. We can use MongoDB's query capabilities to return a list of flights between airports on a given day, sorted by departure and arrival time. The following queries are in *ch04/mongo.js* (*http://bit.ly/2oNlOTr*):

```
$ mongo agile_data_science
```

```
> db.on_time_performance.find(
    {Origin: 'ATL', Dest: 'SFO', FlightDate: '2015-01-01'}).sort(
    {DepTime: 1, ArrTime: 1}) // Slow or broken
```

You may see this error:

```
error: {
    "$err" : "too much data for sort() with no index.  add an index or specify a
            smaller limit",
    "code" : 10128
}
```

If not, this query may still take a long time to complete, so let's add another index for it. In general, we'll need to add an index for each access pattern in our application, so always remember to do so up front in order to save yourself trouble with performance in the future:

```
> db.on_time_performance.ensureIndex({Origin: 1, Dest: 1, FlightDate: 1})
```

Now that our index on origin, destination, and date is in place, we can get the flights between ATL and SFO on January 1, 2015:

```
> db.on_time_performance.find(
    {Origin: 'ATL', Dest: 'SFO',
    FlightDate: '2015-01-01'}).sort(
    {DepTime: 1, ArrTime: 1})
    // Fast
```

Our Flask stub works the same as before—except this time it passes an array of flights instead of one flight. This time, we're using slugs in the URL for our web controller.[1] A slug puts arguments in between forward slashes, instead of as query parameters. Check out this excerpt from *ch04/web/on_time_flask_template.py* (*http://bit.ly/2nRRk3E*):

```
# Controller: Fetch all flights between cities on a given day and display them
@app.route("/flights/<origin>/<dest>/<flight_date>")
def list_flights(origin, dest, flight_date):

    flights = client.agile_data_science.on_time_performance.find(
      {
        'Origin': origin,
        'Dest': dest,
        'FlightDate': flight_date
      },
      sort = [
        ('DepTime', 1),
        ('ArrTime', 1),
      ]
    )
    flight_count = flights.count()

    return render_template('flights.html', flights=flights,
      flight_date=flight_date, flight_count=flight_count)
```

Our templates are pretty simple too, owing to Bootstrap's snazzy presentation of tables. Tables are often scoffed at by designers when used for layout, but this is tabular data, so their use is appropriate. To be extra snazzy, we've included the number of flights that day, and since the date is constant for all records, it is a field in the title of the page instead of a column:

---

[1] For more on controllers, see Alex Coleman's blog post on MVC in Flask (*http://bit.ly/2oN5CSe*).

```
{% extends "layout.html" %}
{% block body %}
  <div>
    <p class="lead">{{flight_count}} Flights on {{flight_date}}</p>
    <table class="table table-condensed table-striped">
      <thead>
        <th>Airline</th>
        <th>Flight Number</th>
        <th>Origin</th>
        <th>Destination</th>
        <th>Departure Time</th>
        <th>Tail Number</th>
        <th>Air Time</th>
        <th>Distance</th>
      </thead>
      <tbody>
        {% for flight in flights %}
        <tr>
          <td>{{flight.Carrier}}</td>
          <td>
<a href="/on_time_performance?Carrier=
  {{flight.Carrier}}&FlightDate=
    {{flight.FlightDate}}&FlightNum=
      {{flight.FlightNum}}">{{flight.FlightNum}}</a></td>
          <td>{{flight.Origin}}</td>
          <td>{{flight.Dest}}</td>
          <td>{{flight.DepTime}}</td>
          <td>{{flight.TailNum}}</td>
          <td>{{flight.AirTime}}</td>
          <td>{{flight.Distance}}</td>
        </tr>
        {% endfor %}
      </tbody>
    </table>
  </div>
{% endblock %}
```

We can bind as many variables to a template as we want. Note that we also link from
the list page (Figure 4-6) to the individual record pages, constructing the links out of
the airline carrier, flight number, and flight date.

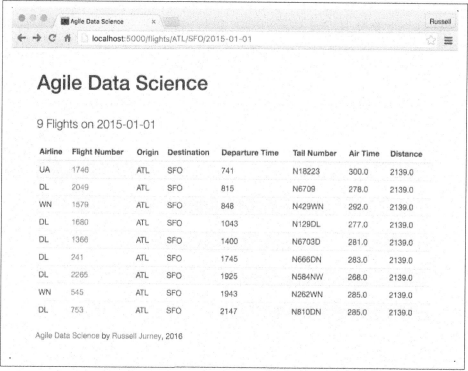

Figure 4-6. Presenting a list of flights

Paginating Data

Now that we can list the flights on a given day between cities, our users say, "What if I want to see lots of flights and there are so many on one page that it crashes my browser?" Listing hundreds of records is not a good presentation, and this will happen for other types of data. Shouldn't there be a previous/next button to scroll forward and back in time? Yes. That is what we'll add next.

So far we've glossed over how we're creating these templates, subtemplates, and macros. Now we're going to dive in by creating a macro and a subtemplate for pagination.

Reinventing the wheel?

Why are we building our own pagination? Isn't that a solved problem?

The first answer is that it makes a good example to connect the browser with the data directly. In Agile Data Science, we try to process the data into the very state it takes on a user's screen with minimal manipulation between the backend and an image in a browser. Why? We do this because it decreases complexity in our systems, because it unites data scientists and designers around the same vision, and because this philosophy embraces the nature of distributed systems in that it doesn't rely on joins or other tricks that work best on "big iron," or legacy systems.

Keeping the model consistent with the view is critical when the model is complex, as in a predictive system. We can best create value when the interaction design around a feature is cognizant of and consistent with the underlying data model. Data scientists must bring understanding of the data to the rest of the team, or the team can't build to a common vision. The principle of building a view to match the model ensures this from the beginning.

In practice, we cannot predict at which layer a feature will arise. It may first appear as a burst of creativity from a web developer, designer, data scientist, or platform engineer. To validate it, we must ship it in an experiment as quickly as possible, and so the implementation layer of a feature may in fact begin at any level of our stack. When this happens, we must take note and ticket the feature as containing technical debt. As the feature stabilizes, if it is to remain in the system, we move it further back in the stack as time permits.

A full-blown application framework like Rails or Django would likely build in this functionality. However, when we are building an application around derived data, the mechanics of interactions often vary in both subtle and dramatic ways. Most web frameworks are optimized around CRUD operations (*http://bit.ly/1G4WdV1*). In big data exploration and visualization, we're only doing the read part of CRUD, and we're doing relatively complex visualization as part of it. Frameworks offer less value in this situation, where their behavior must likely be customized. Also note that while MongoDB happens to include the ability to select and return a range of sorted records, the NoSQL store you use may or may not provide this functionality, or it may not be possible to use this feature because publishing your data in a timely manner requires a custom service. You may have to precompute the data periodically and serve the list yourself. NoSQL gives us options, and web frameworks are optimized for relational databases. We must often take matters into our own hands.

Serving paginated data

To start, we'll need to change our controller for flights to use pagination via MongoDB (*https://api.mongodb.org/python/current/api/pymongo/cursor.html*). There is a little math to do, since MongoDB pagination uses `skip` and `limit` instead of `start` and `end`. We need to compute the width of the query by subtracting the start from the end, then applying this width in a `limit` call:

```
# Controller: Fetch all flights between cities on a given day and display them
@app.route("/flights/<origin>/<dest>/<flight_date>")
def list_flights(origin, dest, flight_date):

  start = request.args.get('start') or 0
  start = max(int(start) - 1, 0)
  end = request.args.get('end') or 20
  end = int(end)
  width = end - start

  flights = client.agile_data_science.on_time_performance.find(
    {
      'Origin': origin,
      'Dest': dest,
      'FlightDate': flight_date
    },
    sort = [
      ('DepTime', 1),
      ('ArrTime', 1),
    ]
  ).skip(start).limit(width)
  flight_count = flights.count()

  return render_template('flights.html', flights=flights,
    flight_date=flight_date, flight_count=flight_count)
```

Prototyping back from HTML

In order to implement pagination in our templates, we need to prototype back from
HTML. We're all familiar with next/previous buttons from browsing flights on airline
websites. We'll need to set up the same thing for listing flights. We need links at the
bottom of the flight list page (Figure 4-7) that allow you to paginate forward and
back.

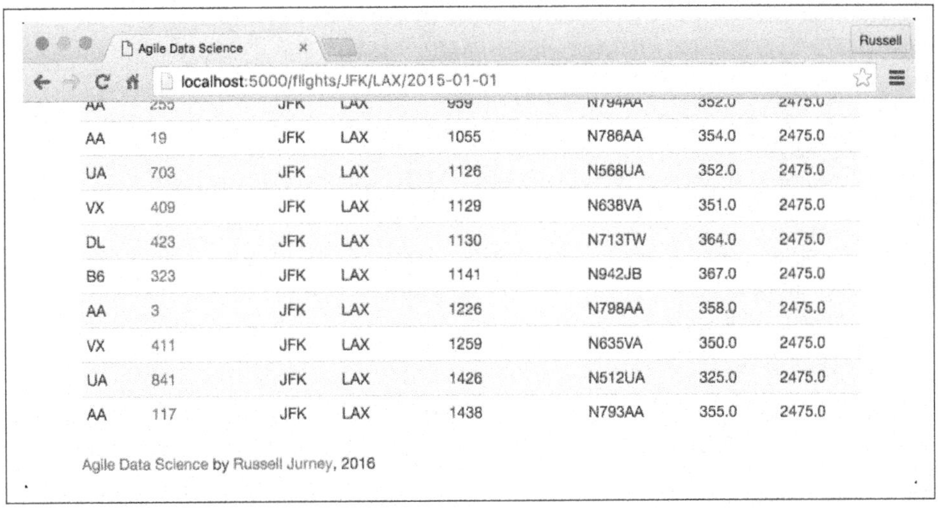

AA	255	JFK	LAX	959	N794AA	352.0	2475.0
AA	19	JFK	LAX	1055	N786AA	354.0	2475.0
UA	703	JFK	LAX	1126	N568UA	352.0	2475.0
VX	409	JFK	LAX	1129	N638VA	351.0	2475.0
DL	423	JFK	LAX	1130	N713TW	364.0	2475.0
B6	323	JFK	LAX	1141	N942JB	367.0	2475.0
AA	3	JFK	LAX	1226	N798AA	358.0	2475.0
VX	411	JFK	LAX	1259	N635VA	350.0	2475.0
UA	841	JFK	LAX	1426	N512UA	325.0	2475.0
AA	117	JFK	LAX	1438	N793AA	355.0	2475.0

Agile Data Science by Russell Jurney, 2016

Figure 4-7. Missing next/previous links

More specifically, we need a link to an incremented/decremented offset range for the path */flights/<origin>/<dest>/<date>?start=N&end=N*. Let's prototype the feature based on these requirements by appending static forward and back links against our flight list API (Figure 4-8).

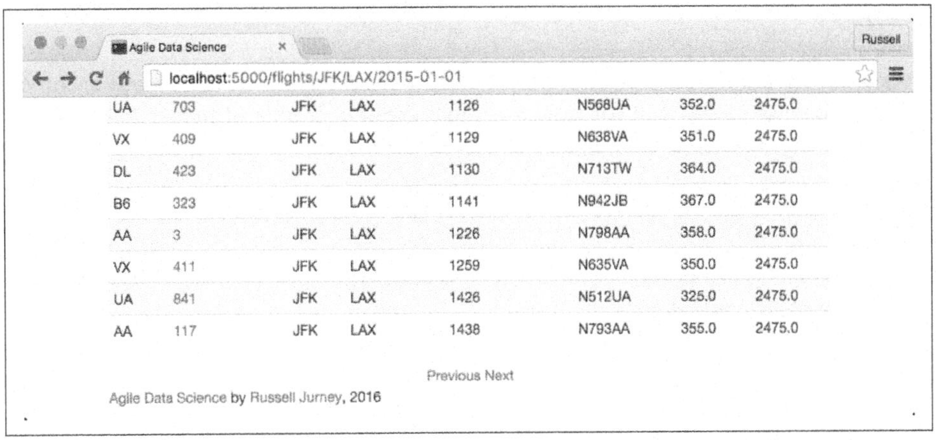

UA	703	JFK	LAX	1126	N568UA	352.0	2475.0
VX	409	JFK	LAX	1129	N638VA	351.0	2475.0
DL	423	JFK	LAX	1130	N713TW	364.0	2475.0
B6	323	JFK	LAX	1141	N942JB	367.0	2475.0
AA	3	JFK	LAX	1226	N798AA	358.0	2475.0
VX	411	JFK	LAX	1259	N635VA	350.0	2475.0
UA	841	JFK	LAX	1426	N512UA	325.0	2475.0
AA	117	JFK	LAX	1438	N793AA	355.0	2475.0

Previous Next

Agile Data Science by Russell Jurney, 2016

Figure 4-8. Simple next/previous links

For example, we want to dynamically render this HTML, corresponding to the URL /flights/JFK/LAX/2015-01-01?start=20&end=40:

```
# /ch04/templates/partials/flights.html
...
  <div style="text-align: center">
    <a href="/flights/{{origin}}/{{dest}}/{{flight_date}}?start=0&end=20">
        Previous
    </a>
    <a href="/flights/{{origin}}/{{dest}}/{{flight_date}}?start=20&end=40">
        Next
    </a>
  </div>
{% endblock -%}
```

Pasting and navigating to the links, such as *http://localhost:5000/flights/JFK/LAX/2015-01-01?start=20&end=40*, demonstrates that the feature works with our data.

Now let's generalize it. Macros are convenient, but we don't want to make our template too complicated, so we compute the increments in a Python helper (we might consider a model class) and make a macro to render the offsets.

For starters, let's use this opportunity to set up a simple config file to set variables like the number of records to display per page (embedding these in code will cause headaches later):

```
# ch04/web/config.py, a configuration file for index.py
RECORDS_PER_PAGE = 20
```

Let's also create a simple helper to calculate record offsets. In time this will become a full-blown class model, but for now, we'll just create a couple of helper methods in /ch04/web/on_time_flask_template.py (*http://bit.ly/2nRRk3E*):

```
# Process Elasticsearch hits and return flight records
def process_search(results):
  records = []
  if results['hits'] and results['hits']['hits']:
    total = results['hits']['total']
    hits = results['hits']['hits']
    for hit in hits:
      record = hit['_source']
      records.append(record)
  return records, total

# Calculate offsets for fetching lists of flights from MongoDB
def get_navigation_offsets(offset1, offset2, increment):
  offsets = {}
  offsets['Next'] = {'top_offset': offset2 + increment, 'bottom_offset':
  offset1 + increment}
  offsets['Previous'] = {'top_offset': max(offset2 - increment, 0),
  'bottom_offset': max(offset1 - increment, 0)} # Don't go < 0
  return offsets
```

```
# Strip the existing start and end parameters from the query string
def strip_place(url):
  try:
    p = re.match('(.+)&start=.+&end=.+', url).group(1)
  except AttributeError, e:
    return url
  return p
```

The controller now employs the helper to generate and then bind the navigation variables to the template, because we are now passing both the list of flights and the calculated offsets for the navigation links. Check out *ch04/web/ on_time_flask_template.py* (*http://bit.ly/2p44qGT*):

```
# Controller: Fetch all flights between cities on a given day and display them
@app.route("/flights/<origin>/<dest>/<flight_date>")
def list_flights(origin, dest, flight_date):

    start = request.args.get('start') or 0
    start = int(start)
    end = request.args.get('end') or 20
    end = int(end)
    width = end - start

    nav_offsets = get_navigation_offsets(start, end, config.RECORDS_PER_PAGE)

    flights = client.agile_data_science.on_time_performance.find(
      {
        'Origin': origin,
        'Dest': dest,
        'FlightDate': flight_date
      },
      sort = [
        ('DepTime', 1),
        ('ArrTime', 1),
      ]
    )
    flight_count = flights.count()
    flights = flights.skip(start).limit(width)

    return render_template(
      'flights.html',
      flights=flights,
      flight_date=flight_date,
      flight_count=flight_count,
      nav_path=request.path,
      nav_offsets=nav_offsets

    )
```

Our flight list template, *ch04/web/templates/flights.html* (*http://bit.ly/2ocK3KK*), calls a macro to render our data. Note the use of |safe to ensure our HTML isn't escaped:

```
{% import "macros.jnj" as common %}
{% if nav_offsets and nav_path -%}
  {{ common.display_nav(nav_offsets, nav_path, flight_count, query)|safe }}
{% endif -%}
```

We place this in our Jinja2 macros file, further breaking up the task as the drawing of two links inside a div:

```
ch04/web/templates/macros.jnj
<!-- Display two navigation links for previous/next page in the flight list -->
{% macro display_nav(offsets, path, count, query) -%}
  <div style="text-align: center;">
    {% for key, values in offsets.items() -%}
      {%- if values['bottom_offset'] >= 0 and values['top_offset'] >
      0 and count > values['bottom_offset'] -%}
        <a style="margin-left: 20px; margin-right: 20px;"
          href="{{ path }}?start={{ values
          ['bottom_offset'] }}&end={{ values['top_offset']
           }}{%- if query -%}?search=
          {{query}}{%- endif -%}">{{ key }}</a>
      {% else -%}
        {{ key }}
      {% endif %}
    {% endfor -%}
  </div>
{% endmacro -%}
```

And we're done. We can now paginate through our list of flights as we would in any other flight website. We're one step closer to providing the kind of user experience that will enable real user sessions, and we've extended a graph connecting flights over the top of our individual records. This additional structure will enable even more structure later on, as we climb the data-value pyramid.

Searching for Flights

Browsing through a list of flights certainly beats manually looking up message_ids, but it's hardly as efficient as searching for flights of interest. Let's use our data platform to add search.

Creating Our Index

Before we can store our documents in Elasticsearch, we need to create a search index for them to reside in. Check out *elastic_scripts/create.sh* (*http://bit.ly/2oBJvMm*). Note that we create only a single shard with a single replica. In production, you would want to distribute the workload around a cluster of multiple machines with multiple shards, and to achieve redundancy and high availability with multiple replicas of each shard. For our purposes, one of each is fine!

```
#!/usr/bin/env bash

curl -XPUT 'http://localhost:9200/agile_data_science/' -d '{
    "settings" : {
        "index" : {
            "number_of_shards" : 1,
            "number_of_replicas" : 1
        }
    }
}'
```

Go ahead and run the script, before we move on to publishing our on-time performance records to Elasticsearch:

```
elastic_scripts/create.sh
```

Note that if you want to start over, you can blow away the `agile_data_science` index with:

```
elastic_scripts/drop.sh
```

And just like the create script, it calls `curl`:

```
#!/usr/bin/env bash

curl -XDELETE 'http://localhost:9200/agile_data_science/'
```

Publishing Flights to Elasticsearch

Using the recipe we created in Chapter 2, it is easy to publish our on-time performance flight data to Elasticsearch. Check out *ch04/pyspark_to_elasticsearch.py* (*http://bit.ly/2pGuAjy*):

```
# Load the Parquet file
on_time_dataframe = spark.read.parquet('data/on_time_performance.parquet')

# Save the DataFrame to Elasticsearch
on_time_dataframe.write.format("org.elasticsearch.spark.sql")\
    .option("es.resource","agile_data_science/on_time_performance")\
    .option("es.batch.size.entries","100")\
    .mode("overwrite")\
    .save()
```

Note that we need to set `es.batch.size.entries` to 100, down from the default of 1000. This keeps Elasticsearch from being overwhelmed by Spark. You can find other settings to adjust in the configuration guide (*http://bit.ly/2pGLi25*).

Note that this might take some time, as there are several million records to index. You might want to leave this alone to run for a while. You can interrupt it midway and move on; so long as some records are indexed you should be okay. Similarly, if there is an error, you should check the results of the following query; it might be possible to disregard the error and just move on, if enough records have been indexed for the rest of the examples.

Querying our data with `curl` is easy. This time, let's look for flights originating in Atlanta (airport code ATL), the world's busiest airport:

```
curl \
  'localhost:9200/agile_data_science/on_time_performance/ \
    _search?q=Origin:ATL&pretty'
```

The output looks like so:

```
{
  "took": 7,
  "timed_out": false,
  "_shards": {
    "total": 5,
    "successful": 5,
    "failed": 0
  },
  "hits": {
    "total": 379424,
    "max_score": 3.7330098,
    "hits": [
      {
        "_index": "agile_data_science",
        "_type": "on_time_performance",
        "_id": "AVakkdOGX8o-akD569e2",
        "_score": 3.7330098,
        "_source": {
          "Year": 2015,
          "Quarter": 3,
          "Month": 9,
          "DayofMonth": 23,
          "DayOfWeek": 3,
          "FlightDate": "2015-09-23",
          "UniqueCarrier": "DL",
          ...
```

Note the useful information our query returned along with the records found: how long the query took (7 ms) and the total number of records that matched our query (379,424).

Searching Flights on the Web

Next, let's connect our search engine to the web.

First, configure `pyelastic` to point at our Elasticsearch server:

```
# ch04/web/config.py
ELASTIC_URL = 'http://localhost:9200/agile_data_science'
```

Then import, set up, and query Elasticsearch via the */flights/search* path in *ch04/web/ on_time_flask_template.py* (*http://bit.ly/2nRRk3E*):

```python
@app.route("/flights/search")
def search_flights():

  # Search parameters
  carrier = request.args.get('Carrier')
  flight_date = request.args.get('FlightDate')
  origin = request.args.get('Origin')
  dest = request.args.get('Dest')
  tail_number = request.args.get('TailNum')
  flight_number = request.args.get('FlightNum')

  # Pagination parameters
  start = request.args.get('start') or 0
  start = int(start)
  end = request.args.get('end') or config.RECORDS_PER_PAGE
  end = int(end)

  nav_offsets = get_navigation_offsets(start, end, config.RECORDS_PER_PAGE)

  # Build our Elasticsearch query
  query = {
    'query': {
      'bool': {
        'must': []}
    },
    'sort': [
      {'FlightDate': {'order': 'asc', 'ignore_unmapped' : True} },
      {'DepTime': {'order': 'asc', 'ignore_unmapped' : True} },
      {'Carrier': {'order': 'asc', 'ignore_unmapped' : True} },
      {'FlightNum': {'order': 'asc', 'ignore_unmapped' : True} },
      '_score'
    ],
    'from': start,
    'size': config.RECORDS_PER_PAGE
  }
  if carrier:
    query['query']['bool']['must'].append({'match': {'Carrier': carrier}})
  if flight_date:
    query['query']['bool']['must'].append({'match': {'FlightDate': flight_date}})
  if origin:
    query['query']['bool']['must'].append({'match': {'Origin': origin}})
  if dest:
    query['query']['bool']['must'].append({'match': {'Dest': dest}})
  if tail_number:
    query['query']['bool']['must'].append({'match': {'TailNum': tail_number}})
  if flight_number:
    query['query']['bool']['must'].append(\n||||{...}\n||||) # where |
                                                              # is a space
```

```
results = elastic.search(query)
flights, flight_count = process_search(results)

# Persist search parameters in the form template
return render_template(
  'search.html',
  flights=flights,
  flight_date=flight_date,
  flight_count=flight_count,
  nav_path=request.path,
  nav_offsets=nav_offsets,
  carrier=carrier,
  origin=origin,
  dest=dest,
  tail_number=tail_number,
  flight_number=flight_number
  )
```

Generalizing the navigation links, we are able to use a similar template for searching flights as we did for listing them. We'll need a form to search for flights against specific fields, so we create one at the top of the page. We have parameterized the template with all of our search arguments, to persist them through multiple submissions of the form. Check out *ch04/web/templates/search.html* (*http://bit.ly/2oEbvlD*):

```html
<form action="/flights/search" method="get">
  <label for="Carrier">Carrier</label>
  <input name="Carrier" maxlength="3" style="width: 40px; margin-right: 10px;"
      value="{{carrier}}"></input>
  <label for="Origin">Origin</label>
  <input name="Origin" maxlength="3" style="width: 40px; margin-right: 10px;"
      value="{{origin}}"></input>
  <label for="Dest">Dest</label>
  <input name="Dest" maxlength="3" style="width: 40px; margin-right: 10px;"
      value="{{dest}}"></input>
  <label for="FlightDate">FlightDate</label>
  <input name="FlightDate" style="width: 100px; margin-right: 10px;"
      value="{{flight_date}}"></input>
  <label for="TailNum">TailNum</label>
  <input name="TailNum" style="width: 100px; margin-right: 10px;"
      value="{{tail_number}}"></input>
  <label for="FlightNum">FlightNum</label>
  <input name="FlightNum" style="width: 50px; margin-right: 10px;"
      value="{{flight_number}}"></input>
  <button type="submit" class="btn btn-xs btn-default" style="height: 25px;">
    Submit
  </button>
</form>
```

Figure 4-9 shows the result.

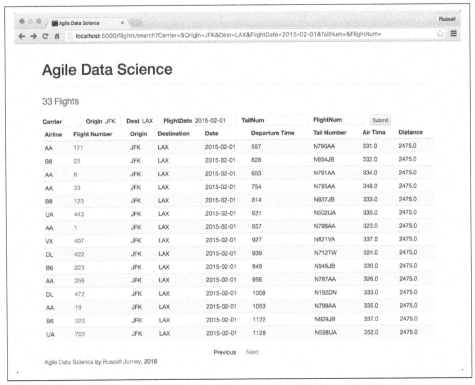

Figure 4-9. Searching for flights

Conclusion

We have now collected, published, indexed, displayed, listed, and searched flight records. They are no longer abstract. We can search for flights, click on individual flights, and explore as we might any other dataset. More importantly, we have piped our raw data through our platform and transformed it into an interactive application.

This application forms the base of our value stack. We will use it as the way to develop, present, and iterate on more advanced features throughout the book as we build value while walking up the data-value pyramid. With the base of the pyramid in place, we can move on to building charts.

## CHAPTER 5

Visualizing Data with Charts and Tables

In the next step, our second agile sprint, we will start building charts from our data (Figure 5-1).

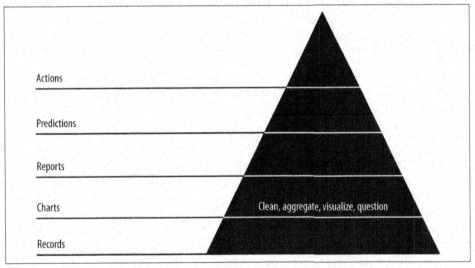

Figure 5-1. Level 2: visualizing with charts

Charts are our first view into our data in aggregate, mapping the properties of many records into visual representations that help us understand and navigate them. Our goals in this step are to publish charts to generate interest in our data and get users interacting with it, to build reusable tools that will help us explore our data interactively in reports in the next step, and to begin extracting structure and entities so that we can create new features and insights with this structure.

Code examples for this chapter are available at *Agile_Data_Code_2/ch05* (*http://bit.ly/ 2ok0YYY*). Clone the repository and follow along!

```
git clone https://github.com/rjurney/Agile_Data_Code_2.git
```

Chart Quality: Iteration Is Essential

A good chart is one that tells a story, that yields insight, and that users find interesting enough to share and respond to. In practice, most charts fail to achieve this, and have little value. Rare is the chart that tells a story. This is because most people make a chart and move on... when in reality, you have to iteratively create and improve charts to achieve useful visualizations. Expect to throw many charts away before you find a few good ones—don't try to specify them up front or you will be disappointed. Instead, try to use your intuition and curiosity to add charts organically, as you engage in ad hoc, interactive exploratory data analysis (*http://bit.ly/2ocx9xs*).

You can create charts in an ad hoc way at first, but as you progress, your workflow should become increasingly automated and reproducible. In Agile Data Science, we take a web-first approach to creating visualizations. While it is easier to create charts as images using matplotlib or R than it is to create web charts, this is changing fast. With modern JavaScript chart libraries, there isn't much overhead to creating a web-based chart, so that is what we do from the beginning.

Well-formed URLs with slugs or query parameters can be made to generalize, so one chart works for different slices of data according to different parameters and options. Once we master charts, in the next chapter, we will improve and extend our successful charts into full-blown interactive reports.

Scaling a Database in the Publish/Decorate Model

A concept related to database normalization (*http://bit.ly/2pM1u38*) that we must understand is how we compute, publish, and consume data for charts and other services, and where we put the data processing. The more processing you do in batch and the less processing you do at the publishing/database layer, the less you have to spend time operating a database. There are several patterns of data access that come with their own methods of data processing and database operations. We will briefly discuss them all and illustrate their operation both in batch and in serving published results in real time.

Which form is right for you depends on your application and data access patterns; your hardware budget; and the volume of your desire to depend on, operate, and tune a database. The less batch processing we do, the less efficient storage form we use, and the more features of a database we depend on, the more we have to tune and operate the database. This could be great, because we like operating databases. Or, from my perspective most of the time, it could be bad, because I'd rather not spend more than a few minutes a week operating a database.

We're going to discuss how to store a time series chart at decreasing levels of scalability and increasing levels of sophistication of the required database. For instance, operating a key/value store like Cassandra or Voldemort is extremely easy. There is no single point of failure, so you have room to sleep and ignore your database. By contrast, when operating a Bigtable clone where you have a master, there is a single point of failure, which is more likely to happen. When your master fails, your application will be down at least momentarily. This will require administration tasks to fix. If you employ an even more featureful database like MongoDB or MySQL, you will have to administer those features you make use of by, for instance, creating indexes to enable efficient access.

Note, though, that any database can be used simply as a key/value store, no matter how many features it offers. MySQL is very featureful, but if you don't employ its features, it makes a very simple and efficient key/value store. You simply store a JSON representation of your data and access it via a SELECT on its primary key. This may make sense for your application if you're a MySQL expert.

The point I want to make is that the more you compute in batch and the less you use database features, the simpler your application will be to operate and the more scalable it will be. Use database features thoughtfully. Prefer batch computing to employing database features and you will have an application that operates itself, instead of one that requires your constant attention.

First Order Form

The most scalable form of data is where you prepare the records for your chart, table, or prediction in their entirety and store those as a single, nested object within a key/value or document store (although technically, you can use any database as a key/value store by encoding the value in JSON and storing the record under its primary key). For instance, to store a time series chart's data, we would compute a sorted list of the values for the chart and encapsulate this list in an object with a primary key, through which we would access the chart's data in one query.

Figure 5-2 shows an example of this kind of prepare/publish model. In this form, we prepare an object containing a table of flights in sorted order inside a field called Flights. The object also has a primary key field called TailNum, which we use to access it.

```
{
        "TailNum" : "N16954"
        "Flights" : [
                [
                        "EV",
                        "2015-01-07",
                        3926,
                        "IAH",
                        "MFE"
                ],
                ...
        ]
}
```

Figure 5-2. An object prepared for a document store

This form is the most scalable of all because you need use only a key/value store to hold the data, and to query this data you use a single, unique key. Serving data from a key/value store is a much simpler problem than most relational databases, for instance, solve. This makes them easy to operate in systems without a single point of failure. This translates into simple operations. Remember: first order form makes operations easy.

Second Order Form

The next most scalable form takes advantage of key range scans (*https://hbase.apache.org/book.html#scan*) in Google Bigtable (*http://bit.ly/18N6Ctq*) clones like Apache HBase (*http://hbase.apache.org/*). Data in HBase tables is stored sorted by key, in alphabetical order. This is a critical feature because it means you can access a range of values very efficiently, the records for similar keys being near (next to) one another on disk.

Key design then becomes the mechanism through which you can perform many operations you might expect from relational databases. Apache Phoenix (*http://phoenix.apache.org/*) provides a SQL abstraction on top of HBase, which means you don't have to employ tricks in Java to make HBase go. Phoenix is the go-to way to use HBase for application developers (who need to get things done quickly). An excellent "Introduction to HBase Schema Design" (*http://bit.ly/2pxRIBo*) by Amandeep Khurana is available if you'd like to dive deeper.

We don't employ HBase in the book, but Figure 5-3 shows what our last example might look like in HBase land. To reproduce the query, we would compose a unique key for our data so that when stored in sorted order and retrieved by a scan against the `TailNum` it would produce a sorted list of flights identical to the one in the previous example.

Key: TailNum + FlightDate + FlightNum + Origin + Dest	Carrier	FlightDate	FlightNum	Origin	Dest	TailNum
N16953-2015-12-31-1241-ATL-SFO	DL	2015-12-31	1241	ATL	SFO	N16953
N16954-2015-01-07-3926-IAH-MFE	EV	2015-01-07	3926	IAH	MFE	N16954
N16954-2015-01-07-3926-MFE-IAH	EV	2015-01-07	3926	MFE	IAH	N16954
...						
N16955-2015-01-01-1611-LAX-LAS	AA	2015-01-01	1611	LAX	LAS	N16955

Figure 5-3. Documents stored in HBase with compound key prepared to enable range scan access pattern

Range scans can be used to handle many types of query through novel key composition. They are surprisingly powerful, and yet they scale surprisingly well. HBase applications handling petabytes of data exist and operate with relative ease. We could easily have employed HBase and Apache Phoenix to produce many of the examples in this book. Remember: if first order form won't work for you, second order form becomes the go-to form.

Third Order Form

The next most efficient way to store data is to summarize it in terms of time or category and store the result in a database like MySQL or MongoDB that employs B-tree (*https://en.wikipedia.org/wiki/B-tree*) indexes (*https://en.wikipedia.org/wiki/Database_index*) to enable efficient lookup of portions of rows in a table, or to facilitate joins. This could replicate a range scan, or it could enable arbitrary, more complex queries that don't resemble a range scan on a sorted table at all. These databases often include the capability to GROUP BY and compute aggregate metrics, similar to what we've done with Spark SQL.

Queries against relational and featureful document stores might compute any given metric at the time of query, or a hybrid approach might occur in which precomputed summaries are delivered by selecting a range of records, similar to a key range scan. We won't demonstrate third order form in this book, but you're probably familiar with it already. It can break the publish/decorate model we've used in this book, or it might simply serve range scans on preaggregated metrics.

Choosing a Form

In general, the lower order form you choose, the easier the system is to scale, and to scale horizontally. But remember: you can always choose a more featureful database and not use its features, except in cases of dire need. For instance, you might use MySQL as a key/value store, or to serve range scans of preaggregated metrics. It will scale easily when used this way. You would have the option, however, of using a GROUP BY if you needed to, in order to more rapidly implement a new feature of your application. You could always scale the feature by moving the processing "back in the stack" to the batch layer if it proves popular.

The key lesson here is to *use database features thoughtfully*, because the more you use them, the more difficult your application will be to scale. Batch computation is relatively easy compared to keeping a large and featureful database instance going under heavy load. You will need to know your database well, and understand the consequences of each feature on the system overall.

Exploring Seasonality

We have to begin somewhere, so let's begin with a question: which is the busiest month for air travel?

This question involves *seasonality*. Seasonality is present when a measure changes repeatedly and consistently, depending on the time of year. For instance, Christmas light sales would display strong seasonality (although I hang them year round), with sales peaking in December every year.

This is a chance to show how SQL and NoSQL dataflows fit together and complement one another. Let's make our first chart, in which we count the total flights by month for the year 2015. Flights by month is very easily expressible as SQL.

Querying and Presenting Flight Volume

```
PYSPARK_DRIVER_PYTHON=ipython pyspark
```

Our PySpark script, *ch05/total_flights.py* (*http://bit.ly/2pe6KPO*), looks like this:

```
# Load the Parquet file
on_time_dataframe = spark.read.parquet('data/on_time_performance.parquet')

# Use SQL to look at the total flights by month across 2015
on_time_dataframe.registerTempTable("on_time_dataframe")
total_flights_by_month = spark.sql(
  """SELECT Month, Year, COUNT(*) AS total_flights
  FROM on_time_dataframe
  GROUP BY Year, Month
  ORDER BY Year, Month"""
)

# This map/asDict trick makes the rows print a little prettier. It is optional.
flights_chart_data = total_flights_by_month.rdd.map(lambda row: row.asDict())
flights_chart_data.collect()
```

This gets us the raw data for our chart:

```
[{'Month': 1, 'Year': 2015, 'total_flights': 469968},
 {'Month': 2, 'Year': 2015, 'total_flights': 429191},
 {'Month': 3, 'Year': 2015, 'total_flights': 504312},
 {'Month': 4, 'Year': 2015, 'total_flights': 485151},
 {'Month': 5, 'Year': 2015, 'total_flights': 496993},
 {'Month': 6, 'Year': 2015, 'total_flights': 503897},
 {'Month': 7, 'Year': 2015, 'total_flights': 520718},
 {'Month': 8, 'Year': 2015, 'total_flights': 510536},
 {'Month': 9, 'Year': 2015, 'total_flights': 464946},
 {'Month': 10, 'Year': 2015, 'total_flights': 486165},
 {'Month': 11, 'Year': 2015, 'total_flights': 467972},
 {'Month': 12, 'Year': 2015, 'total_flights': 479230}]
```

Save it to MongoDB:

```
# Save chart to MongoDB
import pymongo_spark
pymongo_spark.activate()
flights_chart_data.saveToMongoDB('mongodb://localhost:27017/ \
  agile_data_science.flights_by_month')
```

and verify it's there:

```
> db.flights_by_month.find().sort({"Year": 1, "Month": 1})
{ "_id" : ObjectId(
  "56ff1246b050473d23777138"
),
  "total_flights" : 469968,
  "Month" : 1,
  "Year" : 2015
}
{
  "_id" : ObjectId("56ff1246b050473d23777134"),
  "total_flights" : 429191,
  "Month" : 2,
  "Year" : 2015
}
{
  "_id" : ObjectId("56ff1246b050473d23777137"),
  "total_flights" : 504312,
  "Month" : 3,
  "Year" : 2015
}
{
  "_id" : ObjectId("56ff1246b050473d2377713a"),
  "total_flights" : 485151,
  "Month" : 4,
  "Year" : 2015
}
...
```

Now let's set up new Flask controllers to serve our chart's HTML page, and its data as JSON:

```
# Controller: Fetch a flight chart
@app.route("/total_flights")
def total_flights():
  total_flights = client.agile_data_science.flights_by_month.find({},
    sort = [
      ('Year', 1),
      ('Month', 1)
    ])
  return render_template('total_flights.html', total_flights=total_flights)

# Serve the chart's data via an asynchronous request (formerly known as 'AJAX')
@app.route("/total_flights.json")
def total_flights_json():
  total_flights = client.agile_data_science.flights_by_month.find({},
    sort = [
      ('Year', 1),
      ('Month', 1)
    ])
  return json_util.dumps(total_flights, ensure_ascii=False)
```

Note that before we make a chart, we're going to create a simple table, as we did in the last chapter:

```
{% extends "layout.html" %}
{% block body %}
  <div>
    <p class="lead">Total Flights by Month</p>
    <table class="table table-condensed table-striped" style="width: 200px;">
      <thead>
        <th>Month</th>
        <th>Total Flights</th>
      </thead>
      <tbody>
        {% for month in total_flights %}
        <tr>
          <td>{{month.Month}}</td>
          <td>{{month.total_flights}}</td>
        </tr>
        {% endfor %}
      </tbody>
    </table>
  </div>
{% endblock %}
```

Figure 5-4 shows the result.

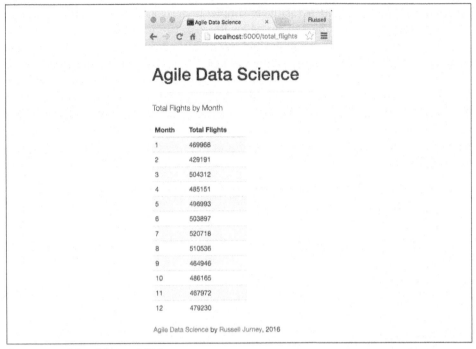

Figure 5-4. Monthly total flights

As far as presenting data in tables, that is it! This is the place to start, but I can't look at that table and notice any trends—can you? Let's use D3 to make a time series chart. We'll start by making a controller in Flask to serve our chart page, and a derivative of our table controller that serves the JSON data for our chart:

```
# Controller: Fetch a flight chart
@app.route("/total_flights_chart")
def total_flights_chart():
  total_flights = client.agile_data_science.flights_by_month.find({},
    sort = [
      ('Year', 1),
      ('Month', 1)
    ])
  return render_template('total_flights_chart.html', total_flights=total_flights)

# Serve the chart's data via an asynchronous request (formerly known as 'AJAX')
@app.route("/total_flights.json")
def total_flights_json():
  total_flights = client.agile_data_science.flights_by_month.find({},
    sort = [
      ('Year', 1),
      ('Month', 1)
    ])
  return json_util.dumps(total_flights, ensure_ascii=False)
```

The template for our chart is relatively simple: it starts as a paste from an example (*https://bost.ocks.org/mike/bar/3/*) by Mike Bostock (*https://bost.ocks.org/mike/*). In the last edition we started with an example by Mike, and then showed how you might have built it from the ground up—but we did not build it from the ground up (we did credit Mike's example). You never build them from the ground up, so in this edition I'm going to tell the truth about D3: nearly all D3 charts begin as examples from Mike Bostock. Taking examples and adapting them to your needs is a skill fundamental not just to visualization, but to all data science and programming in general. Nobody knows everything, and the job involves a lot of figuring things out. This edition aims to teach you to do that.

Our template reproduces the CSS style code from the example:

```
{% extends "layout.html" %}
{% block body %}
<style>

.chart rect {
  fill: steelblue;
}

.chart text {
  fill: white;
  font: 10px sans-serif;
  text-anchor: middle;
}

</style>

  <div>
    <p class="lead">Total Flights by Month</p>
    <div id="chart"><svg class="chart"></svg></div>
  </div>
  <script src="/static/app.js"></script>
  <script>

  </script>
{% endblock %}
```

It also puts the JavaScript from the same example into *ch05/web/static/app.js* (*http://bit.ly/2opErZZ*), with a few changes. *d3.tsv* won't work for us, unless we copy the example's data over. We need to edit just a few things to get the example working. Changed lines are highlighted in bold:

```
var width = 960,
    height = 350;

var y = d3.scale.linear()
    .range([height, 0]);
    // We define the domain once we get our data in d3.json, below
```

```
var chart = d3.select(".chart")
    .attr("width", width)
    .attr("height", height);

d3.json("/total_flights.json", function(data) {
  y.domain([0, d3.max(data, function(d) { return d.total_flights; })]);

  var barWidth = width / data.length;

  var bar = chart.selectAll("g")
      .data(data)
      .enter()
      .append("g")
      .attr("transform", function(d, i) {
          return "translate(" + i * barWidth + ",0)"; });

  bar.append("rect")
      .attr("y", function(d) { return y(d.total_flights); })
      .attr("height", function(d) { return height - y(d.total_flights); })
      .attr("width", barWidth - 1);

  bar.append("text")
      .attr("x", barWidth / 2)
      .attr("y", function(d) { return y(d.total_flights) + 3; })
      .attr("dy", ".75em")
      .text(function(d) { return d.total_flights; });
});
```

The first step is pointing the script at our data using the d3.json (*http://bit.ly/ 2p3T2Ld*) method, and pointing it at our server at */total_flights.json*. After that, we just need to change the value field from y to total_flights throughout the file, and we're done! This produces a chart detailing how flight volume changes per month (Figure 5-5).

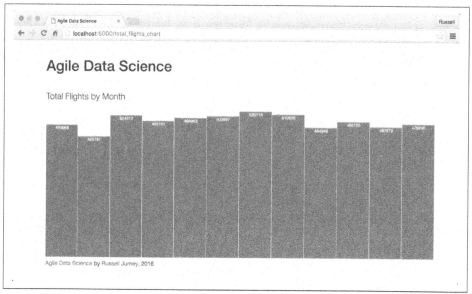

Figure 5-5. The resulting chart after adapting an example from Mike Bostock

We've created a simple chart in D3. Note that we haven't gotten fancy, and when you first create a chart you shouldn't. Start with something that simply visualizes the data, and then add bells and whistles once you've found a chart that merits it.

Iterating on our first chart

True to our introduction, we're going to iterate on this chart to help answer our original question, "Which is the busiest month for air travel?" Can you tell by looking at this chart what the answer to that question is? Looking very carefully, I see it's July, but I can't easily tell at a glance.

What our question is really asking is, for a given year, what month is the mode? Wikipedia defines *mode* as "the value that appears most often in a set of data." We can improve our chart by highlighting the mode, since it isn't obvious from the bars alone. Let's edit *app.js* to highlight the mode, so it is apparent at a glance. We need to create a function called `varColor`, which will return a different color when the value is the maximum. We apply this to the chart's bar/rectangle selection using D3's `style` (*https://github.com/d3/d3-selection#selection_style*) method:

```
d3.json("/total_flights.json", function(data) {

    var defaultColor = 'steelblue';
    var modeColor = '#4CA9F5';

    var maxY = d3.max(data, function(d) { return d.total_flights; });
    y.domain([0, maxY]);
```

```
var varColor = function(d, i) {
    if(d['total_flights'] == maxY) { return modeColor; }
    else { return defaultColor; }
}
var barWidth = width / data.length;
var bar = chart.selectAll("g")
    .data(data)
    .enter()
    .append("g")
    .attr("transform", function(d, i) {
        return "translate(" + i * barWidth + ",0)"; });

bar.append("rect")
    .attr("y", function(d) { return y(d.total_flights); })
    .attr("height", function(d) { return height - y(d.total_flights); })
    .attr("width", barWidth - 1)
    .style("fill", varColor);

bar.append("text")
    .attr("x", barWidth / 2)
    .attr("y", function(d) { return y(d.total_flights) + 3; })
    .attr("dy", ".75em")
    .text(function(d) { return d.total_flights; });
});
```

The result makes the answer to our question readily apparent (see Figure 5-6).

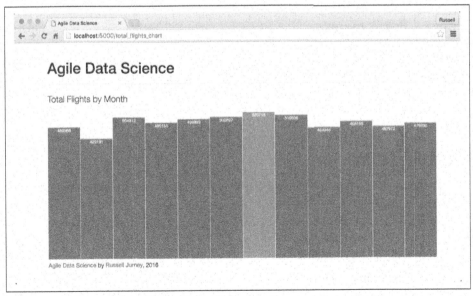

Figure 5-6. The second iteration of our chart

This completes the titular element of the second level of the data-value pyramid. Now let's explore another element: entity extraction.

Extracting Metal (Airplanes [Entities])

There is another element to the charts layer of the data-value pyramid: entity extraction. Entity extraction is implicit during chart creation, in the sense that we are grouping atomic records on properties to produce aggregates. Entities often emerge as a next step in our analysis. For instance, having listed and searched flights in the previous chapter and having aggregated flights in this one, it is natural to dig into some other aspects of the flights themselves: airplanes, airlines, and airports. Figure 5-7 shows the entities we might want to extract.

Carrier	Origin	Dest	FlightDate		TailNum N18223	FlightNum	Submit		
Airline	Flight Number		Origin	Destination	Date	Departure Time	Tail Number	Air Time	Distance
UA	1104		ANC	DEN	2015-01-01	1	N18223	268.0	2405.0
UA	1746		ATL	SFO	2015-01-01	741	N18223	300.0	2139.0
UA	1451		SFO	ORD	2015-01-01	1106	N18223	231.0	1846.0
UA	1623		ORD	ANC	2015-01-01	1844	N18223	407.0	2846.0
UA	1250		DEN	MCO	2015-01-02	807	N18223	181.0	1546.0
UA	1262		MCO	EWR	2015-01-02	1416	N18223	124.0	937.0
UA	1191		EWR	SFO	2015-01-02	1833	N18223	367.0	2565.0
UA	1204		SFO	IAH	2015-01-02	2328	N18223	210.0	1635.0

Figure 5-7. Entities emerge!

Let's focus on one entity to start: airplanes. An airplane is referred to as the "metal" of a flight, and a tail number is a unique identifier for an airplane. We're going to extract airplanes by their tail number, in order to demonstrate how to extract entities from raw data. We will create a new entity for each tail number, and it will list all flights for that plane.

Extracting Tail Numbers

We start by creating an index of all flights for a given airplane, represented by its TailNum field. We'll create a tuple with a tail number as the first field, and every unique flight that tail number made in 2015 as the second field, sorted by date.

Data processing: batch or realtime?

We are now presented with a choice: where to implement this feature. This decision is a common one you will experience in the field working on real data applications. The general rule is to prototype anywhere, at any layer from Spark to HTML mocks, but to push to batch processing as you are able.

The first option in this case is using PySpark to group flights by tail number. This method puts all of our processing at the far backend in batch, which would be desirable for very large data. The second method is to use a MongoDB query or Elasticsearch facets to query our flight record index just as we have before, but with different handling in our web application.

In this instance, we choose to group flights in PySpark and store them in MongoDB. We do this because we intend to use this data in other analyses via joins, and while we can read data from Elasticsearch in PySpark, it is important to have a copy of intermediate data on reliable bulk storage, where it is truly persistent and easily accessible. We know we can easily and arbitrarily scale operations in Spark, so doing data processing in this layer is conservative.

Grouping and sorting data in Spark

We'll need to group by tail number to get a list of flights per airplane, identified by carrier, date, origin/destination, and flight number. Note that for round-trip flights, where a plane turns around and goes directly back to where it came from, there are often two flights per day with the same carrier and flight number; one for coming and one for going.

Check out *ch05/extract_airplanes.py (http://bit.ly/2pP9i3i)*. First we load the data, and then we filter down to the fields we need. Dropping unneeded, extra fields is always a good idea to keep things performant:

```
# Load the Parquet file
on_time_dataframe = spark.read.parquet('data/on_time_performance.parquet')

# Filter down to the fields we need to identify and link to a flight
flights = on_time_dataframe.rdd.map(lambda x:
  (x.Carrier, x.FlightDate, x.FlightNum, x.Origin, x.Dest, x.TailNum)
  )
```

Now, we group flights by tail number and then sort these flights by date, flight number, then origin/destination airport codes. Note that the first step in achieving this is to create a tuple where the first field is the tail number, and the second field is a one-tuple list. What good is a one-tuple list? Lists in Python can be added like so:

```
a = [0]
b = [1]
c = a + b
print(c)
```

The result is:

```
    [0, 1]
```

Here we will add lists in our reduce step, so we need to initialize them in our map step:

```
flights_per_airplane = flights\
    .map(lambda nameTuple: (nameTuple[5], [nameTuple[0:5]]))\
```

Also note that we drop the last field, TailNum, in the list of tuples. TailNum is the same for all records in a group and is stored as the key, so it is redundant. This is a style option; you can leave TailNum in if you like.

Next, we aggregate a list per key by adding them in a reduce step:

```
    .reduceByKey(lambda a, b: a + b)\
```

Finally, we produce a dict we can store in Mongo. We also sort the list of flights we just aggregated by date, flight number, then origin and destination:

```
    .map(lambda tuple:
        {
          'TailNum': tuple[0],
          'Flights': sorted(tuple[1], key=lambda x: (x[1], x[2], x[3], x[4]))
        }
      )
```

Check out what we've created (this may take a few minutes):

```
> db.flights_per_airplane.first()
```

```
{'Flights': [(u'AA', u'2015-01-01', 262, u'RSW', u'DFW'),
  (u'AA', u'2015-01-01', 2414, u'DFW', u'EWR'),
  (u'AA', u'2015-01-02', 1060, u'LAX', u'TPA'),
  (u'AA', u'2015-01-02', 1161, u'MIA', u'TPA'),
  (u'AA', u'2015-01-02', 1161, u'TPA', u'MIA'),
  (u'AA', u'2015-01-02', 1205, u'EWR', u'MIA'),
  (u'AA', u'2015-01-02', 1370, u'MIA', u'ORD'),
  (u'AA', u'2015-01-02', 2271, u'ORD', u'LAX'),
  (u'AA', u'2015-01-03', 346, u'ORD', u'LGA'),
  (u'AA', u'2015-01-03', 1192, u'LAX', u'ORD'),
  (u'AA', u'2015-01-03', 1209, u'TPA', u'LAX'),
  ...],
 'TailNum': u'N3MDAA'}
```

Publishing airplanes with Mongo

Finally, we store these records to MongoDB, where we can fetch them by tail number:

```
import pymongo_spark
pymongo_spark.activate()
flights_per_airplane.saveToMongoDB(
  'mongodb://localhost:27017/agile_data_science.flights_per_airplane'
  )
```

Now we'll check on our data in MongoDB:

```
mongo agile_data_science
```

```
> db.flights_per_airplane.findOne()
```

```
{
        "_id" : ObjectId("5700092b8821240a5941fed2"),
        "TailNum" : "N249AU",
        "Flights" : [
                [
                        "US",
                        "2015-01-03",
                        837,
                        "STT",
                        "PHL"
                ],
    ...
        ]
}
```

Serving airplanes with Flask

We can see how to query airplanes by tail number, which is an important access pattern given that the tail number is a unique identifier for an airplane. *This kind of data is foundational—it lets us add features to a page by directly rendering precomputed data.* We'll start by displaying these flights as list via the */airplane/flights* controller in *ch05/web/chart_flask.py* (*http://bit.ly/2pPyOFG*):

```
# Controller: Fetch a flight and display it
@app.route("/airplane/flights/<tail_number>")
def flights_per_airplane(tail_number):
  flights = client.agile_data_science.flights_per_airplane.find_one(
    {'TailNum': tail_number}
)
  return render_template(
    'flights_per_airplane.html', flights=flights, tail_number=tail_number
)
```

Our template is simple. It extends our application layout and relies on Bootstrap for styling the table. Once again, we link to the individual flight record page from the flight number in our table:

```
{% extends "layout.html" %}
{% block body %}
  <div>
    <p class="lead">Flights by Tail Number {{tail_number}}</p>
    <table class="table table-condensed table-striped">
      <thead>
        <th>Carrier</th>
        <th>Date</th>
        <th>Flight Number</th>
        <th>Origin</th>
        <th>Destination</th>
      </thead>
      <tbody>
        {% for flight in flights['Flights'] %}
        <tr>
```

```
      <td>{{flight[0]}}</td>
      <td>{{flight[1]}}</td>
      <td>{{flight[2]}}</td>
      <td>
        <a href="/on_time_performance?Carrier={{flight[0]}}
&FlightDate={{flight[1]}}
&FlightNum={{flight[2]}}">{{flight[2]}}</a>
      </td>
      <td>{{flight[3]}}</td>
      <td>{{flight[4]}}</td>
    </tr>
    {% endfor %}
  </tbody>
</table>
</div>
{% endblock %}
```

The result is a page for an airplane detailing its flights for the year (Figure 5-8).

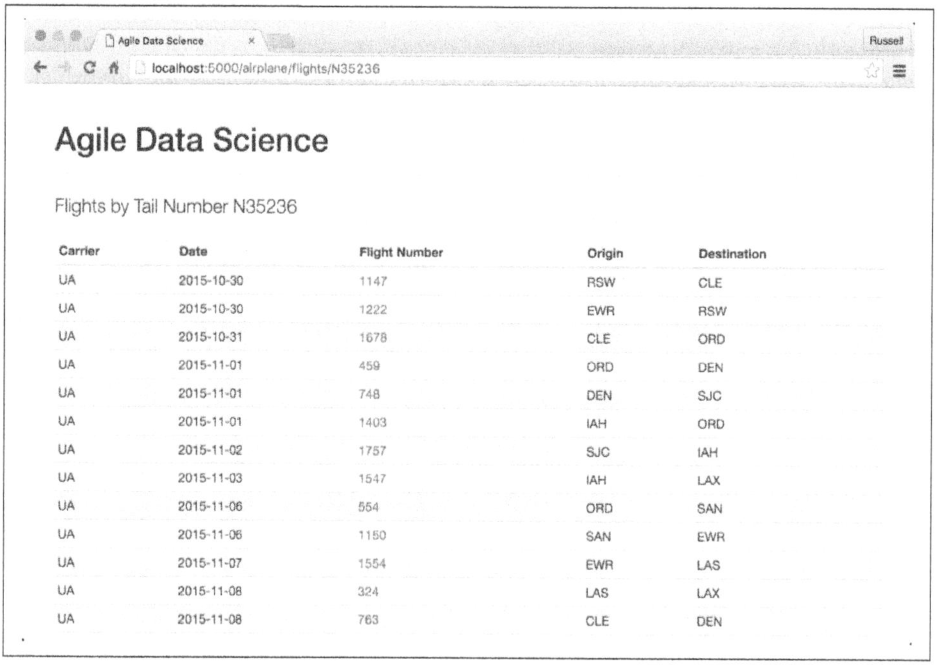

Figure 5-8. Flights by tail number

Ensuring database performance with indexes

However, there is one problem. Our query is slow! We need to add an index to Mongo to improve the lookup of the flight records by tail number. Check out *ch05/mongo.js* (*http://bit.ly/2oJSN9a*).

This is a good time to talk about indexes. Indexes in Mongo are similar to indexes in MySQL or any other relational database. They use B-trees to optimize query lookups. When queries are slow, indexes come in handy.

First, we use explain (*http://bit.ly/2pP9PSA*) to verify that the query is not using an index. The output shows that 13,533 objects are being scanned to return one record, using a BasicCursor (*https://docs.mongodb.com/v3.0/core/cursors/*) cursor:

```
> db.flights_per_airplane.find({"TailNum": "N361VA"}).explain()

{
        "cursor" : "BasicCursor",
        "isMultiKey" : false,
        "n" : 4,
        "nscannedObjects" : 13533,
        "nscanned" : 13533,
        "nscannedObjectsAllPlans" : 13533,
        "nscannedAllPlans" : 13533,
        "scanAndOrder" : false,
        "indexOnly" : false,
        "nYields" : 105,
        "nChunkSkips" : 0,
        "millis" : 28,
        "server" : "Russells-MacBook-Pro-OLD-506.local:27017",
        "filterSet" : false
}
```

Then we add an index with ensureIndex (*http://bit.ly/2qWvEjN*). Creating indexes is simple—just select the fields you will query with, and put them as keys in a JSON object with a value of 1:

```
> db.flights_per_airplane.ensureIndex({"TailNum": 1})

{
        "createdCollectionAutomatically" : false,
        "numIndexesBefore" : 1,
        "numIndexesAfter" : 2,
        "ok" : 1
}
```

Finally, we explain again to make sure the query is using an index:

```
> db.flights_per_airplane.find({"TailNum": "N361VA"}).explain()

{
        "cursor" : "BtreeCursor TailNum_1",
        "isMultiKey" : false,
        "n" : 4,
        "nscannedObjects" : 4,
        "nscanned" : 4,
        "nscannedObjectsAllPlans" : 4,
        "nscannedAllPlans" : 4,
        "scanAndOrder" : false,
```

```
            "indexOnly" : false,
            "nYields" : 0,
            "nChunkSkips" : 0,
            "millis" : 3,
            "indexBounds" : {
                    "TailNum" : [
                            [
                                    "N361VA",
                                    "N361VA"
                            ]
                    ]
            },
            "server" : "Russells-MacBook-Pro-OLD-506.local:27017",
            "filterSet" : false
    }
```

Now our query uses the `TailNum_1` index, and only scans four objects. Thus, it returns instantly, and our app will perform well.

You should always add indexes when you create new collections. If you forget, you may sometimes notice and sometimes not. This is because even if a query has to scan an entire table to return a result, it will still be fast enough if there are only a few users. When there are many users, though, these things come to light, so it is best to create an index when you create the collection.

Linking back in to our new entity

We've got one more thing to do: link to a tail number page from a flight's page. We'll need to edit *ch05/web/templates/flight.html* (*http://bit.ly/2oSixlM*) and *ch05/web/templates/search.html* (*http://bit.ly/2pemdzp*):

```
{% extends "layout.html" %}
{% block body %}
  <div>
    <p class="lead">Flight {{flight.FlightNum}}</p>
    <table class="table">
      <thead>
        <th>Airline</th>
        <th>Origin</th>
        <th>Destination</th>
        <th>Tail Number</th>
        <th>Date</th>
        <th>Air Time</th>
        <th>Distance</th>
      </thead>
      <tbody>
        <tr>
          <td>{{flight.Carrier}}</td>
          <td>{{flight.Origin}}</td>
          <td>{{flight.Dest}}</td>
          <td><a href="/airplane/flights/{{flight.TailNum}}">{{flight.TailNum}}
```

```
      </a>
    </td>
    <td>{{flight.FlightDate}}</td>
    <td>{{flight.AirTime}}</td>
    <td>{{flight.Distance}}</td>
  </tr>
      </tbody>
    </table>
  </div>
{% endblock %}
```

This produces the result in Figure 5-9.

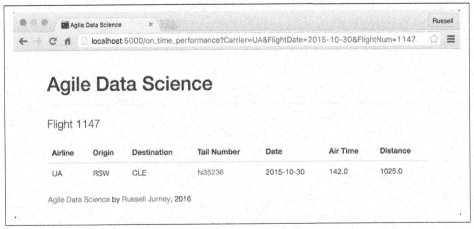

Figure 5-9. Linking back to airplane pages from the flight page

Information architecture

Now that our airplanes are on the web, we've got a place to put any interesting data tables, charts, and recommendations we create as we climb the data-value pyramid. We're creating good information architecture (*http://bit.ly/2pyB9p2*), which Wikipedia defines as "the structural design of shared information environments." As we build up our *shared information environment* (our web application and, within the team, our deep storage), if we have a logical structure to the application we make it naturally browsable and shareable. It will make sense to our users, who will pivot between the entities we've created as they ask questions and find answers.

Assessing Our Airplanes

Now that we're thinking about airplanes, let's assess the *intermediate dataset* we've just created. Just how many airplanes are there? We can get a count by running *ch05/assess_airplanes.py* (*http://bit.ly/2oSjYkc*):

```
# Load the Parquet file
on_time_dataframe = spark.read.parquet('data/on_time_performance.parquet')
on_time_dataframe.registerTempTable("on_time_performance")

# Dump the unneeded fields
tail_numbers = on_time_dataframe.map(lambda x: x.TailNum)
tail_numbers = tail_numbers.filter(lambda x: x != '')

# distinct() gets us unique tail numbers
unique_tail_numbers = tail_numbers.distinct()

# Now we need a count() of unique tail numbers
airplane_count = unique_tail_numbers.count()
print("Total airplanes: {}".format(airplane_count))
```

Which gives us:

```
Total airplanes: 4897
```

Wow, that's a lot of airplanes! Now I'm wondering things like: Which airplanes are they? Who made them? How much are all those airplanes worth in total? To answer that first question, we'll need to *enrich* our data with another source: the FAA Registry.

Data Enrichment

Now that we have tail numbers of airplanes, we want more information about the planes! This information is not contained in the on-time flight performance records, so we need to *enrich* our dataset with another. Techopedia (*http://bit.ly/2pwWiTp*) defines data enrichment as a "term that refers to processes used to enhance, refine or otherwise improve raw data." When we say *enrich*, we mean bring in another dataset that enhances what we've already got—in other words, a join and some additional processing called *munging*.

Reverse Engineering a Web Form

The data we need is contained in the FAA Registry (*http://bit.ly/2oSrDit*) for airplanes. Check out all the cool stuff in the registry: manufacturer, model, year manufactured, owner, and even the engine manufacturer and model! This opens up many possibilities for our analysis. We need this data.

There's just one problem: the data is not available for download. This is often the case, and this is one reason for the saying about 90% of data science being "munging." To get this dataset, we'll need to *scrape* it, or extract it from the web, one N-Number at a time. We can easily do this in Python.

We are not including a script for these operations in the code examples, because we don't want numerous readers to scrape the FAA Registry (which might result in a service disruption from overload). You can copy and paste or type out code from the book to get started scraping other pages, but please *don't scrape the FAA Registry.*

Before we can start coding, we need to inspect the result of the inquiry form (Figure 5-10). The URL for our search for N933EV is *http://bit.ly/2pPnQQm* (see Figure 5-11). You can see that the N-Number is encoded in the URL query parameters as *NNumbertxt*, which means this form uses an HTTP GET request. If somehow you're unfamiliar with how the web works, check out the method definitions in section 9 of RFC 2616 (*http://bit.ly/2oINiJM*). Anyone not familiar with web forms should skim sections 3 and 4 of the RFC. The other type of form is a POST form, but we'll get to those later. Scraping a GET form is simple.

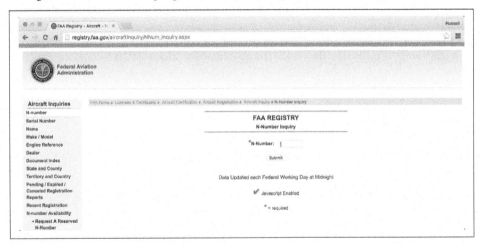

Figure 5-10. FAA Registry N-Number inquiry

Figure 5-11. FAA Registry results

Gathering Tail Numbers

In order to use what we've learned about the inquiry form, we need to create a list of tail numbers for our scraper to read and use as the `NNumbertxt` value.

We do this with *ch05/save_tail_numbers.py* (*http://bit.ly/2oJTQGn*):

```
# Load the Parquet file
on_time_dataframe = spark.read.parquet('data/on_time_performance.parquet')
on_time_dataframe.registerTempTable("on_time_performance")

# Dump the unneeded fields
tail_numbers = on_time_dataframe.map(lambda x: x.TailNum)
tail_numbers = tail_numbers.filter(lambda x: x != '')

# distinct() gets us unique tail numbers
unique_tail_numbers = tail_numbers.distinct()

# Store as JSON objects via a dataframe. Repartition to 1 to get 1 JSON file.
unique_records = unique_tail_numbers.map(lambda x: {'TailNum': x})
unique_records.toDF().repartition(1).write.json("data/tail_numbers.json")
```

Now, from bash, run:

```
$ ls data/tail_numbers.json/part*
data/tail_numbers.json/part-r-00000-1f29285f-55b2-4092-8c40-9d4b4c957f90
```

Let's take a look:

```
$ head -5 data/tail_numbers.json/part*
```

This results in:

```
{"TailNum":"N933EV"}
{"TailNum":"N917WN"}
{"TailNum":"N438WN"}
{"TailNum":"N3CHAA"}
{"TailNum":"N875AA"}
```

Let's change that filename to something easier to remember:

```
cp data/tail_numbers.json/part* data/tail_numbers.jsonl
```

Now we're ready to start scraping!

Automating Form Submission

The Python `requests` (*http://docs.python-requests.org/en/master/*) package is excellent at fetching web pages. (The other way to scrape in Python is to use Selenium (*http://www.seleniumhq.org/*), which automates web browsers; we'll get to this later). The Python `BeautifulSoup` (*https://www.crummy.com/software/BeautifulSoup/*) package handily parses HTML for extraction.

Stringing them together to scrape data is simple. Let's take a look at our scraper script, step by step.

First we need to load the JSON file we generated in PySpark, using the utilities we saw in Chapter 3:

```
import sys, os, re
import time

sys.path.append("lib")
import utils

import requests
from bs4 import BeautifulSoup

tail_number_records = utils.read_json_lines_file('data/tail_numbers.jsonl')
```

Next we loop through our tail numbers, remembering to sleep before loading a single page, per the */robots.txt* guidelines (*http://www.robotstxt.org/guidelines.html*). If you fail to sleep first, you may end up skipping your sleep call later inadvertently and bringing down a site by flooding it:

```
aircraft_records = []
# Loop through the tail numbers, fetching
for tail_number_record in tail_number_records:
    time.sleep(0.1) # essential to sleep FIRST in loop or you will flood sites
    ...
```

When developing scripts with loops, don't write the operations inside the loop. Instead, pick the first element off the loop in iPython and run each operation on that element once. For instance:

```
tail_number_record = tail_number_records[0]
```

And then %paste the loop's operations, which will handle the indentation correctly.

Next, we build our URL using the tail number, submit our request, and parse the resulting HTML:

```
# Parameterize the URL with the tail number
BASE_URL =
    'http://registry.faa.gov/aircraftinquiry/NNum_Results.aspx?NNumbertxt={}'
tail_number = tail_number_record['TailNum']
url = BASE_URL.format(tail_number)

# Fetch the page, parse the HTML
r = requests.get(url)
```

Now our form is being submitted automatically!

Extracting Data from HTML

Next up, we need to extract and parse the HTML from our request:

```
html = r.text
soup = BeautifulSoup(html)
```

Now we have to inspect the web page (Figure 5-12) and find the corresponding structure in BeautifulSoup.

Figure 5-12. FAA Registry table inspection

It turns out that this page relies heavily on HTML tables (*http://www.w3schools.com/html/html_tables.asp*), which is excellent. The data we are interested in is in tables 5, 6, and 7 in the document. Let's take a look at table 5, the aircraft description:

```
...
# The table structure is constant for all pages that contain data
try:
    aircraft_description = soup.find_all('table')[4]
    craft_tds = aircraft_description.find_all('td')
    serial_number = craft_tds[1].text.strip()
    manufacturer = craft_tds[5].text.strip()
    model = craft_tds[9].text.strip()
    mfr_year = craft_tds[25].text.strip()
```

Using BeautifulSoup's find_all (*http://bit.ly/2oQrWY1*), we fetch the list of tables on the page, focusing on table 5 (the 4th index from 0). Next, we fetch the list of td elements in this table into craft_tds, which we then print to discover the structure of the fields. Note that we call the text method to get the text within the td element and then we str.strip this value.

We work similarly with the other two tables:

```
...
registered_owner = soup.find_all('table')[5]
reg_tds = registered_owner.find_all('td')
owner = reg_tds[1].text.strip()
owner_state = reg_tds[9].text.strip()

airworthiness = soup.find_all('table')[6]
worthy_tds = airworthiness.find_all('td')
engine_manufacturer = worthy_tds[1].text.strip()
engine_model = worthy_tds[5].text.strip()
```

Finally, we form a record and add it to our list:

```
aircraft_record = {
    'TailNum': tail_number,
    'serial_number': serial_number,
    'manufacturer': manufacturer,
    'model': model,
    'mfr_year': mfr_year,
    'owner': owner,
    'owner_state': owner_state,
    'engine_manufacturer': engine_manufacturer,
    'engine_model': engine_model,
}
aircraft_records.append(
  aircraft_record
)
print(aircraft_record)
```

The only other thing to handle in this script is when a record isn't available. After operating our script for a few iterations, you will see it die from an exception. This always happens when scraping data—it's part of the process; you never get 100%. After inspecting the reason the script died, depending on the problem, you can likely simply catch it as an exception and print an error, and simply accept some loss in the join to this operation:

```
...
except IndexError, e:
  print("Missing {} record: {}".format(tail_number, e))
```

Note that you can print one record per line as JSON, or write it all at the end as we do here:

```
utils.write_json_lines_file(
  aircraft_records, 'data/faa_tail_number_inquiry.jsonl'
)
```

Evaluating Enriched Data

Now that we've got our tail number data in *data/faa_tail_number_inquiry.jsonl*, let's take a look. First we want to know how many records did we successfully achieve, both in raw form and as a percent?

In bash, run:

```
head -5 data/faa_tail_number_inquiry.jsonl
```

Which results in:

```
{
  "engine_model": "CF34 SERIES",
  "engine_manufacturer": "GE",
  "owner_state": "GEORGIA",
  "serial_number": "8022",
  "owner": "DELTA AIR LINES INC",
  "TailNum": "N933EV",
  "model": "CL-600-2B19",
  "mfr_year": "2005",
  "manufacturer": "BOMBARDIER INC"
}
{
  "engine_model": "CFM56-7B24",
  "engine_manufacturer": "CFM INTL",
  "owner_state": "TEXAS",
  "serial_number": "36624",
  "owner": "SOUTHWEST AIRLINES CO",
  "TailNum": "N917WN",
  "model": "737-7H4",
  "mfr_year": "2008",
  "manufacturer": "BOEING"
}
...
```

We can count the number of records via `wc`, as in `wc -l data/faa_tail_number_inquiry.jsonl`:

```
4272 data/faa_tail_number_inquiry.jsonl
```

Now, back in PySpark, let's load the data and count it as we would if this dataset were large:

```
# Load the FAA N-Number Inquiry Records
faa_tail_number_inquiry = spark.read.json('data/faa_tail_number_inquiry.jsonl')
faa_tail_number_inquiry.show()

# Count the records
faa_tail_number_inquiry.count()
```

Which results in: 4272.

To see how the two datasets work together, let's join this data to our unique tail numbers and see how many hits we get:

```
# Load our unique tail numbers
unique_tail_numbers = spark.read.json('data/tail_numbers.jsonl')
unique_tail_numbers.show()

# Left outer join tail numbers to our inquries to see how many came through
tail_num_plus_inquiry = unique_tail_numbers.join(
  faa_tail_number_inquiry,
  unique_tail_numbers.TailNum == faa_tail_number_inquiry.TailNum,
  'left_outer'
)
tail_num_plus_inquiry.show()

# Now compute the total records and the successfully joined records
total_records = tail_num_plus_inquiry.count()
join_hits = tail_num_plus_inquiry.filter(
  tail_num_plus_inquiry.owner.isNotNull()
).count()

# This being Python, we can now compute and print a join percent...
hit_ratio = float(join_hits)/float(total_records)
hit_pct = hit_ratio * 100
print("Successful joins: {:.2f}%".format(hit_pct))
```

Which results in `Successful joins: 83.65%`. To continue the example, we might next inquire into the structure of the records that were missed by the join to see if they seem random and can be ignored, or if they tend to be one kind of record or another in terms of the values of their fields, in which case we would need to consider that the join has bias in our analysis hereafter.

We have now enriched our dataset with some interesting new data, which we will dive into in the next chapter.

Conclusion

In this chapter, we've started to tease structure from our data with tables and charts. We have also begun to enrich our data with outside datasets to give us new axes across which to pivot and analyze. In doing so, we have gone further than the preceding chapter in cataloging our data assets. We'll take what we've learned with us as we proceed up the data-value pyramid.

Now we move on to the next step of the data-value stack: *reports*.

## CHAPTER 6

Exploring Data with Reports

In the next step, our third agile sprint, we'll extend our chart pages into full-blown reports. In this step, charts become interactive, static pages become dynamic, and our data becomes explorable through networks of linked, related entities with tables and charts. These are the characteristics of the reports stage of the data-value pyramid (Figure 6-1).

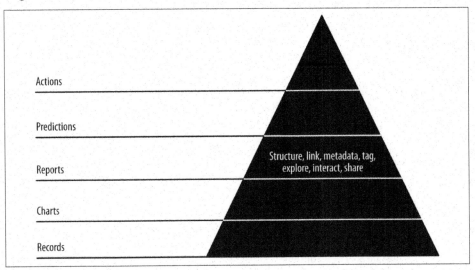

Figure 6-1. Level 3: exploring with reports

Code examples for this chapter are available at *Agile_Data_Code_2/tree/master/ch06* (*http://bit.ly/2qX1ltm*). Clone the repository and follow along!

```
git clone https://github.com/rjurney/Agile_Data_Code_2.git
```

Extracting Airlines (Entities)

To build a report, we need to compose multiple views of our dataset. Building these views corresponds with enumerating entities. The entity we created in the previous chapter, *airplanes*, will serve as a foundation as we increase the number of entities and the corresponding links between them to create reports. As with the last chapter, before we can start creating different views on our data, we need a web page to put our charts and tables into. So let's create another entity, *airlines*, and give each a page of its own.

We start by gathering all tail numbers for a given airline in a table on its entity page. Every commercial flight has an airline it operates under, and each airline has a fleet of beautifully branded airplanes that, along with airport facilities and staff, are the key assets of its business. We already created a page for each airplane, so we'll leverage this data asset to create a list of all tail numbers for each airline.

Defining Airlines as Groups of Airplanes Using PySpark

We begin by preparing the lists of tail numbers for each airline code, in *ch06/extract_airlines.py* (*http://bit.ly/2pyUINP*). These will form the basis for our airline pages:

```
# Load the on-time Parquet file
on_time_dataframe = spark.read.parquet('data/on_time_performance.parquet')

# The first step is easily expressed as SQL: get all unique tail numbers for
# each airline
on_time_dataframe.registerTempTable("on_time_performance")
carrier_airplane = spark.sql(
  "SELECT DISTINCT Carrier, TailNum FROM on_time_performance"
  )

# Now we need to store a sorted list of tail numbers for each carrier, along
# with a fleet count
airplanes_per_carrier = carrier_airplane.rdd\
  .map(lambda nameTuple: (nameTuple[0], [nameTuple[1]]))\
  .reduceByKey(lambda a, b: a + b)\
  .map(lambda tuple:
    {
      'Carrier': tuple[0],
      'TailNumbers': sorted(
        filter(
          lambda x: x != '', tuple[1] # empty string tail numbers were
                                       # getting through
        )
      ),
      'FleetCount': len(tuple[1])
    }
  )
```

```
airplanes_per_carrier.count() # 14

# Save to Mongo in the airplanes_per_carrier relation
import pymongo_spark
pymongo_spark.activate()
airplanes_per_carrier.saveToMongoDB(
  'mongodb://localhost:27017/agile_data_science.airplanes_per_carrier'
)
```

Querying Airline Data in Mongo

Next we verify that the data is in Mongo with: db.airplanes_per_carrier.find(),
which gets us:

```
{"_id": ..., "TailNumbers": ["N502NK", ...], "Carrier": "NK", "FleetCount": 79 }
{"_id": ..., "TailNumbers": ["N0EGMQ", ...], "Carrier": "MQ", "FleetCount": 204 }
{"_id": ..., "TailNumbers": ["N281VA", ...], "Carrier": "VX", "FleetCount": 57 }
```

Building an Airline Page in Flask

Next we'll create a controller for our airline page. Our Flask controller is simple. It
accepts an airline carrier code and returns a page with a list of airplanes, by tail number, from Mongo:

```
@app.route("/airline/<carrier_code>")
def airline(carrier_code):
  airline_airplanes = client.agile_data_science.airplanes_per_carrier.find_one(
    {'Carrier': carrier_code}
  )
  return render_template(
    'airlines.html',
    airline_airplanes=airline_airplanes,
    carrier_code=carrier_code
  )
```

Our template code creates an HTML bullet for each tail number. Check out *ch06/web/
templates/airlines.html* (*http://bit.ly/2pPkg8I*):

```
{% extends "layout.html" %}
{% block body %}
  <p class="lead">Airline {{carrier_code}}</p>
  <h4>Fleet: {{airline_airplanes.FleetCount}} Planes</h4>
  <ul class="nav nav-pills">
    {% for tail_number in airline_airplanes.TailNumbers -%}
    <li class="button">
      <a href="/airplane/{{tail_number}}">{{tail_number}}</a>
    </li>
    {% endfor -%}
  </ul>
{% endblock %}
```

The result is the start of an airline page detailing its entire fleet (Figure 6-2). Don't worry, we'll dress this up later. It is absolutely necessary to ship something ugly before you ship something sharp!

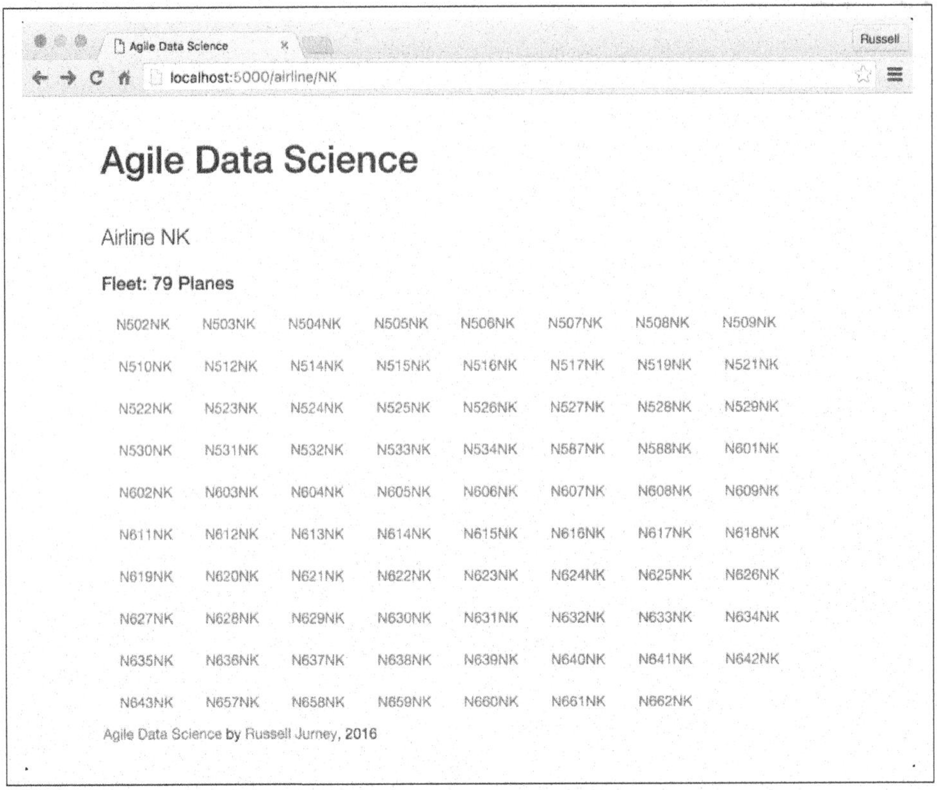

Figure 6-2. Airline page

Linking Back to Our Airline Page

Having created the airline entity page type, we will now link back to it from the airplane page we created, and the search and flight pages in from Chapter 5. We do this by editing the templates for the airplane, flight, and search pages.

We'll link back to our airline pages in *ch06/web/templates/flights_per_airplane.html* (*http://bit.ly/2oKiOoP*):

```
<tbody>
  {% for flight in flights['Flights'] %}
  <tr>
    <td><a href="/airline/{{flight[0]}}">{{flight[0]}}</a></td>
    <td>{{flight[1]}}</td>
    <td><a href="/on_time_performance?Carrier={{flight[0]}}&FlightDate=
      {{flight[1]}}&FlightNum={{flight[2]}}">{{flight[2]}}</a></td>
```

```
      <td>{{flight[3]}}</td>
      <td>{{flight[4]}}</td>
    </tr>
    {% endfor %}
  </tbody>
```

in *ch06/web/templates/flight.html* (*http://bit.ly/2oq4Erf*):

```
<tbody>
  <tr>
    <td><a href="/airline/{{flight.Carrier}}">{{flight.Carrier}}</a></td>
    <td>{{flight.Origin}}</td>
    <td>{{flight.Dest}}</td>
    <td><a href="/airplane/flights/{{flight.TailNum}}">
      {{flight.TailNum}}</a></td>
    <td>{{flight.FlightDate}}</td>
    <td>{{flight.AirTime}}</td>
    <td>{{flight.Distance}}</td>
  </tr>
</tbody>
```

and in *ch06/web/templates/search.html* (*http://bit.ly/2oKrJXD*):

```
{% for flight in flights %}
  <tr>
    <td><a href="/airline/{{flight.Carrier}}">{{flight.Carrier}}</a></td>
    <td><a href="/on_time_performance?Carrier={{flight.Carrier}}&FlightDate=
      {{flight.FlightDate}}&FlightNum={{flight.FlightNum}}">{{flight.FlightNum}}
        </a></td>
    <td>{{flight.Origin}}</td>
    <td>{{flight.Dest}}</td>
    <td>{{flight.FlightDate}}</td>
    <td>{{flight.DepTime}}</td>
    <td><a href="/airplane/{{flight.TailNum}}">{{flight.TailNum}}</a></td>
    <td>{{flight.AirTime}}</td>
    <td>{{flight.Distance}}</td>
  </tr>
{% endfor %}
```

Creating an All Airlines Home Page

But who knows airline carrier codes (okay, other than me)? We need a way to get users started browsing, so let's create a home page listing all the airlines operating in the US.

Our controller is simple, just six lines of code. We're able to reuse the `air lines_per_carrier` MongoDB collection, this time ignoring the tail numbers and only querying the carrier codes using a `find`. Let's also direct users to this page by default, as our *index.html* for this application:

```
@app.route("/")
@app.route("/airlines")
@app.route("/airlines/")
def airlines():
  airlines = client.agile_data_science.airplanes_per_carrier.find()
  return render_template('all_airlines.html', airlines=airlines)
```

Our template is similar to the one for an individual airline:

```
{% extends "layout.html" %}
{% block body %}
  <!-- Navigation guide -->
  / <a href="/airlines">Airlines</a>

  <p class="lead">US Domestic Airlines</p>
  <ul class="nav nav-pills">
    {% for airline in airlines -%}
    <li class="button">
      <a href="/airline/{{airline.Carrier}}">{{airline.Carrier}}</a>
    </li>
    {% endfor -%}
  </ul>
{% endblock %}
```

The result is a simple but effective way to get users browsing the world of aviation (Figure 6-3).

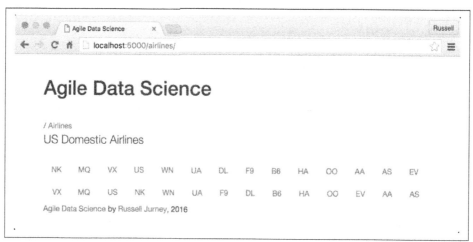

Figure 6-3. Airlines home page

Curating Ontologies of Semi-structured Data

We can now explore airlines, airplanes, and flights endlessly! Big deal, right? Maybe not, but it is a good start. Let's extend this by making airplanes and airlines clickable in our flight pages.

Now we can look at airplanes and airlines, their properties, and their relationships as we view flights (Figure 6-4). This kind of pivot offers insight, and is a form of simple recommendation.

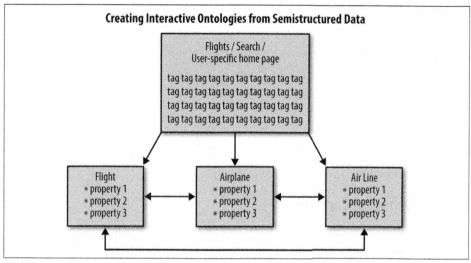

Figure 6-4. Page structure

What we're doing can be described as creating interactive ontologies of semi-structured data. Breaking up our process around building this kind of structure does several things for us. First, it creates small batches of work—one per entity—that break efficiently into agile sprints. This enables a kind of data agility, and also extends our application into a more and more browsable state. This in turn enables users to click around and explore our dataset, which connects the team into the ground truth or reality of the data—which, as you know by now, is a theme in Agile Data Science.

Improving Airlines

Now that we've got airline pages, let's improve them with some multimedia content: text and images. To begin, let's get a list of the carrier codes in our primary dataset:

```
# Load the on-time Parquet file
on_time_dataframe = spark.read.parquet('data/on_time_performance.parquet')

# The first step is easily expressed as SQL: get all unique tail numbers
# for each airline
on_time_dataframe.registerTempTable("on_time_performance")
carrier_codes = spark.sql(
  "SELECT DISTINCT Carrier FROM on_time_performance"
  )
carrier_codes.collect()
```

Which results in a list of the airline carrier codes that appear in the on-time performance data:

```
[Row(Carrier=u'AA'),
 Row(Carrier=u'NK'),
 Row(Carrier=u'HA'),
 Row(Carrier=u'AS'),
 Row(Carrier=u'B6'),
 Row(Carrier=u'UA'),
 Row(Carrier=u'US'),
 Row(Carrier=u'OO'),
 Row(Carrier=u'VX'),
 Row(Carrier=u'WN'),
 Row(Carrier=u'DL'),
 Row(Carrier=u'EV'),
 Row(Carrier=u'F9'),
 Row(Carrier=u'MQ')]
```

Adding Names to Carrier Codes

In order to link more data to our carriers, we need to get the name of each along with the carrier code. This data is available in the airlines database we downloaded from OpenFlights (*http://openflights.org/data.html*) in Chapter 5. Let's inspect *airlines.dat*, which we've renamed *airlines.csv*:

```
cat data/airlines.csv | grep '"DL"\|"NW"\|"AA"'
```

This shows us some of our airlines are listed:

```
24,"American Airlines",\N,"AA","AAL","AMERICAN","United States","Y"
2009,"Delta Air Lines",\N,"DL","DAL","DELTA","United States","Y"
3731,"Northwest Airlines",\N,"NW","NWA","NORTHWEST","United States","Y"
```

OpenFlights lists the fieldnames as Airline ID, Name, Alias, 2-Letter IATA Code, 3-Letter ICAO Code, Callsign, Country, and Active. Let's open and inspect this data in PySpark. Check out *ch06/add_name_to_airlines.py* (*http://bit.ly/2okRE75*):

```
airlines = spark.read.format('com.databricks.spark.csv')\
  .options(header='false', nullValue='\N')\
  .load('data/airlines.csv')
airlines.show()
```

This results in:

```
+---+--------------------+----+---+---+---------------+---------------+---+
| C0|                  C1| C2| C3| C4|             C5|             C6| C7|
+---+--------------------+----+---+---+---------------+---------------+---+
|  1|      Private flight|null|  -|N/A|               |               |  Y|
|  2|         135 Airways|null|   |GNL|        GENERAL|  United States|  N|
|  3|        1Time Airline|null| 1T|RNX|        NEXTIME|   South Africa|  Y|
|  4|2 Sqn No 1 Elemen...|null|   |WYT|               | United Kingdom|  N|
...
```

And this:

```
# Is Delta around?
airlines.filter(airlines.C3 == 'DL').show()
```

produces the following result:

```
+----+----------------+----+---+---+-----+-------------+---+
| C0|              C1| C2| C3| C4|   C5|           C6| C7|
+----+----------------+----+---+---+-----+-------------+---+
|2009|Delta Air Lines|null| DL|DAL|DELTA|United States|  Y|
+----+----------------+----+---+---+-----+-------------+---+
```

Now let's filter this data down to just the airline names and two-letter carrier codes, and join it to the unique carrier codes from the on-time performance dataset:

```
# Drop fields except for C1 as name, C3 as carrier code
airlines.registerTempTable("airlines")
airlines = spark.sql("SELECT C1 AS Name, C3 AS CarrierCode from airlines")

# Join our 14 carrier codes to the airlines table to get our set of airlines
our_airlines = carrier_codes.join(
  airlines, carrier_codes.Carrier == airlines.CarrierCode
)
our_airlines = our_airlines.select('Name', 'CarrierCode')
our_airlines.show()
```

This results in:

```
+--------------------+-----------+
|                Name|CarrierCode|
+--------------------+-----------+
|   American Airlines|         AA|
|     Spirit Airlines|         NK|
|   Hawaiian Airlines|         HA|
|     Alaska Airlines|         AS|
|     JetBlue Airways|         B6|
|     United Airlines|         UA|
|          US Airways|         US|
|            SkyWest |         OO|
|     Virgin America |         VX|
|  Southwest Airlines|         WN|
|     Delta Air Lines|         DL|
|Atlantic Southeas...|         EV|
|    Frontier Airlines|        F9|
|American Eagle Ai...|         MQ|
+--------------------+-----------+
```

Finally, let's store this intermediate data as JSON:

```
our_airlines.repartition(1).write.json("data/our_airlines.json")
```

and again, copy it into a JSON Lines file:

```
cp data/our_airlines.json/part* data/our_airlines.jsonl
```

Then we can take a peek with `cat data/our_airlines.jsonl`:

```
{"Name":"American Airlines","CarrierCode":"AA"}
{"Name":"Spirit Airlines","CarrierCode":"NK"}
{"Name":"Hawaiian Airlines","CarrierCode":"HA"}
{"Name":"Alaska Airlines","CarrierCode":"AS"}
{"Name":"JetBlue Airways","CarrierCode":"B6"}
{"Name":"United Airlines","CarrierCode":"UA"}
{"Name":"US Airways","CarrierCode":"US"}
{"Name":"SkyWest","CarrierCode":"OO"}
{"Name":"Virgin America","CarrierCode":"VX"}
{"Name":"Southwest Airlines","CarrierCode":"WN"}
{"Name":"Delta Air Lines","CarrierCode":"DL"}
{"Name":"Atlantic Southeast Airlines","CarrierCode":"EV"}
{"Name":"Frontier Airlines","CarrierCode":"F9"}
{"Name":"American Eagle Airlines","CarrierCode":"MQ"}
```

Incorporating Wikipedia Content

Now that we have airline names, we can use Wikipedia to get various information about each airline, like a summary, logo, and company website! To do so, we make use of the wikipedia (*https://pypi.python.org/pypi/wikipedia/*) package for Python, which wraps the MediaWiki API (*https://www.mediawiki.org/wiki/API:Main_page*). We'll be using BeautifulSoup (*http://bit.ly/2pwZcYs*) again to parse the page's HTML.

Check out *ch06/enrich_airlines_wikipedia.py* (*http://bit.ly/2peAoVh*):

```python
import sys, os, re
sys.path.append("lib")
import utils

import wikipedia
from bs4 import BeautifulSoup
import tldextract

# Load our airlines...
our_airlines = utils.read_json_lines_file('data/our_airlines.jsonl')

# Build a new list that includes Wikipedia data
with_url = []
for airline in our_airlines:
  # Get the Wikipedia page for the airline name
  wikipage = wikipedia.page(airline['Name'])

  # Get the summary
  summary = wikipage.summary
  airline['summary'] = summary

  # Get the HTML of the page
  page = BeautifulSoup(wikipage.html())

  # Task: get the logo from the right 'vcard' column
```

```
# 1) Get the vcard table
vcard_table = page.find_all('table', class_='vcard')[0]
# 2) The logo is always the first image inside this table
first_image = vcard_table.find_all('img')[0]
# 3) Set the URL to the image
logo_url = 'http:' + first_image.get('src')
airline['logo_url'] = logo_url

# Task: get the company website
# 1) Find the 'Website' table header
th = page.find_all('th', text='Website')[0]
# 2) Find the parent tr element
tr = th.parent
# 3) Find the a (link) tag within the tr
a = tr.find_all('a')[0]
# 4) Finally, get the href of the a tag
url = a.get('href')
airline['url'] = url

# Get the domain to display with the URL
url_parts = tldextract.extract(url)
airline['domain'] = url_parts.domain + '.' + url_parts.suffix

with_url.append(airline)

utils.write_json_lines_file(with_url, 'data/our_airlines_with_wiki.jsonl')
```

Publishing Enriched Airlines to Mongo

Note that we skipped Mongo in this section—we went from our original dataset to two stages of enriched, intermediate datasets without storing to Mongo at all. This is fine! In Agile Data Science we use databases to *publish* data, not always to persist it in its intermediate state.

Now, however, we want to include our enriched airlines in the airline web pages we created earlier. To get it there, we need to send it through Mongo. Since we already have a JSON file prepared, we can use the mongoimport (*http://bit.ly/2oKydFW*) command to load it into Mongo:

```
mongoimport -d agile_data_science -c airlines \
    --file data/our_airlines_with_wiki.jsonl
```

Verify the data is there:

```
$ mongo agile_data_science

> db.airlines.findOne();

{
        "_id" : ObjectId("57c0e656818573ed12d584d1"),
        "CarrierCode" : "AA",
        "url" : "http://www.aa.com",
        "logo_url" : "http://upload.wikimedia.org/.../300px-American...
                       _2013.svg.png",
        "Name" : "American Airlines",
        "summary" : "American Airlines, Inc. (AA), commonly referred to as
                       American..."
}
```

Enriched Airlines on the Web

Now that our enriched airline records are in Mongo, we can alter our Flask controller for */airline* to include this data. Check out *ch06/web/report_flask.py* (*http://bit.ly/ 2o0z73K*):

```python
# Controller: Fetch an airplane entity page
@app.route("/airline/<carrier_code>")
def airline(carrier_code):
  airline_summary = client.agile_data_science.airlines.find_one(
    {'CarrierCode': carrier_code}
  )
  airline_airplanes = client.agile_data_science.airplanes_per_carrier.find_one(
    {'Carrier': carrier_code}
  )
  return render_template(
    'airlines.html',
    airline_summary=airline_summary,
    airline_airplanes=airline_airplanes,
    carrier_code=carrier_code
  )
```

Next we alter our template, *ch06/web/templates/airlines.html* (*http://bit.ly/2pPkg8I*), to include the Wikipedia data:

```html
{% extends "layout.html" %}
{% block body %}
  <!-- Navigation guide -->
  / <a href="/airlines">Airlines</a>
    / <a href="/airline/{{carrier_code}}">{{carrier_code}}</a>

  <!-- Logo -->
  <img src="{{airline_summary.logo_url}}" style="float: right;"/>

  <p class="lead">
    <!-- Airline name and website-->
```

```
    {{airline_summary.Name}}
    / <a href="{{airline_summary.url}}">{{airline_summary.domain}}</a>
  </p>

  <!-- Summary -->
  <p style="text-align: justify;">{{airline_summary.summary}}</p>
  <h4>Fleet: {{airline_airplanes.FleetCount}} Planes</h4>
  <ul class="nav nav-pills">
    {% for tail_number in airline_airplanes.TailNumbers -%}
    <li class="button">
      <a href="/airplane/{{tail_number}}">{{tail_number}}</a>
    </li>
    {% endfor -%}
  </ul>
{% endblock %}
```

And for our labors, we get a greatly improved airline page (Figure 6-5). The point of this enrichment? While your data may not be so easily enhanced from a public dataset like Wikipedia, this example shows how to combine data from different sources, some private, some public, to compose better entity pages.

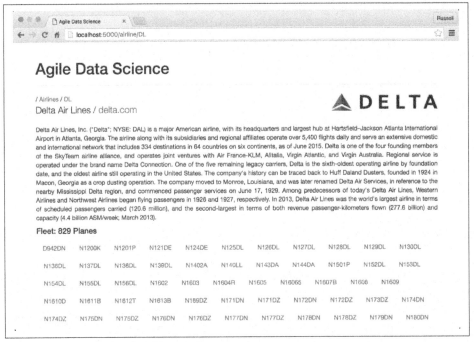

Figure 6-5. Enriched airline home page

Investigating Airplanes (Entities)

In Chapter 5, we were just getting into some interesting data that we will now look at once again. To begin, let's store our enriched airplanes in their own intermediate dataset. Check out *ch06/prepare_airplanes.py* (*http://bit.ly/2pxk5T1*):

```
# Load the FAA N-Number inquiry records
faa_tail_number_inquiry = spark.read.json('data/faa_tail_number_inquiry.jsonl')
faa_tail_number_inquiry.show()

# Count the records
faa_tail_number_inquiry.count()

# Load our unique tail numbers
unique_tail_numbers = spark.read.json('data/tail_numbers.jsonl')
unique_tail_numbers.show()

# Join tail numbers to our inquries
tail_num_plus_inquiry = unique_tail_numbers.join(
  faa_tail_number_inquiry,
  unique_tail_numbers.TailNum == faa_tail_number_inquiry.TailNum,
)
tail_num_plus_inquiry = tail_num_plus_inquiry.drop(unique_tail_numbers.TailNum)
tail_num_plus_inquiry.show()

# Dump extra field and store tail_numbers plus inquiry
tail_num_plus_inquiry.registerTempTable("tail_num_plus_inquiry")
airplanes = spark.sql("""SELECT
  TailNum AS TailNum,
  engine_manufacturer AS EngineManufacturer,
  engine_model AS EngineModel,
  manufacturer AS Manufacturer,
  mfr_year AS ManufacturerYear,
  model AS Model,
  owner AS Owner,
  owner_state AS OwnerState,
  serial_number AS SerialNumber
FROM
  tail_num_plus_inquiry""")

airplanes.repartition(1).write.json('data/airplanes.json')
```

As before, we can copy this directory of data into a single file for convenient access outside of Spark—note that this is not a good idea for very large files, but in this case our airplanes data is less than one megabyte:

```
$ cat data/airplanes.json/part-* >> data/airplanes.jsonl

$ head -5 data/airplanes.jsonl

{
  "TailNum": "N933EV",
  "EngineManufacturer": "GE",
```

```
    "EngineModel": "CF34 SERIES",
    "Manufacturer": "BOMBARDIER INC",
    "ManufacturerYear": "2005",
    "Model": "CL-600-2B19",
    "Owner": "DELTA AIR LINES INC",
    "OwnerState": "GEORGIA",
    "SerialNumber": "8022"
}
```

Let's begin our analysis by asking a question: Boeing versus Airbus—who manufactures more airplanes in the US commercial fleet? Check out *ch06/ analyze_airplanes.py* (*http://bit.ly/2oKlliP*):

```
airplanes = spark.read.json('data/airplanes.json')

# How many airplanes are made by each manufacturer?
airplanes.registerTempTable("airplanes")
manufacturer_counts = spark.sql("""SELECT
  Manufacturer,
  COUNT(*) AS Total
FROM
  airplanes
GROUP BY
  Manufacturer
ORDER BY
  Total DESC, Manufacturer"""
)
manufacturer_counts.show(30) # show top 30
```

Note that we ORDER BY both the Total and the Manufacturer. Always employ an additional "tiebreaker" sort key like this, so that your results are repeatable. Without a second sort key, the order of the results is not specified by the query and is at the mercy of the SQL interpreter. Here are the results:

```
+--------------------+-----+
|        Manufacturer|Total|
+--------------------+-----+
|              BOEING| 2095|
|              AIRBUS|  550|
|      BOMBARDIER INC|  460|
|    AIRBUS INDUSTRIE|  451|
|             EMBRAER|  366|
|   MCDONNELL DOUGLAS|  122|
|MCDONNELL DOUGLAS...|  105|
|         EMBRAER S A|   47|
...
```

Interesting, Boeing planes outnumber Airbus planes by 4 to 1! I had no idea; I thought it was much closer than this. However, what I really want to know is who has what share of the market (without having to compute a ratio in my head). In other words, I'd like to see this data as a percentage.

SQL Subqueries Versus Dataflow Programming

This is a good way to illustrate the difference between SQL subqueries and dataflow programming. SQL is declarative, in that you specify what you want without saying how to get it. Imperative dataflow programming, on the other hand, involves the step-wise computation of data that you link and compose into dataflows.

First we'll implement the percentage totals using imperative dataflows, and then we'll do so using declarative SQL subqueries. You'll see that in this case subqueries are more convenient, but there is a limit to the utility of subqueries—they can get obscure fast. It is better to create a series of simple SQL or dataflow statements that compose into the computation you desire rather than to try to specify it all in one large, deeply nested subquery.

Dataflow Programming Without Subqueries

Subqueries weren't supported in Spark SQL until 2.0. Instead, given our manufacturer airplane counts, we would need to calculate the total airplane count, join that to our existing totals, and then divide the manufacturer subtotals by the overall total. We'll reuse the `manufacturer_counts` relation we computed in the previous program listing:

```
# How many airplanes total?
total_airplanes = spark.sql(
  """SELECT
  COUNT(*) AS OverallTotal
  FROM airplanes"""
)
print("Total airplanes: {}".format(total_airplanes.collect()[0].OverallTotal))

mfr_with_totals = manufacturer_counts.join(total_airplanes)
mfr_with_totals = mfr_with_totals.rdd.map(
  lambda x: {
    'Manufacturer': x.Manufacturer,
    'Total': x.Total,
    'Percentage': round(
      (
        float(x.Total)/float(x.OverallTotal)
      ) * 100,
      2
    )
  }
)
mfr_with_totals.toDF().show()
```

Which results in:

```
+--------------------+----------+-----+
|        Manufacturer|Percentage|Total|
+--------------------+----------+-----+
|              BOEING|     49.04| 2095|
|              AIRBUS|     12.87|  550|
|      BOMBARDIER INC|     10.77|  460|
|    AIRBUS INDUSTRIE|     10.56|  451|
|             EMBRAER|      8.57|  366|
|   MCDONNELL DOUGLAS|      2.86|  122|
|MCDONNELL DOUGLAS...|      2.46|  105|
|         EMBRAER S A|       1.1|   47|
...
```

This is clearly an out-of-the-way method of calculating percentage totals, but it illustrates how dataflow programming works in more complex examples as well.

Subqueries in Spark SQL

Subqueries are handy, and computing the percentage share of the aircraft manufacturers is easy using them:

```
relative_manufacturer_counts = spark.sql("""SELECT
  Manufacturer,
  COUNT(*) AS Total,
  ROUND(
    100 * (
      COUNT(*)/(SELECT COUNT(*) FROM airplanes)
    ),
    2
  ) AS PercentageTotal
FROM
  airplanes
GROUP BY
  Manufacturer
ORDER BY
  Total DESC, Manufacturer"""
)
relative_manufacturer_counts.show(30) # show top 30
```

The result is identical to the previous section's result:

```
+--------------------+-----+--------------+
|        Manufacturer|Total|PercentageTotal|
+--------------------+-----+--------------+
|             BOEING| 2095|         49.04|
|             AIRBUS|  550|         12.87|
|     BOMBARDIER INC|  460|         10.77|
|   AIRBUS INDUSTRIE|  451|         10.56|
|            EMBRAER|  366|          8.57|
|   MCDONNELL DOUGLAS|  122|          2.86|
|MCDONNELL DOUGLAS...|  105|          2.46|
|        EMBRAER S A|   47|           1.1|
...
```

Creating an Airplanes Home Page

Now I want to see this data as a chart on a web page, which means we need some-where to put the chart. This is a good time to create an */airplanes* home page—a page that analyzes the fleet as a whole.

Let's create a Flask controller for */airplanes*. Check out *ch06/web/report_flask.py* (*http://bit.ly/2o0z73K*), which simply loads the data from Mongo and passes it to a template, *all_airplanes.html* (*http://bit.ly/2pyFUie*):

```
@app.route("/airplanes")
@app.route("/airplanes/")
def airplanes():
    mfr_chart = client.agile_data_science.manufacturer_totals.find_one()
    return render_template('all_airplanes.html',mfr_chart=mfr_chart)
```

The beginning of *all_airplanes.html* and the resulting page are also simple:

```
{% extends "layout.html" %}
{% block body %}
  <!-- Navigation guide -->
  / <a href="/airplanes">Airplanes</a>

  <p class="lead">
    <!-- Airline name and website-->
    US Commercial Fleet
  </p>
{% endblock %}
```

The result is shown in Figure 6-6.

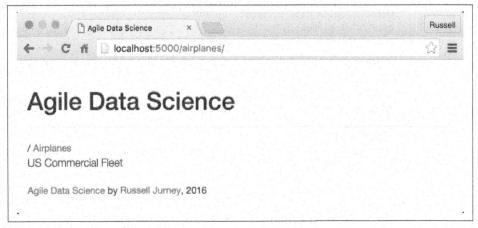

Figure 6-6. Airplanes home page

Adding Search to the Airplanes Page

The */airplanes* page is a great place to implement search for the airplane records we've created. To do this, first we'll need to index our airplane documents in Elasticsearch via PySpark:

```
# Load our airplanes
airplanes = spark.read.json("data/airplanes.json")
airplanes.show()

airplanes.write.format("org.elasticsearch.spark.sql")\
  .option("es.resource","agile_data_science/airplanes")\
  .mode("overwrite")\
  .save()
```

We can verify our documents are there with a quick search:

```
curl -XGET 'localhost:9200/agile_data_science/airplanes/_search?q=*'
```

which should return 4,272 results:

```
{
  "took": 3,
  "timed_out": false,
  "_shards": {
    "total": 5,
    "successful": 5,
    "failed": 0
  },
  "hits": {
    "total": 4272,
    "max_score": 1,
    "hits": [
      {
```

```
      "_index": "agile_data_science",
      "_type": "airplanes",
      "_id": "AVbYpad6tuTlhookKT6d",
      "_score": 1,
      "_source": {
        "EngineManufacturer": "ROLLS-ROYC",
        "EngineModel": "RB.211 SERIES",
        "Manufacturer": "BOEING",
        "ManufacturerYear": "1999",
        "Model": "757-224",
        "Owner": "UNITED AIRLINES INC",
        "OwnerState": "ILLINOIS",
        "SerialNumber": "29284",
        "TailNum": "N41135"
      }
    },
    ...
  ]
  }
}
```

Now we can add search capability to our */airplanes* controller. Recall that we we did this in Chapter 5 for flight search, and that it took several pages of code. This time, we are going to build a reusable component for searching and displaying records in a Flask application.

Code versus configuration

There are varying opinions on how much code duplication is acceptable before factoring it out, and this varies greatly by context and across programming disciplines. Data science has a higher tolerance for ugly, duplicated code than does general software engineering. This is for the simple reason that most code a data scientist writes is discarded immediately after it is run. Most data scientists are doing well to commit all their code to a repository at all (an absolute must!). But when code persists and we share the result, as in our application, cleanliness starts to matter.

This is the second time we've been tasked with implementing search, and when repeating oneself at length, it is a good time to take pause and see if one can't reduce some of the redundant code necessary to reproduce a feature. (Because most code is throwaway in data science, it is important to wait until you repeat yourself to factor out duplicate code and generalize capabilities, as we have done here.)

Being tasked with generalizing code, we have to split our code into two elements: algorithms and configuration. Algorithms define the behavior of what we're building; configuration defines what an instance of that algorithm is like.

To take one extreme, it is possible in programming to remove all redundancy in code, to the point that everything becomes a configuration file or an algorithm implementing the behavior of a configuration. This extreme, however, is not maintainable and isn't compatible with a data scientist's workload, where we have to remember lots of things at once and can't dive deep into each component just to edit or make use of it. As usual in Agile Data Science, we choose the middle path, where we remove the worst of the redundancy without reducing everything to its most generalized, reusable form.

Configuring a search widget

Our search configuration is simple. It lays out the fields we will search and display, and an optional label we would like to use in the user interface:

```
search_config = [
  {'field': 'TailNum', 'label': 'Tail Number'},
  {'field': 'Owner'},
  {'field': 'OwnerState', 'label': 'Owner State'},
  {'field': 'Manufacturer'},
  {'field': 'Model'},
  {'field': 'ManufacturerYear', 'label': 'MFR Year'},
  {'field': 'SerialNumber', 'label': 'Serial Number'},
  {'field': 'EngineManufacturer', 'label': 'Engine MFR'},
  {'field': 'EngineModel', 'label': 'Engine Model'}
]
```

Building an Elasticsearch query programmatically

Our pagination works as before, but we've got a new configuration item for `AIRPLANE_RECORDS_PER_PAGE`:

```
# Pagination parameters
start = request.args.get('start') or 0
start = int(start)
end = request.args.get('end') or config.AIRPLANE_RECORDS_PER_PAGE
end = int(end)

# Navigation path and offset setup
nav_path = search_helpers.strip_place(request.url)
nav_offsets = search_helpers.get_navigation_offsets(
  start, end, config.AIRPLANE_RECORDS_PER_PAGE
)
```

With our search config in hand, we need only define the base of the Elasticsearch query and flesh it out based on the search arguments we receive. Our base query looks like this:

```
# Build the base of our Elasticsearch query
query = {
  'query': {
    'bool': {
      'must': []}
  },
  'sort': [
```

```
        {'Owner': {'order': 'asc', 'ignore_unmapped': True}},
        {'Manufacturer': {'order': 'asc', 'ignore_unmapped' : True} },
        {'ManufacturerYear': {'order': 'asc', 'ignore_unmapped' : True} },
        {'SerialNumber': {'order': 'asc', 'ignore_unmapped' : True} },
        '_score'
    ],
    'from': start,
    'size': config.AIRPLANE_RECORDS_PER_PAGE
}
```

And we parameterize it like so:

```
arg_dict = {}
for item in search_config:
  field = item['field']
  value = request.args.get(field)
  arg_dict[field] = value
  if value:
    query['query']['bool']['must'].append({'match': {field: value}})
```

We submit the query as before:

```
# Query Elasticsearch, process to get records and count
results = elastic.search(query)
airplanes, airplane_count = search_helpers.process_search(results)
```

In our call to render our template, we now include the search_config and arg_dict,
which will generate our content in the template:

```
# Persist search parameters in the form template
return render_template(
  'all_airplanes.html',
  search_config=search_config,
  args=arg_dict,
  airplanes=airplanes,
  airplane_count=airplane_count,
  nav_path=nav_path,
  nav_offsets=nav_offsets
)
```

Our template, *all_airplanes.html* (*http://bit.ly/2pyFUie*), is derived from *search.html*
(*http://bit.ly/2okK2Br*). Using search_config and the request arguments, we programmatically build all the content we manually specified before in *search.html*. We
can reuse this code now to re-create any search controller:

```
{% extends "layout.html" %}
{% block body %}

  / <a href="/airplanes">Airplanes</a>

  <p class="lead">
    <!-- Airline name and website-->
    US Commercial Fleet
  </p>
```

```
<!-- Generate form from search_config and request args -->
<form action="/airplanes" method="get">
  {% for item in search_config %}
    {% if 'label' in item %}
      <label for="{{item['field']}}">{{item['label']}}</label>
    {% else %}
      <label for="{{item['field']}}">{{item['field']}}</label>
    {% endif %}
      <input name="{{item['field']}}"
             value="{{args[item['field']] if args[item['field']] else ''}}">
      </input>
  {% endfor %}
  <button type="submit" class="btn btn-xs btn-default" style="height: 25px">
    Submit
  </button>
</form>

<table class="table table-condensed table-striped">

  <!-- Create table header, based on search_config -->
  <thead>
    {% for item in search_config %}
      {% if 'label' in item %}
        <th>{{item['label']}}</th>
      {% else %}
        <th>{{item['field']}}</th>
      {% endif %}
    {% endfor %}
  </thead>


<!--
  Create table content, based on airplanes for each <tr> and
  search_config for each <td>
  -->
  <tbody>
    {% for airplane in airplanes %}
    <tr>
      {% for item in search_config %}
        <td>{{airplane[item['field']]}}</td>
      {% endfor %}
    </tr>
    {% endfor %}
  </tbody>
</table>

{% import "macros.jnj" as common %}
{% if nav_offsets and nav_path -%}
  {{ common.display_nav(nav_offsets, nav_path, airplane_count)|safe }}
{% endif -%}
{% endblock %}
```

Creating a Manufacturers Bar Chart

Now that we've got a place to put our chart, let's get down to creating it!

Continuing with our script, *ch06/analyze_airplanes.py* (*http://bit.ly/2oKlliP*), we store the data for the chart in Mongo:

```
#
# Now get these things on the web
#
relative_manufacturer_counts = relative_manufacturer_counts.rdd.map(
  lambda row: row.asDict()
)
grouped_manufacturer_counts = relative_manufacturer_counts.groupBy(lambda x: 1)

# Save to Mongo in the airplanes_per_carrier relation
import pymongo_spark
pymongo_spark.activate()
grouped_manufacturer_counts.saveToMongoDB(
  'mongodb://localhost:27017/agile_data_science.airplane_manufacturer_totals'
)
```

Next, check that the data is in Mongo:

```
> db.manufacturer_totals.find()
{
   "_id":1,
   "maxindex":35,
   "data":[
      {
         "PercentageTotal":49.04,
         "Manufacturer":"BOEING",
         "Total":2095
      },
      {
         "PercentageTotal":12.87,
         "Manufacturer":"AIRBUS",
         "Total":550
      },
      ...
   ]
}
```

The rest is similar to the bar chart from Chapter 5. We add a controller to *report_flask.py* (*http://bit.ly/2o0z73K*) where we grab the chart from Mongo, and return it as JSON:

```
@app.route("/airplanes/chart/manufacturers.json")
@app.route("/airplanes/chart/manufacturers.json")
def airplane_manufacturers_chart():
  mfr_chart = client.agile_data_science.manufacturer_totals.find_one()
  return json.dumps(mfr_chart)
```

Then we edit the *all_airplanes.html* (*http://bit.ly/2pyFUie*) template to call *airplane.js*, which draws the chart.

This time we want x- and y-axes for our bar chart, so we're going to draw from an example that includes them. Mike Bostock's example Bar Chart IIIc (*https://bl.ocks.org/mbostock/7441121*) is concise and straightforward. Let's begin by titling our page and calling our chart script, *airplane.js* (*http://bit.ly/2oSI3Yi*):

```
<div>
  <p class="lead">Total Flights by Month</p>
  <div id="chart"><svg class="chart"></svg></div>
</div>
<script src="/static/airplane.js"></script>
```

/static/airplane.js has a few changes to make the example work for our chart's data, and they are emboldened in the following code. Aside from plugging in the `Total` and `Manufacturer` field names and passing through the `data.data` field, we haven't changed anything except the dimensions of the chart:

```
var margin = {top: 20, right: 30, bottom: 30, left: 40},
    width = 900 - margin.left - margin.right,
    height = 300 - margin.top - margin.bottom;

var x = d3.scale.ordinal()
    .rangeRoundBands([0, width], .1);
var y = d3.scale.linear()
    .range([height, 0]);

var xAxis = d3.svg.axis()
    .scale(x)
    .orient("bottom");

var yAxis = d3.svg.axis()
    .scale(y)
    .orient("left");

var chart = d3.select(".chart")
    .attr("width", width + margin.left + margin.right)
    .attr("height", height + margin.top + margin.bottom)
    .append("g")
    .attr("transform", "translate(" + margin.left + "," + margin.top + ")");

console.log("HELLO");
d3.json("/airplanes/chart/manufacturers.json", function(error, data) {
    var data = data.data;

    x.domain(data.map(function(d) { return d.Manufacturer; }));
    y.domain([0, d3.max(data, function(d) { return d.Total; })]);

    chart.append("g")
        .attr("class", "x axis")
```

```
        .attr("transform", "translate(0," + height + ")")
        .call(xAxis);

    chart.append("g")
        .attr("class", "y axis")
        .call(yAxis);

    chart.selectAll(".bar")
        .data(data)
        .enter().append("rect")
        .attr("class", "bar")
        .attr("x", function(d) { return x(d.Manufacturer); })
        .attr("y", function(d) { return y(d.Total); })
        .attr("height", function(d) { return height - y(d.Total); })
        .attr("width", x.rangeBand());
});
```

And for our trouble, we get a beautiful chart (Figure 6-7).

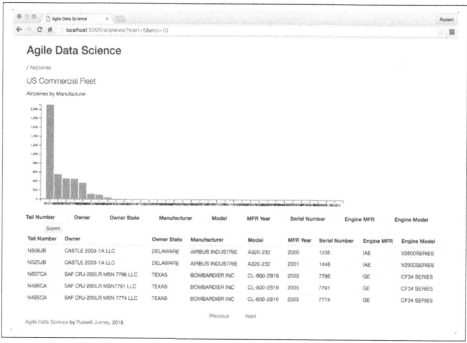

Figure 6-7. Airlines home page with our new chart

Iterating on the Manufacturers Bar Chart

Wait a minute, something is wrong! Remember when we said iteration is essential? Let's debug this chart. We need to infer from the chart what might be going on. Why are the bars so thin? Why are they shoved to the left?

Recall that we sorted the data by `Total` in descending order:

```
relative_manufacturer_counts = spark.sql("""SELECT
  Manufacturer,
  COUNT(*) AS Total,
  ROUND(
    100 * (
      COUNT(*)/(SELECT COUNT(*) FROM airplanes)
    ),
    2
  ) AS PercentageTotal
FROM
  airplanes
GROUP BY
  Manufacturer
ORDER BY
  Total DESC, Manufacturer"""
)
```

This means that the largest values are on the left, and the smallest values are on the right... so what must be happening is that there are simply too many small values to make the chart readable! We can improve the chart by removing some of these smaller values, since they are insignificant. Note that this won't always be the case, so think carefully before discarding data!

We can fix up our chart by recomputing the data using a SQL `LIMIT` command. First, we need to drop the stale data from Mongo:

```
mongo agile_data_science
```
```
> db.airplane_manufacturer_totals.drop()
```

Now go back to *analyze_airplanes.py* (*http://bit.ly/2oKlliP*) and add a `LIMIT 10` to get the top 10 manufacturers:

```
relative_manufacturer_counts = spark.sql("""SELECT
  Manufacturer,
  COUNT(*) AS Total,
  ROUND(
    100 * (
      COUNT(*)/(SELECT COUNT(*) FROM airplanes)
    ),
    2
  ) AS PercentageTotal
FROM
  airplanes
GROUP BY
  Manufacturer
ORDER BY
  Total DESC, Manufacturer
LIMIT 10"""
)
```

Running our new script and pushing our new data to Mongo results in something that clearly shows the trend of Boeing dominating the market, trailed by several other manufacturers (Figure 6-8). Note that we also created a function called `truncate` to shorten long manufacturer names in the x-axis, so these labels do not overlap. We call this function from the `tickFormat` method on our `xAxis` object:

```
function truncate(d, l) {
    if(d.length > l)
        return d.substring(0,l)+'...';
    else
        return d;
}

var xAxis = d3.svg.axis()
    .scale(x)
    .orient("bottom")
    .tickFormat(function(d) {
        return truncate(d, 14);
    });
```

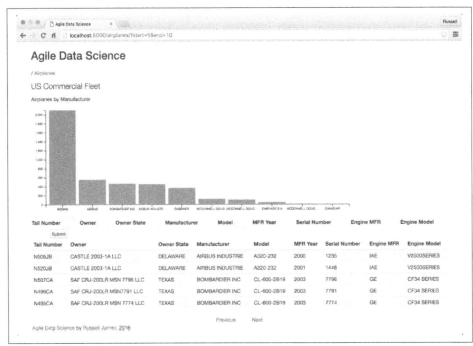

Figure 6-8. Airlines home page with improved chart

Entity Resolution: Another Chart Iteration

However, there is another problem with the chart—the column names are duplicated, which is distorting the values of manufacturers Airbus, McDonnel Douglas, and Embraer. We need to iterate yet again! This time we'll be tackling entity resolution.

Entity resolution in 30 seconds

The problem we have encountered is that there are several forms of the manufacturers' names used in the registrations of various airplanes. Addressing this problem is called entity resolution, which is defined in a tutorial (*http://bit.ly/2pxK8d1*) by Lise Getoor and Ashwin Machanavajjhala as "[the] problem of identifying and linking/grouping different manifestations of the same real world object." Entity resolution is the process by which AIRBUS is identified as the same thing as AIRBUS INDUSTRIE.

There are many methods of entity resolution, including complicated means employing statistical inference. We will only explore a simple heuristic-based approach, because it turns out that in this case that is simply good enough. Don't allow your curiosity to distract you into employing machine learning and statistical techniques whenever you can. Get curious about *results*, instead.

Resolving manufacturers in PySpark

Let's begin by inspecting the different ways the Manufacturer field appears in the airplane records. We can use SQL to SELECT DISTINCT(Manufacturer) AS Manufacturer and then see similar records next to one another with ORDER BY Manufacturer. Then we need only print the data in a left-justified manner, and see what we've got!

```
airplanes = spark.read.json('data/airplanes.json')

airplanes.registerTempTable("airplanes")
manufacturer_variety = spark.sql(
"""SELECT
  DISTINCT(Manufacturer) AS Manufacturer
FROM
  airplanes
ORDER BY
  Manufacturer"""
)
manufacturer_variety_local = manufacturer_variety.collect()

# We need to print these left-justified
for mfr in manufacturer_variety_local:
    print(mfr.Manufacturer)
```

This results in a list that allows us to easily visualize the variety of values of Manufacturer:

```
...
AIRBUS
AIRBUS INDUSTRIE
...
EMBRAER
EMBRAER S A
...
GULFSTREAM AEROSPACE
GULFSTREAM AEROSPACE CORP
...
MCDONNELL DOUGLAS
MCDONNELL DOUGLAS AIRCRAFT CO
MCDONNELL DOUGLAS CORPORATION
...
```

It turns out that we don't have very much variety at all: only 35 distinct values. Reconciling the `Manufacturer` field of these records could be done manually, with a simple table elaborating the matches in two columns. One column would contain the raw value, and the other would contain the value to map to (the "standard" you have chosen). Against this table you can then `LEFT JOIN` and, if there is a match, replace the value of the field, in order to get a common identifier between records.

If you encounter 35 values for a field in your work, do yourself a favor: make the table manually as CSV and load it in Spark and do the join. Here we will go further to illustrate how to create such a mapping table in an automated way, and how to `JOIN` it and effect the mapping. We do this to give you experience in how to problem solve and "munge" your way out of these situations when you can without having to turn to more complex (and thus time-consuming) statistical techniques.

A more sophisticated approach would be to inspect the data and see if we can infer a rule to use to decide if records are identical. In looking at our duplicates, it seems that whenever there is a duplicate, there is a lot of overlap at the start of the strings. This is common among company names in the wild, where trailing symbols like "Incorporated" are shortened to "Inc," "Inc.," "INC," "Corp," etc. We might then formulate a strategy: if fields between records contain more than N characters in common at the start of the string, they are identical. We would choose the longest common substring as the "standard" value among those records, and use this rule to create our mapping table.

To employ this strategy, we need to compare all unique values of `Manufacturer` with one another. This is feasible with 35 unique values, but keep in mind that this may not always be the case when resolving entities. Sometimes it is impossible to compare all records with one another, because the square of the number of unique records is too big, even for Spark! In this case we're only resolving one field, which keeps the cardinality low by enabling us to use the unique values of just that one field. When records have numerous fields that identify them, the number of unique records explodes. That situation is (thankfully) beyond the scope of this book, but I've had good experiences with the Swoosh algorithms (*http://infolab.stanford.edu/serf/swoosh_vldbj.pdf*), which are implemented in the SERF (*http://infolab.stanford.edu/serf/*) project from Stanford.

Check out *ch06/resolve_airplane_manufacturers.py* (*http://bit.ly/2oT2sg1*). Here we prepare a mapping table for similar `Manufacturer` values, using the assumption that strings whose beginnings overlap by more than five characters are the same. Note that this assumption is naive and would not work for most datasets. Nonetheless, it shows how you can munge your way out of sticky situations by learning your dataset and actually *looking at the data*, record by sorted, unique record.

Continuing from the last code example where we computed `manufacturer_variety`, check out the inline comments that describe the computation here:

```
# Detect the longest common beginning string in a pair of strings
def longest_common_beginning(s1, s2):
  if s1 == s2:
    return s1
  min_length = min(len(s1), len(s2))
  i = 0
  while i < min_length:
    if s1[i] == s2[i]:
      i += 1
    else:
      break
  return s1[0:i]

# Compare two manufacturers, returning a tuple describing the result
def compare_manufacturers(mfrs):
  mfr1 = mfrs[0]
  mfr2 = mfrs[1]
  lcb = longest_common_beginning(mfr1, mfr2)
  len_lcb = len(lcb)
  record = {
    'mfr1': mfr1,
    'mfr2': mfr2,
    'lcb': lcb,
    'len_lcb': len_lcb,
    'eq': mfr1 == mfr2
  }
  return record

# Pair every unique instance of Manufacturer field with every
# other for comparison
comparison_pairs = manufacturer_variety.join(manufacturer_variety)

# Do the comparisons
comparisons = comparison_pairs.rdd.map(compare_manufacturers)

# Matches have > 5 starting chars in common
matches = comparisons.filter(lambda f: f['eq'] == False and f['len_lcb'] > 5)
```

```
#
# Now we create a mapping of duplicate keys from their raw value
# to the one we're going to use
#

# 1) Group the matches by the longest common beginning ('lcb')
common_lcbs = matches.groupBy(lambda x: x['lcb'])

# 2) Emit the raw value for each side of the match along with the key, our 'lcb'
mfr1_map = common_lcbs.map(
  lambda x: [(y['mfr1'], x[0]) for y in x[1]]).flatMap(lambda x: x)
mfr2_map = common_lcbs.map(
  lambda x: [(y['mfr2'], x[0]) for y in x[1]]).flatMap(lambda x: x)

# 3) Combine the two sides of the comparison's records
map_with_dupes = mfr1_map.union(mfr2_map)

# 4) Remove duplicates
mfr_dedupe_mapping = map_with_dupes.distinct()

# 5) Convert mapping to dataframe to join to airplanes dataframe
mapping_dataframe = mfr_dedupe_mapping.toDF()

# 6) Give the mapping column names
mapping_dataframe.registerTempTable("mapping_dataframe")
mapping_dataframe = spark.sql(
  "SELECT _1 AS Raw, _2 AS NewManufacturer FROM mapping_dataframe"
)
```

Now we can employ the mapping table we have created. Note that this table could have been prepared manually, given the small number of records, and in that case this is the point at which you would load the mapping table as CSV (and run the next code block):

```
# JOIN our mapping left outer...
airplanes_w_mapping = airplanes.join(
  mapping_dataframe,
  on=airplanes.Manufacturer == mapping_dataframe.Raw,
  how='left_outer'
)
# Now replace Manufacturer with NewManufacturer where needed
airplanes_w_mapping.registerTempTable("airplanes_w_mapping")
resolved_airplanes = spark.sql("""SELECT
  TailNum,
  SerialNumber,
  Owner,
  OwnerState,
  IF(NewManufacturer IS NOT null,NewManufacturer,Manufacturer) AS Manufacturer,
  Model,
  ManufacturerYear,
  EngineManufacturer,
```

```
    EngineModel
FROM
    airplanes_w_mapping""")

# Store for later use, in place of airplanes.json
resolved_airplanes.repartition(1).write.mode("overwrite") \
    .json("data/resolved_airplanes.json")
```

Again, for convenience, let's create a single JSON Lines file:

```
cat data/resolved_airplanes.json/part* >> data/resolved_airplanes.jsonl
```

Now we need to update our chart!

Updating our chart

We need to run *ch06/analyze_airplanes_again.py* (*http://bit.ly/2oKArFn*), which is just a copy of the original *ch06/analyze_airplanes.py* (*http://bit.ly/2oKlliP*) with the new path for our resolved airplanes plugged in. Once you've done that, check out */ airplanes* to see the updated chart (Figure 6-9).

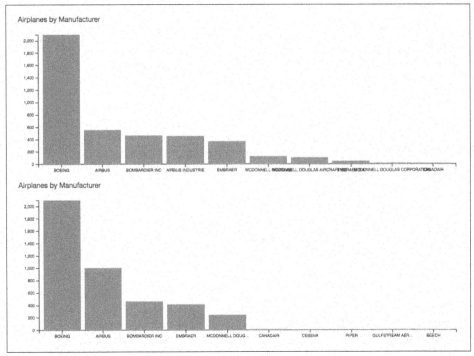

Figure 6-9. Old chart (top) versus deduplicated chart (bottom)

The chart has changed quite a bit now that we've deduplicated manufacturers! Airbus isn't so far behind as we had thought. Now I'm wondering precisely how much market share each manufacturer has using the new `airplanes` dataframe.

Boeing versus Airbus revisited

To find out precisely how much market share Boeing and Airbus have, let's run the percentages again. Check out *ch06/analyze_airplanes_again.py* (*http://bit.ly/2oKArFn*):

```
airplanes = spark.read.json('data/resolved_airplanes.json')
airplanes.registerTempTable("airplanes")

relative_manufacturer_counts = spark.sql("""SELECT
  Manufacturer,
  COUNT(*) AS Total,
  ROUND(
    100 * (
      COUNT(*)/(SELECT COUNT(*) FROM airplanes)
    ),
    2
  ) AS PercentageTotal
FROM
  airplanes
GROUP BY
  Manufacturer
ORDER BY
  Total DESC, Manufacturer
LIMIT 10"""
)
relative_manufacturer_counts.show(10)
```

This produces the following result:

```
+--------------------+-----+---------------+
|        Manufacturer|Total|PercentageTotal|
+--------------------+-----+---------------+
|              BOEING| 2095|          49.04|
|              AIRBUS| 1001|          23.43|
|       BOMBARDIER INC|  460|          10.77|
|             EMBRAER|  413|           9.67|
|   MCDONNELL DOUGLAS|  241|           5.64|
|            CANADAIR|   11|           0.26|
|              CESSNA|    8|           0.19|
|               PIPER|    7|           0.16|
|GULFSTREAM AEROSPACE|    6|           0.14|
|               BEECH|    5|           0.12|
+--------------------+-----+---------------+
```

It turns out that Boeing has 49% of the market, versus Airbus with 23.4%. Go Boeing! (Or, in case you're in Europe... go Airbus!)

Cleanliness: Benefits of entity resolution

Raw data is always dirty. Once you dive in and start working with data and look at it in raw form, when you visualize it in web pages in tables and charts and make it searchable, problems with the data emerge. Resolving these problems as you work with the data enables you to see trends clearly, without distortion. As your visualizations benefit, so will your models. This "cleaning" sets you up for success in building effective statistical models in the next level of the data-value pyramid: *predictions*.

Conclusion

Here's a summary of what we've done so far:

1. Create interesting, interconnected records. The bar for "interesting" is initially low. We will improve it over time based on user feedback, traffic analysis, and noodling.

2. Store these records as objects in a document store, like so:

   ```
   key => {property1, property2, links => [key1, key2, key3]}
   ```

   Split records as properties increase and become complex to avoid deep nesting, or go at it as a document. Both approaches are valid if they fit your data.

3. Use a lightweight web framework like Flask or Sinatra to emit the key/value data as JSON, or use a document store that returns JSON in the first place.

In the next chapter, we'll take what we've learned about our data to make a prediction with lots of practical relevance: will our flight be late? And if so, by how much?

CHAPTER 7

Making Predictions

Now that we have interactive reports exposing different aspects of our data, we're ready to make our first prediction. This forms our fourth agile sprint (Figure 7-1).

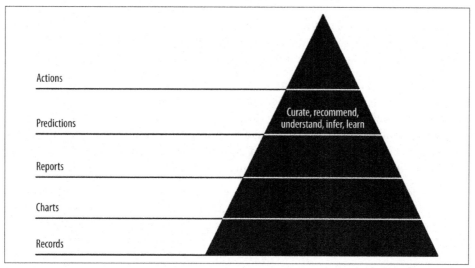

Figure 7-1. Level 4: making predictions

When making predictions, we take what we know about the past and use it to infer what will happen in the future. In doing so, we transition from batch processing of historical data to real-time extrapolation about the future. In real terms, our task in this chapter is to take historical flight records and use them to predict things about future flights.

Code examples for this chapter are available at *Agile_Data_Code_2/ch07* (*http://bit.ly/ 2orM563*). Clone the repository and follow along!

```
git clone https://github.com/rjurney/Agile_Data_Code_2.git
```

The Role of Predictions

We are all used to predictions in life. Some forecasts are based on statistical inference, and some are simply the opinions of pundits. Statistical inference is increasingly involved in predictions of all kinds. From weather forecasts to insurance actuaries determining rates to the point spread in sports betting or odds in poker, statistical predictions are a part of modern life. Sometimes forecasts are accurate, and sometimes they are inaccurate.

For instance, as I was working on this edition of the book, pundits repeatedly dismissed Donald Trump's presidential candidacy as a joke, even as he gained on, pulled ahead of, and ultimately defeated all opponents in the primary and edged closer to Hillary Clinton as the election approached. Pundits are usually wrong, but accurate predictions in elections have emerged thanks to Nate Silver of FiveThirtyEight (*http://53eig.ht/2omLMdA*). He uses an advanced statistical model called a 538 regression (*http://53eig.ht/2oLaffq*) to predict election results state-by-state, and combines these predictions into a model that was highly accurate in 2008 and 2012 (although, as it turns out, Silver—along with every rational member of the world with faith in the American voter—failed to predict Trump's election... to be fair, though, he did predict a 29% chance for Trump, which was about double what others predicted).

We'll be making predictions using statistical inference through a technique called *machine learning*. According to TechTarget (*http://whatis.techtarget.com/definition/machine-learning*), machine learning (ML for short) is "a type of artificial intelligence (AI) that provides computers with the ability to learn without being explicitly programmed." Another way of explaining it is to say that machine learning handles tasks that would be impossibly complex for humans to program manually themselves.

Machine learning is an intimidating topic, an advanced field of study. Mastering all aspects of it can take many years. However, in practice, getting started with machine learning is easy, thanks to some of the libraries we'll be using in this chapter. Once we explain the fundamentals, we'll get on with some simple code.

Predict What?

In this chapter we will employ machine learning to build a predictive analytics application using the dataset we've been visualizing so far. The prediction we'll be making is one with great practical importance for anyone who travels by air. We'll be predicting *flight delays*. Specifically, we'll be predicting the arrival delay, or how late a flight is when arriving at the gate at its destination airport.

First, let's cover the fundamentals of predictive analytics.

Introduction to Predictive Analytics

According to Wikipedia (*https://en.wikipedia.org/wiki/Predictive_analytics*) "Predictive analytics encompasses a variety of statistical techniques from predictive modeling, machine learning, and data mining that analyze current and historical facts to make predictions about future or otherwise unknown events."

Predictive analytics requires training data. Training data is composed of examples of the entity we are trying to predict. Examples are made up of one or more features. *Dependent features* are the values we are trying to predict. *Independent features* are features describing the things we want to predict that *relate* to the dependent features. For instance, our training data for predicting flight delays is our atomic records: our flight delay records. A flight with its delay is an example of a record with a dependent variable. Our independent features are other things we can associate with flights—in other words, all the entities and their properties we've been working with in the preceding chapters! The independent features are the *other* properties of flights—things like the departure delay, the airline, the origin and destination cities, the day of the week or year, etc.

We've been analyzing our data to better understand the features that make up a flight. We know a lot about flight delays, and about flights themselves and those things that combine to produce a flight: airplanes, airlines, airports, etc. This will enable us to effectively engage in *feature engineering*, which is the critical part of making predictions. Interactive visualization and exploratory data analysis as a part of feature engineering is the heart of Agile Data Science. It drives and organizes our efforts.

Now that the groundwork is laid, let's learn the mechanics of making actual predictions.

Making Predictions

There are two ways to approach most predictions: regression and classification. A *regression* takes examples made up of features as input and produces a numeric output. *Classification* takes examples as input and produces a categorical classification. The example dataset that serves as input to a statistical prediction and that enables the machine to learn is called the *training data*.

Whether to build a regression or a classification depends on our business need. The type of response variable often determines which to build. If we need to predict a continuous variable, we build a regression. If we need to predict a nominal/categorical variable, we build a classification.

This decision can be more complex than that, however, taking into account the user interface where we'll present our prediction. For instance, if we were creating an API we were going to sell access to that predicts flight delays, we would probably want to use a regression to produce a numeric prediction. On the other hand, if we were presenting flight delays to users in a mobile application, usability considerations apply that might mean a classification might be better.

In this book, we'll create both a regression and a classification of flight delays using decision trees (*https://en.wikipedia.org/wiki/Decision_tree_learning*), which can both classify and regress.

Features

A feature is what it sounds like: a feature of an example. In software terminology: if examples are objects, features are fields or properties of those objects. Two or more features make up the training data of a statistical prediction—two being the minimum because one field is required as the one to predict, and at least one additional feature is required to make an inference about in order to create a prediction.

Sometimes features are already a part of the training data in question, in their own fields. Sometimes we have to perform feature engineering to derive the training values we need from the ones the data includes.

The models we'll be using employ decision trees. Decision trees are important for a few reasons. First, they can both classify and regress. It requires literally one line of code to switch between the two models just described, from a classification to a regression. Second, they are able to determine and share the *feature importance* of a given training set.

Feature importances tell us which features in the training data were most important in creating an accurate model. This is invaluable, because it gives us insight into what features we should engineer and the approach we should take to improving performance. It also gives us insight into the underlying data, by telling us which features have relationships with the predicted feature.

Regression

The simplest kind of regression analysis is a linear regression. Stat Trek (*http://bit.ly/2omSErf*) defines linear regression as follows:

> In a cause and effect relationship, the independent variable is the cause, and the dependent variable is the effect. Least squares linear regression is a method for predicting the value of a dependent variable Y, based on the value of an independent variable X.

A linear regression is a trend line. We've all seen them in Excel (if you haven't, check out North Carolina State University's Excel regression tutorial (*http://bit.ly/2omYlp8*)). Given a set of variables that characterize a flight, a linear regression might predict how early or late the flight will be, in minutes.

Classification

The second way to solve the problem is to define a set of categories and to classify a flight into one of those categories. Flight delays are a continuous distribution, so they don't naturally yield to classification. The trick here is to define the categories so they simplify the continuous distribution of flight delays into two or more categories. For instance, we might formulate categories similar to the buckets we will use for the weather delay distribution (0–15, 15–60, and 60+), and then classify into these three categories.

Exploring Flight Delays

Our topic for this chapter is flight delays. If we want to predict the feature, we must first understand it. Let's lay the groundwork by creating a delay entity in our application and fleshing it out.

We'll begin by exploring the magnitude of the problem. Just how often are flights late? It feels like "all the time," but is it? This dataset is exciting in that it can answer questions like this one! Check out *ch07/explore_delays.py* (*http://bit.ly/2oV4BaG*):

```
# Load the on-time Parquet file
on_time_dataframe = spark.read.parquet('data/on_time_performance.parquet')
on_time_dataframe.registerTempTable("on_time_performance")
total_flights = on_time_dataframe.count()

# Flights that were late leaving...
late_departures = on_time_dataframe.filter(on_time_dataframe.DepDelayMinutes > 0)
total_late_departures = late_departures.count()

# Flights that were late arriving...
late_arrivals = on_time_dataframe.filter(on_time_dataframe.ArrDelayMinutes > 0)
total_late_arrivals = late_arrivals.count()

# Flights that left late but made up time to arrive on time...
on_time_heros = on_time_dataframe.filter(
  (on_time_dataframe.DepDelayMinutes > 0)
  &
  (on_time_dataframe.ArrDelayMinutes <= 0)
)
total_on_time_heros = on_time_heros.count()

# Get the percentage of flights that are late, rounded to 1 decimal place
pct_late = round((total_late_arrivals / (total_flights * 1.0)) * 100, 1)

print("Total flights:   {:,}".format(total_flights))
print("Late departures: {:,}".format(total_late_departures))
print("Late arrivals:   {:,}".format(total_late_arrivals))
print("Recoveries:      {:,}".format(total_on_time_heros))
print("Percentage Late: {}%".format(pct_late))
```

Which results in:

```
Total flights:     5,819,079
Late departures:   2,125,618
Late arrivals:     2,086,896
Recoveries:          606,902
Percentage Late:   35.9%
```

Wow, flights arrive late 35.9% of the time! The problem is as big as it seems. But how late is the average flight?

```
# Get the average minutes late departing and arriving
spark.sql("""
SELECT
  ROUND(AVG(DepDelay),1) AS AvgDepDelay,
  ROUND(AVG(ArrDelay),1) AS AvgArrDelay
FROM on_time_performance
"""
).show()
```

```
+-----------+-----------+
|AvgDepDelay|AvgArrDelay|
+-----------+-----------+
|        9.4|        4.4|
+-----------+-----------+
```

Flights are 9.4 minutes late departing and 4.4 minutes late arriving on average. Why the constant tardiness? Are the airlines incompetent (as we often angrily suspect), or is the problem weather? Weather is presently out of human control, so that would let the airlines off the hook. Should we be mad at the airlines or angry with the god(s)? (Personally, I'm fearful of Zeus!)

Let's take a look at some delayed flights, and specifically the fields that specify the kinds of delay. We want to be sure to use a random sample, which we can obtain via Spark's DataFrame.sample (*http://bit.ly/2os5rrE*) function. In the first rendition of this chapter, I did not use a random sample and was deceived by what appeared to be constant weather delays, when these are actually not very common. Don't be lazy—it's very easy to insert a .sample(False, 0.01) before every one of your .show functions:

```
late_flights = spark.sql("""
SELECT
  FlightDate,
  ArrDelayMinutes,
  WeatherDelay,
  CarrierDelay,
  NASDelay,
  SecurityDelay,
  LateAircraftDelay
FROM
  on_time_performance
WHERE
```

```
    WeatherDelay IS NOT NULL
    OR
    CarrierDelay IS NOT NULL
    OR
    NASDelay IS NOT NULL
    OR
    SecurityDelay IS NOT NULL
    OR
    LateAircraftDelay IS NOT NULL
ORDER BY
    FlightDate
""")

late_flights.sample(False, 0.01).show()
```

This results in:

ArrDelayMinutes	WeatherDelay	CarrierDelay	NASDelay	SecurityDelay	LateAircraftDelay
21.0	0.0	0.0	21.0	0.0	0.0
17.0	0.0	0.0	17.0	0.0	0.0
27.0	0.0	2.0	25.0	0.0	0.0
19.0	0.0	0.0	19.0	0.0	0.0
157.0	0.0	155.0	2.0	0.0	0.0
19.0	0.0	8.0	11.0	0.0	0.0
24.0	0.0	14.0	0.0	0.0	10.0
105.0	0.0	0.0	0.0	0.0	105.0
46.0	0.0	16.0	15.0	0.0	15.0
22.0	0.0	0.0	20.0	0.0	2.0
35.0	0.0	11.0	24.0	0.0	0.0
67.0	0.0	35.0	32.0	0.0	0.0
39.0	0.0	15.0	5.0	0.0	19.0
21.0	0.0	0.0	21.0	0.0	0.0
204.0	0.0	8.0	0.0	0.0	196.0
31.0	0.0	0.0	0.0	0.0	31.0
16.0	0.0	0.0	16.0	0.0	0.0
50.0	0.0	0.0	0.0	0.0	50.0
23.0	0.0	0.0	23.0	0.0	0.0
36.0	0.0	23.0	13.0	0.0	0.0

An explanation of the different kinds of delay is available on the Federal Aviation Administration (FAA) website (*http://aspmhelp.faa.gov/index.php/Types_of_Delay*).

What does this small sample tell us? Carrier delays are constant and sometimes severe. NAS delays—delays under the control of the National Airspace System (NAS) that can be attributed to conditions such as traffic volume and air traffic control—are as common as carrier delays. Security delays appear rare, while late aircraft delays (which result from the propagation of a previous delay) are frequent and sometimes severe.

A small sample is a good way to get familiar with the data, but small samples can be deceptive. We want real answers we can trust, so let's quantify the sources of delay. What percentage of total delay does each source contribute? We'll use arrival delay for our total—a simplification we'll have to live with, since some delay may be on departure and some in flight:

```
# Calculate the percentage contribution to delay for each source
total_delays = spark.sql("""
SELECT
    ROUND(SUM(WeatherDelay)/SUM(ArrDelayMinutes) * 100, 1) AS pct_weather_delay,
    ROUND(SUM(CarrierDelay)/SUM(ArrDelayMinutes) * 100, 1) AS pct_carrier_delay,
    ROUND(SUM(NASDelay)/SUM(ArrDelayMinutes) * 100, 1) AS pct_nas_delay,
    ROUND(SUM(SecurityDelay)/SUM(ArrDelayMinutes) * 100, 1) AS pct_security_delay,
    ROUND(SUM(LateAircraftDelay)/SUM(ArrDelayMinutes) * 100, 1) AS
        pct_late_aircraft_delay
FROM on_time_performance
""")
total_delays.show()
```

Which results in (formatted to fit the page):

pct_weather_delay	pct_carrier_delay	pct_nas_delay	pct_security_delay	pct_late_aircraft_delay
4.5	29.2	20.7	0.1	36.1

Our result isn't perfect—the sources of delay don't total to 100%. This is a result of our aforementioned simplification regarding arrival/departing delays. Nevertheless, we do get a sense of things; our sample is informative. Most delay is from previous delays with the same airplane, which have a cascading effect on the rest of the schedule. Of delays originating during a flight's operations, most are carrier delays. Specifically, 29% of delays are carrier delays, versus 21% for air traffic control delays and only 4.5% for weather delays.

The answer to our earlier question is clear: we should usually be mad at the airline. However, not all carrier delays are because of mistakes the carrier makes. The FAA website (*http://aspmhelp.faa.gov/index.php/Types_of_Delay*) explains:

> Examples of occurrences that may determine carrier delay are: aircraft cleaning, aircraft damage, awaiting the arrival of connecting passengers or crew, baggage, bird strike, cargo loading, catering, computer, outage-carrier equipment, crew legality (pilot or attendant rest), damage by hazardous goods, engineering inspection, fueling, handling disabled passengers, late crew, lavatory servicing, maintenance, oversales, potable water servicing, removal of unruly passenger, slow boarding or seating, stowing carry-on baggage, weight and balance delays.

In other words, sometimes shit happens and the carrier didn't do anything wrong. We don't have data to determine how often the carrier is really to blame. Importantly for our problem in this chapter, predicting flight delays, the best we'll be able to do is to characterize the overall carrier delay of each airline. We won't be modeling bird strikes or unruly passengers.

Having familiarized ourselves with flight delays, now let's plug some of the features we've discovered into a simple classification and regression.

Extracting Features with PySpark

To use features, we need to extract them from the broader dataset. Let's begin by extracting just a few features from our dataset using PySpark, along with the time delays themselves. In order to do this, we need to decide which feature we're going to predict. There are two delay fields listed in minutes: `ArrDelayMinutes` and `DepDelay Minutes`. Which are we to predict?

In thinking about our use case, it seems that our users want to know both things: whether and how late a flight will depart, and whether and how late it will arrive. Let's include both in our training data. In terms of other features to extract, a little thought tells me that a few things are certain to matter. For instance, some airports have more delays than others, so departing and arriving airport is a no brainer. Flights are probably more often delayed in the hurricane and snow seasons, so the month of the year makes sense. Some carriers are more punctual than others. Finally, some routes must have more delays than others, so the flight number makes sense too.

We'll also include the last of the unique identifiers for the flight, the flight date. Flights are uniquely identified by `FlightDate`, `Carrier`, `FlightNum`, and `Origin` and `Dest`. Always include all of the fields that uniquely identify a record, as it makes debugging easier.

That is all the features we will start with. The more features you use, the more complex wrangling them can get, so keep it simple and use just a few features at first. Once you have a pipeline set up with `sklearn` where you can iterate quickly and determine what helps and what doesn't, you can add more.

All these features are simple and tabular, so it is easy to select them and store them as JSON for our model to read.

Let's pick out and check our features. Check out *ch07/extract_features.py* (*http://bit.ly/ 2pRS6dt*):

```
import sys, os, re
import iso8601
import datetime

# Load the on-time Parquet file
on_time_dataframe = spark.read.parquet('data/on_time_performance.parquet')
on_time_dataframe.registerTempTable("on_time_performance")
```

```
# Select a few features of interest
simple_on_time_features = spark.sql("""
SELECT
  FlightNum,
  FlightDate,
  DayOfWeek,
  DayofMonth AS DayOfMonth,
  CONCAT(Month, '-',  DayofMonth) AS DayOfYear,
  Carrier,
  Origin,
  Dest,
  Distance,
  DepDelay,
  ArrDelay,
  CRSDepTime,
  CRSArrTime
FROM on_time_performance
""")
simple_on_time_features.show()
```

This results in the following (truncated to fit on the page):

FlightNum	FlightDate	...	Carrier	Origin	Dest	Distance	DepDelay	ArrDelay	CRSDepTime	CRSArrTime
1519	...-01	...	AA	DFW	MEM	432.0	-3.0	-6.0	1345	1510
1519	...-01	...	AA	MEM	DFW	432.0	-4.0	-9.0	1550	1730
2349	...-01	...	AA	ORD	DFW	802.0	0.0	26.0	1845	2115
1298	...-01	...	AA	DFW	ATL	731.0	100.0	112.0	1820	2120
1422	...-01	...	AA	DFW	HDN	769.0	78.0	78.0	0800	0925
1422	...-01	...	AA	HDN	DFW	769.0	332.0	336.0	1005	1320
2287	...-01	...	AA	JAC	DFW	1047.0	-4.0	21.0	0800	1200
1080	...-01	...	AA	EGE	ORD	1007.0	null	null	1415	1755
1080	...-01	...	AA	ORD	EGE	1007.0	null	null	1145	1335
2332	...-01	...	AA	DFW	ORD	802.0	null	null	0740	0955
194	...-01	...	AA	DFW	ATL	731.0	null	null	1150	1445
356	...-01	...	AA	ATL	DFW	731.0	-5.0	1.0	1640	1805
356	...-01	...	AA	DFW	ATL	731.0	-4.0	-11.0	1300	1600
2396	...-01	...	AA	DFW	ATL	731.0	76.0	86.0	1955	2250
1513	...-01	...	AA	ATL	DFW	731.0	-2.0	-7.0	1045	1215
1513	...-01	...	AA	DFW	ATL	731.0	-5.0	-25.0	0700	1005
937	...-01	...	AA	DFW	EGE	721.0	35.0	17.0	1600	1720
937	...-01	...	AA	EGE	LAX	748.0	10.0	-12.0	1805	1920
1212	...-01	...	AA	DFW	SDF	733.0	null	null	1145	1440
1212	...-01	...	AA	SDF	DFW	733.0	null	null	1520	1640

Looks like a few flights don't have delay information. Let's filter those, and sort the data before saving it as a single JSON file:

```
# Filter nulls, they can't help us
filled_on_time_features = simple_on_time_features.filter(
  simple_on_time_features.ArrDelay.isNotNull()
  &
  simple_on_time_features.DepDelay.isNotNull()
)
```

Now we need to convert all our dates and times (datetimes (*https://docs.python.org/3.5/library/datetime.html*)) from a string representation to a mathematical one—otherwise, our predictive algorithms can't understand them in their proper and most useful contexts. To do so, we need some utility functions:

```
# We need to turn timestamps into timestamps, and not strings or numbers
def convert_hours(hours_minutes):
  hours = hours_minutes[:-2]
  minutes = hours_minutes[-2:]

  if hours == '24':
    hours = '23'
    minutes = '59'

  time_string = "{}:{}:00Z".format(hours, minutes)
  return time_string

def compose_datetime(iso_date, time_string):
  return "{} {}".format(iso_date, time_string)

def create_iso_string(iso_date, hours_minutes):
  time_string = convert_hours(hours_minutes)
  full_datetime = compose_datetime(iso_date, time_string)
  return full_datetime

def create_datetime(iso_string):
  return iso8601.parse_date(iso_string)

def convert_datetime(iso_date, hours_minutes):
  iso_string = create_iso_string(iso_date, hours_minutes)
  dt = create_datetime(iso_string)
  return dt

def day_of_year(iso_date_string):
  dt = iso8601.parse_date(iso_date_string)
  doy = dt.timetuple().tm_yday
  return doy

def alter_feature_datetimes(row):
  flight_date = iso8601.parse_date(row['FlightDate'])
  scheduled_dep_time = convert_datetime(row['FlightDate'], row['CRSDepTime'])
  scheduled_arr_time = convert_datetime(row['FlightDate'], row['CRSArrTime'])
```

```
# Handle overnight flights
if scheduled_arr_time < scheduled_dep_time:
  scheduled_arr_time += datetime.timedelta(days=1)

doy = day_of_year(row['FlightDate'])

return {
  'FlightNum': row['FlightNum'],
  'FlightDate': flight_date,
  'DayOfWeek': int(row['DayOfWeek']),
  'DayOfMonth': int(row['DayOfMonth']),
  'DayOfYear': doy,
  'Carrier': row['Carrier'],
  'Origin': row['Origin'],
  'Dest': row['Dest'],
  'Distance': row['Distance'],
  'DepDelay': row['DepDelay'],
  'ArrDelay': row['ArrDelay'],
  'CRSDepTime': scheduled_dep_time,
  'CRSArrTime': scheduled_arr_time,
}
```

In practice, these functions were worked out iteratively over the course of an hour. Employing them is then simple:

```
timestamp_features = filled_on_time_features.rdd.map(alter_feature_datetimes)
timestamp_df = timestamp_features.toDF()
```

Always explicitly sort your data before vectorizing it. Don't leave the sort up to the system. If you do so, a software version change or some other unknown cause might ultimately change the sort order of your training data as compared with your result data. This would be catastrophic and confusing and should be avoided at all costs. Explicitly sorting training data in a way that avoids arbitrary sorting is essential:

```
# Explicitly sort the data and keep it sorted throughout.
# Leave nothing to chance.
sorted_features = timestamp_df.sort(
  timestamp_df.DayOfYear,
  timestamp_df.Carrier,
  timestamp_df.Origin,
  timestamp_df.Dest,
  timestamp_df.FlightNum,
  timestamp_df.CRSDepTime,
  timestamp_df.CRSArrTime,
)
```

Let's copy the file into a JSON Lines file and check it out:

```
# Store as a single JSON file and bzip2 it
sorted_features.repartition(1).write.mode("overwrite") \
  .json("data/simple_flight_delay_features.json")
os.system("cp data/simple_flight_delay_features.json/part*
```

```
  data/simple_flight_delay_features.jsonl")
os.system("bzip2 --best data/simple_flight_delay_features.jsonl")
os.system("bzcat data/simple_flight_delay_features.jsonl.bz2 >>
  data/simple_flight_delay_features.jsonl")
```

Now take a look at the result:

```
$ bzcat data/simple_flight_delay_features.jsonl.bz2 | head -5
```

```
{"FlightNum":"1024",
 ...
 "Carrier":"AA",
 "Origin":"ABQ",
 "Dest":"DFW",
 "DayOfYear":"1-1",
 "Distance":569.0,
 "DepDelay":14.0,
 "ArrDelay":13.0
}
{"FlightNum":"1184",
 ...
 "Carrier":"AA",
 "Origin":"ABQ",
 "Dest":"DFW",
 "DayOfYear":"1-1",
 "Distance":569.0,
 "DepDelay":14.0,
 "ArrDelay":17.0
}
{"FlightNum":"336",
 ...
 "Carrier":"AA",
 "Origin":"ABQ",
 "Dest":"DFW",
 "DayOfYear":"1-1",
 "Distance":569.0,
 "DepDelay":-2.0,
 "ArrDelay":36.0
}
{"FlightNum":"125",
 ...
 "Carrier":"AA",
 "Origin":"ATL",
 "Dest":"DFW",
 "DayOfYear":"1-1",
 "Distance":731.0,
 "DepDelay":-1.0,
 "ArrDelay":-21.0
}
{"FlightNum":"1455",
 ...
 "Carrier":"AA",
 "Origin":"ATL",
```

```
  "Dest":"DFW",
  "DayOfYear":"1-1",
  "Distance":731.0,
  "DepDelay":-4.0,
  "ArrDelay":-14.0
}
```

Looking good! Our features are now prepared for vectorization.

Building a Regression with scikit-learn

As we said in Chapter 3, `scikit-learn` is the leading machine learning library for beginners. It also finds widespread use in production applications. As Python has become the lingua franca of data science, `sklearn`, along with `numpy` and `scipy`, has become a foundational part of data science. We will attempt to use `sklearn` to produce a "quick and dirty" predictive model for flight delays in this section—however, we will find its limits. For a Jupyter notebook, 5.4 million flight records is "big data." This will illustrate the limitations of scientific computing on one machine, and will serve as a good introduction to the motivation for using Spark MLlib.

Note that another library is generally recognized as state of the art for classification, and that is `xgboost` (*https://github.com/dmlc/xgboost*). It works similarly to `sklearn`'s `GradientBoosted` classifier and regressor, but some differences in the implementation make it work better than anything else available for the kind of classification task we'll cover. Note that this library is by data science luminary Hadley Wickham (*http://hadley.nz/*), and works with Python, R, Java, Scala, and C++. We'll begin with a linear regression before moving on to a gradient boosted regression.

Loading Our Data

We'll start by loading our data in Python and building our models. Check out *ch07/train_sklearn_model.py* (*http://bit.ly/2pfQ5LU*), or you can follow along using the Jupyter notebook in *ch07/Predicting flight delays with sklearn.ipynb* (*http://bit.ly/2oNRd6c*). Note that in the Jupyter notebook, we have to sample the data down from 5.4 million to 1 million records. To run the notebook locally, run `jupyter notebook` in the project root directory, and then open *ch07/Predicting flight delays with sklearn*.

Our features file is 1.6 GB, so it may take a minute to load. If you're using iPython to paste the code directly, you will want to run this code in a new iPython window, and not one you've used with PySpark. Otherwise, you may run out of RAM. You may also want to stop unneeded programs, to give your system enough RAM to run this example.

If the system doesn't respond for more than 10 minutes, kill the process with Ctrl-C and follow the instructions in the next section to handle the problem by reducing the size of the data being processed. Also note that if you have problems with the Jupyter notebook, you can try running the code in the normal iPython console and see if that works. Part of the point of this section is to explore and discover the limits of Python on a single machine, but you should be able to get through it with 16 GB of RAM.

Now, let's load our features!

```
import sys, os, re
sys.path.append("lib")
import utils

import numpy as np
import sklearn
import iso8601
import datetime
print("Imports loaded...")

# Load and check the size of our training data. May take a minute.
training_data = utils.read_json_lines_file('
  data/simple_flight_delay_features.jsonl'
)
print("Training items: {:,}".format(len(training_data))) # 5,714,008
print("Data loaded...")
```

Note that this is a lot of training data, and it will push the limits of our local machines (presumably with only 16 GB or so of RAM). We will look at ways to address this problem, before moving on to using Spark MLlib.

Let's take a look at a single record as well as the data's size in bytes:

```
# Inspect a record before we alter them
print("Size of training data: {:,} Bytes".format(sys.getsizeof(training_data)))
print(training_data[0])
```

This results in:

```
Size of training data: 50,897,424 Bytes

{'ArrDelay': 13.0, 'DepDelay': 14.0, 'DayOfYear': '1-1', 'FlightNum': '1024',
'FlightDate': '2015-01-01', 'Distance':569.0,
'Carrier': 'AA', 'Origin': 'ABQ', 'Dest': 'DFW'}
```

Sampling Our Data

Here we reach a fork. If you are using the iPython console to run this code, as we have done in other chapters, you can process all of the 5.4 million records without a problem. However, if you're using a Jupyter notebook, this number of records might overwhelm your machine. On my late-model MacBook Pro with 16 GB of RAM, I ran into problems, so I needed to sample the data. In the Jupyter notebook, we run the following code to sample down from 5.4 to 1 million records:

```
# Sample down to 1 million records if not using IPython
training_data = np.random.choice(training_data, 1000000)
print("Sampled items: {:,}".format(training_data))
print("Data sampled...")
```

Which results in:

```
Sampled items: 1,000,000
Data sampled...
```

If you're using the iPython console, you can skip this code unless you run into problems later in this section.

The statistics printed as part of the program output for the rest of the chapter assume you are running without sampling, on all 5.4 million records, using the iPython console. Those for 1 million records would be about 20% of these sizes.

Vectorizing Our Results

Next we need to extract and vectorize the result set (the value we're trying to predict): the flight arrival delays themselves. The way we encode features and results varies between classification and regression, so at this point we have to decide: classification or regression? To classify flight delays, we'll need to map the numeric value of the delay in minutes into categories such as "on time," "late," and "very late." To regress flight delays, we need only use the delay values directly. Because it is simpler, we will begin with a regression.

There are two types of delay, but let's start with arrival delays. We need to extract the arrival delay field from the training data and convert it from a list to a `numpy.array` (*http://bit.ly/2pgM6hY*). In doing so, we are *vectorizing* them in order to serve as the y variable in training our regression:

```
# Separate our results from the rest of the data, vectorize and size up
results = [record['ArrDelay'] for record in training_data]
results_vector = np.array(results)
print("Results vectorized size: {:,} Bytes".format(sys.getsizeof(
    results_vector)))
print("Results vectorized...")
```

This results in:

```
Results vectorized size: 45,712,160 Bytes
Results vectorized...
```

`numpy.array`s are efficient representations of matrices, which are multidimensional arrays of numbers. In this case the value of our data is a float, so there is no more feature extraction necessary. Vectors enable math operations without the inefficiency of loops. They also make possible efficient math using graphics processing units (GPUs). Vectorized, our results are only 45 MB.

Preparing Our Training Data

Now we need to encode the features of our training data. We'll start by removing the arrival delay field, as it is a result and not training data. However, we do include our departure delay as training data in our arrival delay prediction. This means that when we make a prediction, we will include the departure delay as a feature.

We won't be needing the flight date either, as we'll be predicting flights in the future, and these dates do not appear in our historical data. Of course, we can use some features from the date, like day of week, month, and year, and we do so because intuitively we know that flight delays on Christmas day, for example, are worse than on a typical day:

```
# Remove the two delay fields and the flight date from our training data
for item in training_data:
  item.pop('ArrDelay', None)
  item.pop('FlightDate', None)
print("ArrDelay and FlightDate removed from training data...")
```

Next, we need to convert our date/time fields to Unix times (Unix time is defined as the number of seconds since January 1, 1970, in the Greenwich Mean Time zone). This allows our regression to understand the times as numbers, which is the only way it will understand anything (even for nominal features like "departure city ATL," which we'll address later):

```
# Must convert datetime strings to Unix times
for item in training_data:
  if isinstance(item['CRSArrTime'], str):
    dt = iso8601.parse_date(item['CRSArrTime'])
    unix_time = int(dt.timestamp())
    item['CRSArrTime'] = unix_time
  if isinstance(item['CRSDepTime'], str):
    dt = iso8601.parse_date(item['CRSDepTime'])
    unix_time = int(dt.timestamp())
    item['CRSDepTime'] = unix_time
print("CRSArr/DepTime converted to unix time...")
```

Vectorizing Our Features

Now we need to encode and vectorize our features. The numbers, or *continuous* variables, will pass straight through this process as numbers. However, many of our features so far are *nominal*, which just means categorical as opposed to numerical. That is, they are names of things (e.g., ATL represents an airport) and not numbers. Statistical inference is based on vectorized, numeric data, so we need to convert the categories into numbers and build matrices out of the result to feed our regression. If this confuses you, a good guide on types of data (*http://bit.ly/2omEh6d*) is available from Laerd Statistics.

Fortunately for us, sklearn has our back: its DictVectorizer (*http://bit.ly/2omLxPB*) class uses the hashing trick (*http://bit.ly/2pTcI4U*) to convert Python dicts directly into feature vectors (sparse matrices). (There are other, more advanced ways to encode nominal features as well.) This may take a moment and heat your wrists up, as your computer does some heavy lifting:

```
# Use DictVectorizer to convert feature dicts to vectors
from sklearn.feature_extraction import DictVectorizer

print("Original dimensions: [{:,}]".format(len(training_data)))
vectorizer = DictVectorizer()
training_vectors = vectorizer.fit_transform(training_data)
print("Size of DictVectorized vectors: {:,} Bytes".format(
    training_vectors.data.nbytes))
print("Training data vectorized...")
```

The result is:

```
Original dimensions: [5,714,008]
Size of DictVectorized vectors: 500,205,168 Bytes
Training data vectorized...
```

What does fit_transform (*http://bit.ly/2oL8w9y*) do to actually vectorize our data? It is a combination of the fit (*http://bit.ly/2pB0HES*) and transform (*http://bit.ly/2pRhFvc*) methods, which are often used together. First fit creates a list of indices, mapping from the nominal names to a column index in a matrix. Next, transform uses these matrix indices to give each feature its own column, while each instance of a feature, for each example, gets a row. The result is that a dict is converted into a numpy.array. Our data has been transformed from a category to a matrix column representing the presence or absence of that category for each item in the training set (see Figure 7-2).

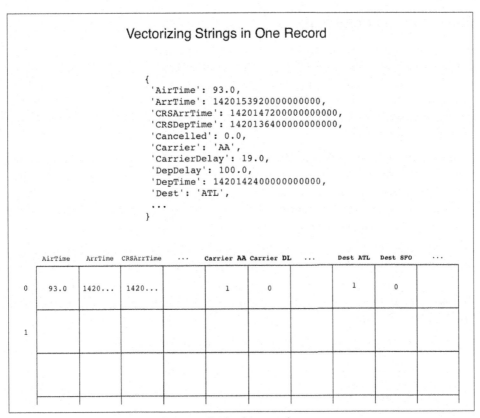

Figure 7-2. Vectorizing records using the hashing trick

Sparse Versus Dense Matrices

Our training data is 500 MB in vectorized form, which is 35% of the size of the original 1.6 GB of JSON, but more than 10 times the size of that data when loaded as
Python variables in RAM. When your data has a lot of nominal (categorical) variables, it can expand in size when vectorized. Note, however, that DictVectorizer
returns a sparse matrix (*http://bit.ly/2pT6C4L*) as opposed to a dense one. The specific matrix employed by DictVectorizer is a scipy.sparse.csr_matrix (*http://
bit.ly/2o5lWyG*), which is a "Compressed Sparse Row matrix."

When used to encode nominal data, sparse matrices don't encode empty elements
with 0s, only full elements with 1s. When data is sparse, as in the case of departures
from ATL, this saves so much space that without the help of sparse matrices, the rest
of this section would be impossible on a MacBook Pro. It is often the case that dense
matrices would make doing math on one machine impossible.

Preparing an Experiment

Before we can train our model, we need to set up an experiment to gauge its accuracy. To do so, we will employ a method called cross-validation (*http://bit.ly/2hKE0pY*). Cross-validation means we split our data into test and training sets, and then train the model on the training set before testing it on the test set. Cross-validation prevents *overfitting*, which is when a model seems quite accurate but fails to actually predict future events well.

If you were to train a model on all your training data without splitting it into training and test sets, you would likely get a good accuracy score since the model would be predicting based on the very input you gave it as training data. But that isn't what we're interested in. What we're interested in is building a statistical model that generalizes to new and unseen data in order to make real predictions about the future.

There is a helpful module in sklearn that can perform cross-validation called sklearn.model_selection (*http://bit.ly/2pRuju5*). We'll employ the test_train_split (*http://bit.ly/2pBIQei*) method to split our data into training and test sets. The test set will be made up of 10% of our total dataset, the other 90% being used for training data:

```
from sklearn.model_selection import train_test_split

X_train, X_test, y_train, y_test = train_test_split(
    training_vectors,
    results_vector,
    test_size=0.1,
    random_state=43
)
print(X_train.shape, X_test.shape)
print(y_train.shape, y_test.shape)
print("Test train split performed...")
```

This results in:

```
(900000, 7420) (100000, 7420)
(900000,) (100000,)
Test train split performed...
```

Training Our Model

With that, we are ready to train our model! First we will train on the training data, and then we will test on the test data to gauge the model's accuracy. The documentation for sklearn.linear_model.LinearRegression (*http://bit.ly/2oUPONt*) is worth a look, as most sklearn classes have usage examples in their documentation. We chose linear regression as the first algorithm to try because it is generally better to have a simpler model if possible, all else being equal (we'll show how easy it is to swap algorithms later):

```
# Train a regressor
from sklearn.linear_model import LinearRegression
from sklearn.model_selection import train_test_split
print("Regressor library and metrics imported...")

regressor = LinearRegression()
print("Regressor instantiated...")

regressor.fit(X_train, y_train)
print("Regressor fit...")
```

There are many different models available in sklearn, and they all work this same way. What power! For instance, we might at this point swap in another algorithm, gradient boosted trees, by importing sklearn.emsemble.GradientBoostingRegres sor (*http://bit.ly/2oL7pa4*) and inserting it in place of sklearn.linear_model.Linear Regression (*http://bit.ly/2oUPONt*):

```
from sklearn.ensemble import GradientBoostingRegressor

regressor = GradientBoostingRegressor
print("Swapped gradient boosting trees for linear regression!")

# Let's go back for now...
regressor = LinearRegression()
print("Swapped back to linear regression!")
```

The fit method takes the training data and results and creates a statistical model mapping one to the other, by inferring how to predict the result from its features:

```
regressor.fit(X_train, y_train)
print("Regressor fitted...")
```

That's all there is to fitting a model in sklearn. Now that we've fitted our model, let's check how accurate it is!

Testing Our Model

To start we need to use our model to make predictions based on our test data. To do so, we use the regressor's predict method, which can take a single item or a matrix of items. The predict method takes the same format as the fit method. This means you will have to transform your features from the textual, object format they probably arrive in into matrices via vectorization before you can make predictions in real time, in the real world, using the model you just fit.

To quantify and visualize our results, we'll need to compare X_test with the model's predictions for X_test. So, we feed X_test to the predict method:

```
predicted = regressor.predict(X_test)
print("Predictions made for X_test...")
```

Once we've got our predictions, we can use some of the many metrics available in `sklearn.metrics` (*http://bit.ly/1ElkZok*). We've chosen the `median_absolute_error` and `r2_score` methods:

```
from sklearn.metrics import median_absolute_error, r2_score

medae = median_absolute_error(y_test, predicted)
print("Median absolute error:    {:.3g}".format(medae))

r2 = r2_score(y_test, predicted)
print("r2 score:                 {:.3g}".format(r2))

Median absolute error:    9.93
r2 score:                 0.829
```

The documentation defines median absolute error as the median of all absolute differences between the target and the prediction (less is better, more indicates a high error between target and prediction). This ranges from 1 to 0, with 1.0 being the best and 0.0 the worst. R2 score is the coefficient of determination, or a measure of how well future samples are likely to be predicted. Taken together, the median absolute error being 9.93 minutes off and the R2 score being 0.829—near to 1—means our model isn't half bad!

Recall that the average lateness in departing is 9.4 minutes, and we have a greater amount of median absolute error. Thats okay, though. Our goal here wasn't to create a great model. Our goal was to plumb our features to our statistical model and then make and test predictions. Remember, we only gave the model a few features off the top of our head. It didn't have a lot to go on! We'll improve our model in Chapter 9. For now, you should learn how to structure a prediction workflow. In Chapter 9, we'll show you how to iteratively improve this model.

Finally, we will plot the values for the arrival lateness in `X_test` against our predicted values for arrival lateness for `X_test`. In other words, we want to visualize how we did so that the actual value is on the x-axis and the predicted value is on the y-axis. We can do so using a scatter plot in `pyplot` (*http://matplotlib.org/api/pyplot_api.html*), with `pyplot.scatter` (*http://bit.ly/2pCQWWJ*):

```
# Plot outputs
import matplotlib.pyplot as plt

plt.scatter(
    y_test,
    predicted,
    color='blue',
    linewidth=1
)

plt.xticks(())
plt.yticks(())
```

```
plt.show()
```

Figure 7-3 shows the result.

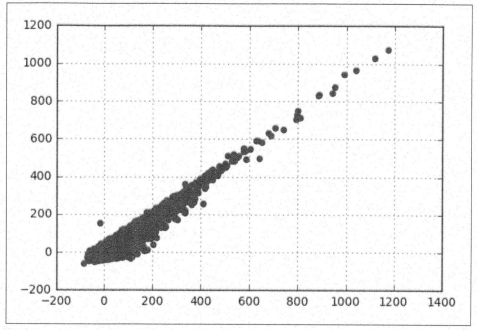

Figure 7-3. Plotting actual versus predicted values

Wow, some flights are almost 20 hours late! And you can see the area left and down of the zeros representing early flights, some of which are as early as over an hour! This is a fascinating chart, and the trend of the plot being up and to the right shows how well it is working.

Conclusion

Note that we had to sample our dataset to make it work in `scikit-learn`. We threw away 80% of our data... but with Spark, we might never have to sample at all! We can use all of our data to make better predictions using a system that scales horizontally across many machines.

Now that we've created a model in `sklearn` and quantified and visualized its accuracy, we're going to move on to building a classifier (*http://bit.ly/2pDU3uN*) in Spark MLlib.

Building a Classifier with Spark MLlib

As we saw in our last example, in order to use `sklearn` to classify or regress all 5.4 million usable flight on-time performance records for 2015, we had to sample down to 1 million records. There simply isn't enough RAM on one typical machine to train the model on all the training data. This is where Spark MLlib comes in. From the Machine Learning Library (MLlib) Guide (*http://spark.apache.org/docs/latest/ml-guide.html*):

> Its goal is to make practical machine learning scalable and easy. At a high level, it provides tools such as:

- ML Algorithms: common learning algorithms such as classification, regression, clustering, and collaborative filtering
- Featurization: feature extraction, transformation, dimensionality reduction, and selection
- Pipelines: tools for constructing, evaluating, and tuning ML Pipelines
- Persistence: saving and load algorithms, models, and Pipelines
- Utilities: linear algebra, statistics, data handling, etc.

MLlib uses Spark DataFrames as the foundation for tables and records. Although some RDD-based methods still remain, they are not under active development.

Note that we are using Spark MLlib because it can work across many machines to handle large volumes of data. We're only using one machine in this book's examples, but the code and the process are identical regardless of the size of the cluster. By learning to build a predictive model with Spark MLlib on a single machine, you are learning to operate a cluster of 1,000 machines. Services like Amazon Elastic Map-Reduce (*https://aws.amazon.com/emr/*) make booting a working Spark cluster a matter of point-and-click. We covered doing analytics in the cloud in the first edition, but removed that chapter to make room for other content in this edition.

Now, follow along as we build a classifier using PySpark and Spark MLlib in *ch07/ train_spark_mllib_model.py* (*http://bit.ly/2pCJr1S*).

Loading Our Training Data with a Specified Schema

First we must load our training data back into Spark. When we first loaded our data, Spark SQL had trouble detecting our timestamp and date types, so we must specify a schema for Spark to go on (just like in our `sklearn` model, it is important for our training data to be typed correctly for it to be interpreted for statistical inference):

```
#
# {
#   "ArrDelay":5.0,"CRSArrTime":"2015-12-31T03:20:00.000-08:00",
```

```
#    "CRSDepTime":"2015-12-31T03:05:00.000-08:00",
#    "Carrier":"WN","DayOfMonth":31,"DayOfWeek":4,
#    "DayOfYear":365,"DepDelay":14.0,"Dest":"SAN",
#    "Distance":368.0, "FlightDate":"2015-12-30T16:00:00.000-08:00",
#    "FlightNum":"6109","Origin":"TUS"
# }
#

from pyspark.sql.types import StringType,
IntegerType, FloatType, DateType, TimestampType
from pyspark.sql.types import StructType, StructField

schema = StructType([
  StructField("ArrDelay", FloatType(), True),       # "ArrDelay":5.0
  StructField("CRSArrTime", TimestampType(), True), # "CRSArrTime":"2015-12..."
  StructField("CRSDepTime", TimestampType(), True), # "CRSDepTime":"2015-12..."
  StructField("Carrier", StringType(), True),       # "Carrier":"WN"
  StructField("DayOfMonth", IntegerType(), True),   # "DayOfMonth":31
  StructField("DayOfWeek", IntegerType(), True),    # "DayOfWeek":4
  StructField("DayOfYear", IntegerType(), True),    # "DayOfYear":365
  StructField("DepDelay", FloatType(), True),       # "DepDelay":14.0
  StructField("Dest", StringType(), True),          # "Dest":"SAN"
  StructField("Distance", FloatType(), True),       # "Distance":368.0
  StructField("FlightDate", DateType(), True),      # "FlightDate":"2015-12..."
  StructField("FlightNum", StringType(), True),     # "FlightNum":"6109"
  StructField("Origin", StringType(), True),        # "Origin":"TUS"
])

features = spark.read.json(
  "data/simple_flight_delay_features.jsonl.bz2",
  schema=schema
)
features.first()
```

This results in:

```
Row(
  ArrDelay=13.0,
  CRSArrTime=datetime.datetime(2015, 1, 1, 10, 10),
  CRSDepTime=datetime.datetime(2015, 1, 1, 7, 30),
  Carrier='AA',
  DayOfMonth=1,
  DayOfWeek=4,
  DayOfYear=1,
  DepDelay=14.0,
  Dest='DFW',
  Distance=569.0,
  FlightDate=datetime.date(2014, 12, 31),
  FlightNum='1024',
  Origin='ABQ'
)
```

With our data loaded, now we need to prepare our data for classification.

Addressing Nulls

Before we can use the tools that PySpark's MLlib provides us, we must eliminate null values from fields in rows of our DataFrames. Otherwise our code will crash as we start to employ tools from pyspark.ml.features (*http://spark.apache.org/docs/latest/ml-features.html*).

To detect null values in columns, we need only loop through our columns and inspect them with pyspark.sql.Column.isNull (*http://bit.ly/2pCZ4Xf*):

```
null_counts = [(column, features.where(features[column].isNull()).count()) \
    for column in features.columns]
cols_with_nulls = filter(lambda x: x[1] > 0, null_counts)
print(list(cols_with_nulls))
```

If null values are found, we need only employ DataFrame.na.fill (*http://bit.ly/2osCqMy*) to fill them. Supply fillna with a dict with the column name as the key and the column's fill value as the value, and it will fill in the column name with that value:

```
filled_features = features.na.fill({'column_name': 'missing_replacement_value'})
```

In our dataset, no nulls are found, but there usually are some, so take note of this step for the future. It will save you trouble as you start engineering and vectorizing your features.

Replacing FlightNum with Route

At this point it occurs to us that FlightNums will change, but routes do not... so long as we define a route as a pair of cities. So, let's add a column Route, which is defined as the concatenation of Origin, -, and Dest, such as ATL-SFO. This will very simply inform our model whether certain routes are frequently delayed, separately from whether certain airports tend to have delays for inbound or outbound flights.

To add Route, we need to use two utilities from the pyspark.sql.functions (*http://bit.ly/2pBrYHj*) package. The concat (*http://bit.ly/2o35tuF*) function concatenates multiple strings together, and the lit (*http://bit.ly/2o37ZkM*) function is needed to specify a literal string to concatenate:

```
#
# Add a Route variable to replace FlightNum
#
from pyspark.sql.functions import lit, concat
features_with_route = features.withColumn(
  'Route',
  concat(
    features.Origin,
    lit('-'),
    features.Dest
```

```
    )
  )
  features_with_route.select("Origin", "Dest", "Route").show(5)
```

This produces the following result:

```
+------+----+--------+
|Origin|Dest|   Route|
+------+----+--------+
|   ABQ| DFW|ABQ-DFW|
|   ABQ| DFW|ABQ-DFW|
|   ABQ| DFW|ABQ-DFW|
|   ATL| DFW|ATL-DFW|
|   ATL| DFW|ATL-DFW|
+------+----+--------+
```

Note that if we wanted to, we could convert the record to an RDD, where we could run something like the following:

```
def add_route(record):
  record = record.asDict()
  record['Route'] = record['Origin'] + "-" + record['Dest']
  return record

features_with_route_rdd = features.rdd.map(add_route)
```

The reason to use DataFrames is that they are much, much faster than RDDs, even if the API is slightly more complex.

Bucketizing a Continuous Variable for Classification

Classification does not work to predict a continuous variable like flight delays (in minutes); classifications predict two or more categories. Therefore, in order to build a classifier for flight delays, we have to create categories our of delays in minutes.

Determining arrival delay buckets

In the first run-through writing the book, we used the same buckets as Bay Area startup FlightCaster (founded in 2009 and acquired in 2011 by Next Jump): on time, slightly late, and very late. The values corresponding to these bins come from a natural split in how people think about time in terms of minutes, hours, and days. One hour is an intuitive value for the high end of slightly late. Over one hour would then be very late. "On time" would be within 15 minutes of the scheduled arrival time. If such natural bins weren't available, you would want to closely analyze the distribution of your continuous variable to determine what buckets to use.

As it turned out, this analysis was necessary in our case too. When writing the book, while debugging an issue with our Spark ML classifier model, we did an analysis where we found that a different set of categories were needed. Check out the Jupyter notebook at *ch09/Debugging Prediction Problems.ipynb* (*http://bit.ly/2pRnjO1*) for details. Note that GitHub supports the display of Jupyter notebooks, which makes them a really powerful way to share data analyses—just commit and push to a GitHub repository and you've got a shared report. When you are doing iterative visualization, notebooks are very handy.

Iterative visualization with histograms. To begin, check out the overall distribution of flight delays, which we compute by converting the features DataFrame to an RDD and then employing RDD.histogram (*http://bit.ly/2o3e2Wm*). RDD.histogram returns two lists: a set of buckets, and the count for each bucket. We then use matplotlib.pyplot (*http://bit.ly/2oMmU1i*) to create a histogram. Note that because our buckets are already counted, we can't use pyplot.hist (*http://bit.ly/2oWzjQQ*). Instead, we employ pyplot.bar (*http://bit.ly/2pSU6ls*) to create a histogram from our precomputed buckets and their corresponding counts.

To gather our data, we select the ArrDelay column, convert the DataFrame to an RDD, and call RDD.flatMap to convert our records into an RDD containing a single list of floats:

```
%matplotlib inline

import numpy as np
import matplotlib.mlab as mlab
import matplotlib.pyplot as plt

# Look at overall histogram
data_tuple = features\
  .select("ArrDelay")\
  .rdd\
  .flatMap(lambda x: x)\
  .histogram([-87.0, -60, -30, -15, 0, 15, 30, 60, 120])
```

Next, we extract the heights of the bars and the bin definitions from the tuple returned by histogram:

```
eights = np.array(data_tuple[1])

# The bins are 1 > length than the values
full_bins = data_tuple[0]
```

Since bars are drawn from the left, we remove the rightmost item in the bins list:

```
# Bars are drawn from the left
mid_point_bins = full_bins[:-1]
```

Next, we use a list comprehension to determine the range between the values defining the buckets, which gives us the width of the bars. We've decided that the bars should be as wide as the data they measure:

```
# The width of a bar should be the range it maps in the data
widths = [abs(i - j) for i, j in zip(full_bins[:-1], full_bins[1:])]
```

Finally, we plot the bar chart, specifying our bar widths (they draw from the left) and coloring our bars blue:

```
# And now the bars should plot nicely
bar = plt.bar(mid_point_bins, heights, width=widths, color='b')
```

We can summarize the previous operations in a function called create_hist, which we will reuse to draw other histograms like this one:

```
def create_hist(rdd_histogram_data):
    """Given an RDD.histogram, plot a pyplot histogram"""
    heights = np.array(rdd_histogram_data[1])
    full_bins = rdd_histogram_data[0]
    mid_point_bins = full_bins[:-1]
    widths = [abs(i - j) for i, j in zip(full_bins[:-1], full_bins[1:])]
    bar = plt.bar(mid_point_bins, heights, width=widths, color='b')
    return bar
```

The result is informative, showing that most flights are slightly early (Figure 7-4). The distribution is fairly normal, with some right skew. Now we must ask ourselves: given how people think about time, the distribution of the arrival delays, and our need to define buckets to categorize flight delays, what are the right bucket definitions?

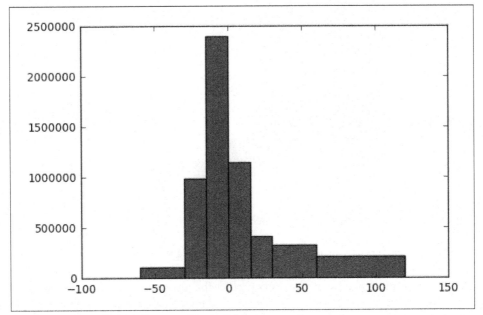

Figure 7-4. Overall distribution of arrival delays

To start, let's visualize the first set of buckets we considered: –87 to 15, 15 to 60, and 60 to 200. Note that the first item in the bucket definition, –87, comes from the minimum delay in the dataset. We use 200 to keep from distorting the chart, although the maximum delay is actually 1,971 minutes:

```
%matplotlib inline

buckets = [-87.0, 15, 60, 200]
rdd_histogram_data = features\
  .select("ArrDelay")\
  .rdd\
  .flatMap(lambda x: x)\
  .histogram(buckets)

create_hist(rdd_histogram_data)
```

The result is shown in Figure 7-5.

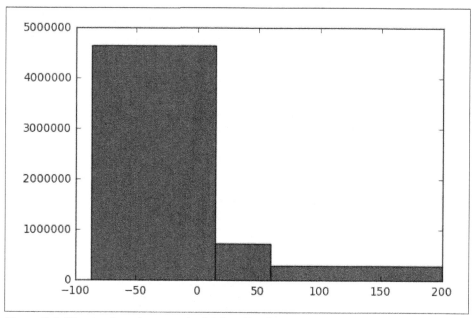

Figure 7-5. First bucket scheme arrival delay distribution

Wow. This is a very distorted distribution. We have created an imbalanced class set from one that should ideally be balanced. This is a problem, because imbalanced classes can produce classifiers that only predict the most common value, and yet still seem fairly accurate. At best, this label set would have made things hard for our classifier when there is no benefit to doing so. We need to rethink our labels.

Let's try something a little more granular and check the distribution using the set of buckets: [-87.0, -30, -15, 0, 15, 30, 120]:

```
%matplotlib inline

buckets = [-87.0, -30, -15, 0, 15, 30, 120]
rdd_histogram_data = features\
    .select("ArrDelay")\
    .rdd\
    .flatMap(lambda x: x)\
    .histogram(buckets)

create_hist(rdd_histogram_data)
```

This produces the result in Figure 7-6.

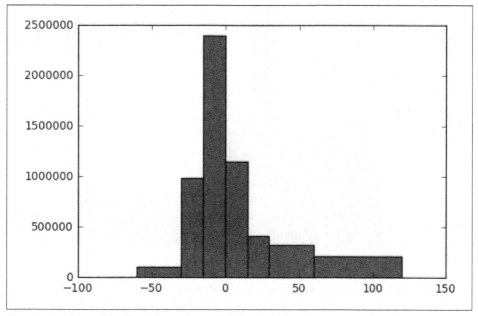

Figure 7-6. Second bucket scheme arrival delay distribution

Hmm... this looks better, but the leftmost and rightmost buckets look too small. Let's combine the −87 to −30 and −30 to −15 buckets, and try again:

```
%matplotlib inline

buckets = [-87.0, -15, 0, 15, 30, 120]
rdd_histogram_data = features\
  .select("ArrDelay")\
  .rdd\
  .flatMap(lambda x: x)\
  .histogram(buckets)

create_hist(rdd_histogram_data)
```

Figure 7-7 shows the result.

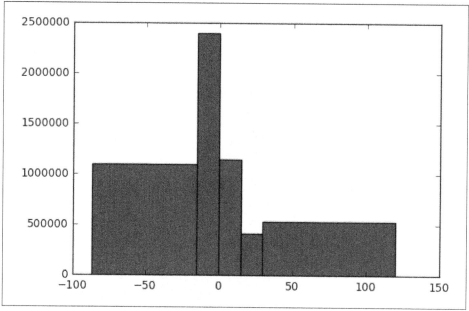

Figure 7-7. Third bucket scheme arrival delay distribution

This looks better! However, the 15–30 bucket seems too small. Let's merge this bucket with the 0–15 bucket and try again:

```
%matplotlib inline

buckets = [-87.0, -15, 0, 30, 120]
rdd_histogram_data = features\
  .select("ArrDelay")\
  .rdd\
  .flatMap(lambda x: x)\
  .histogram(buckets)

create_hist(rdd_histogram_data)
```

The result of this fourth attempt is in Figure 7-8.

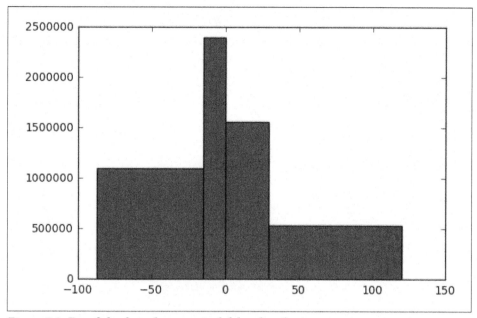

Figure 7-8. Fourth bucket scheme arrival delay distribution

Ah-ha! That looks pretty good. The buckets end up being "very early" (> 15 minutes early), "early" (0–15 minutes early), "late" (0–30 minutes late), and "very late" (30+ minutes late). These aren't perfect in terms of usability, but I think they can work. Ideally the distribution in the buckets would be equal, but they are close enough.

Bucket quest conclusion. We have now determined the right bucket scheme for converting a continuous variable, flight delays, into four categories. Note how we used a Jupyter notebook along with PySpark and PyPlot to iteratively visualize the flights that fell into each bucketing scheme. This notebook is now a shareable asset. This would serve as a great jumping-off point for a discussion involving the data scientist who created the notebook, the product manager for the product, and the engineers working on the project.

Now that we've got our buckets, let's apply them and get on with our prediction!

Bucketizing with a DataFrame UDF

We can bucketize our data in one of two ways: using a DataFrame UDF (*http://bit.ly/2omGIWp*), or with pyspark.ml.feature.Bucketizer (*http://bit.ly/2o3hO2h*).

Let's begin by using a UDF to categorize our data in accordance with the scheme in the preceding section. We'll create a function, bucketize_arr_delay, to achieve the "bucketizing," and then wrap it in a UDF (*http://bit.ly/2omGIWp*) along with a `Struct Field` (*http://bit.ly/2pBFZSr*) of type information—in this case the string `DataType` (*http://bit.ly/2pBeXNW*) `StringType` (*http://bit.ly/2pg9A6S*). Next, we'll apply the UDF to create a new column via `DataFrame.withColumn` (*http://bit.ly/2pBvv5D*). Finally, we'll select `ArrDelay` and `ArrDelayBucket` and see how they compare:

```
#
# Categorize or 'bucketize' the arrival delay field using a DataFrame UDF
#
def bucketize_arr_delay(arr_delay):
  bucket = None
  if arr_delay <= -15.0:
    bucket = 0.0
  elif arr_delay > -15.0 and arr_delay <= 0.0:
    bucket = 1.0
  elif arr_delay > 0.0 and arr_delay <= 30.0:
    bucket = 2.0
  elif arr_delay > 30.0:
    bucket = 3.0
  return bucket

# Wrap the function in pyspark.sql.functions.udf with
# pyspark.sql.types.StructField information
dummy_function_udf = udf(bucketize_arr_delay, StringType())

# Add a category column via pyspark.sql.DataFrame.withColumn
manual_bucketized_features = features_with_route.withColumn(
  "ArrDelayBucket",
  dummy_function_udf(features['ArrDelay'])
)
manual_bucketized_features.select("ArrDelay", "ArrDelayBucket").show()
```

This produces the following result:

```
+--------+--------------+
|ArrDelay|ArrDelayBucket|
+--------+--------------+
|    13.0|           2.0|
|    17.0|           2.0|
|    36.0|           3.0|
|   -21.0|           0.0|
|   -14.0|           1.0|
|    16.0|           2.0|
|    -7.0|           1.0|
|    13.0|           2.0|
|    25.0|           2.0|
+--------+--------------+
```

You can see that `ArrDelay` is mapped to `ArrDelayBucket` as we indicated.

Bucketizing with pyspark.ml.feature.Bucketizer

Creating buckets for classification is simpler using `Bucketizer`. We simply define our splits in a list, instantiate our `Bucketizer`, and then apply a transformation on our features DataFrame. We'll do this transformation for the `ArrDelay` field:

```
#
# Use pysmark.ml.feature.Bucketizer to bucketize ArrDelay
#
from pyspark.ml.feature import Bucketizer

splits = [-float("inf"), -15.0, 0, 30.0, float("inf")]
bucketizer = Bucketizer(
  splits=splits,
  inputCol="ArrDelay",
  outputCol="ArrDelayBucket"
)
ml_bucketized_features = bucketizer.transform(features_with_route)

# Check the buckets out
ml_bucketized_features.select("ArrDelay", "ArrDelayBucket").show()
```

Which results in:

```
+--------+--------------+
|ArrDelay|ArrDelayBucket|
+--------+--------------+
|    13.0|           2.0|
|    17.0|           2.0|
|    36.0|           3.0|
|   -21.0|           0.0|
|   -14.0|           1.0|
|    16.0|           2.0|
|    -7.0|           1.0|
|    13.0|           2.0|
|    25.0|           2.0|
+--------+--------------+
```

You can see the result is the same as with our UDF buckets. Now that we've created the `ArrDelayBucket` fields, we're ready to vectorize our features using tools from `pyspark.ml.feature`.

Feature Vectorization with pyspark.ml.feature

Spark MLlib has an extremely rich library of functions for various machine learning tasks, so it is helpful when using MLlib to have the API documentation (*http://bit.ly/2o4WvNv*) open in a browser tab, along with the DataFrame API documentation (*http://bit.ly/2pDsOQK*). While an RDD-based API (*http://bit.ly/1yCoHox*) does exist, we'll be using the DataFrame-based MLlib routines (*http://bit.ly/2pDuoVK*).

Vectorizing categorical columns with Spark ML

To follow along with this section, open the `pyspark.ml.feature` documentation (*http://bit.ly/2pE51jZ*). First we need to import our tools from `pyspark.ml.feature`:

```
from pyspark.ml.feature import StringIndexer, VectorAssembler
```

Then we need to index our nominal or categorical string columns into sets of vectors made up of binary variables for every unique value found in a given column. To achieve this, for each categorical column (be it a string or number), we need to:

1. Configure and create a `StringIndexer` (*http://bit.ly/2pDEHt4*) to index the column into one number per unique value.

2. Execute `fit` (*http://bit.ly/2pRkbl8*) on the `StringIndexer` to get a `StringIndexerModel`.

3. Run the training data through `StringIndexerModel.transform` (*http://bit.ly/2pg1xHr*) to index the strings into a new column.

The code to implement these steps for each categorical variable column looks like this:

```
# Turn category fields into categoric feature vectors, then drop
# intermediate fields
for column in ["Carrier", "DayOfMonth", "DayOfWeek", "DayOfYear",
               "Origin", "Dest", "Route"]:
  string_indexer = StringIndexer(
    inputCol=column,
    outputCol=column + "_index"
  )
  ml_bucketized_features = string_indexer.fit(ml_bucketized_features)\
                                    .transform(ml_bucketized_features)

# Check out the indexes
ml_bucketized_features.show(6)
```

Having indexed our categorical features, now we combine them with our numeric features into a single feature vector for our classifier.

Vectorizing continuous variables and indexes with Spark ML

As they are already numeric, there isn't much work required to vectorize our continuous numeric features. And now that we have indexes, we have a numeric representation of each string column. Now we simply employ `VectorAssembler` (*http://bit.ly/2pR7Ehm*) to combine the numeric and index columns into a single feature `Vector` (*http://bit.ly/2o3cqfy*). Then we drop the index columns, as they aren't needed anymore:

```
# Handle continuous numeric fields by combining them into one feature vector
numeric_columns = ["DepDelay", "Distance"]
index_columns = ["Carrier_index", "DayOfMonth_index",
                 "DayOfWeek_index", "DayOfYear_index", "Origin_index",
                 "Origin_index", "Dest_index", "Route_index"]
vector_assembler = VectorAssembler(
  inputCols=numeric_columns + index_columns,
  outputCol="Features_vec"
)
final_vectorized_features = vector_assembler.transform(ml_bucketized_features)

# Drop the index columns
for column in index_columns:
  final_vectorized_features = final_vectorized_features.drop(column)

# Check out the features
final_vectorized_features.show()
```

Now we're ready to train our classifier!

Classification with Spark ML

Our features are prepared in a single field, Features_vec, and we're ready to compose the experiment we'll run as part of creating our classifier. To drive our experiment, we require a training dataset and a test dataset. As we discussed earlier, a training dataset is used to train the model and a test set is used to gauge its accuracy. Cross-validation ensures that the models we create in the lab perform well in the real world, and not just on paper.

Test/train split with DataFrames

As before with scikit-learn, we need to cross-validate. This means splitting our data between a training set and a test set.

The DataFrame API makes this easy with DataFrame.randomSplit (*http://bit.ly/2oLdHqe*). This takes an array featuring the ratios of the splits, which should add up to 1:

```
# Test/train split
training_data, test_data = final_vectorized_features.randomSplit([0.8, 0.2])
```

Creating and fitting a model

It takes three lines to import, instantiate, and fit a random forest classifier using our training dataset. Note that we're using a random forest classifier because this is the most accurate decision tree model available in Spark MLlib that can classify into multiple categories. These classifiers also offer feature importances, which we will use in Chapter 9 to improve the model.

Also note that we run the model once, and it throws an exception because we have more than 32 unique values for one feature, the default value for maxBins. We set maxBins to the value suggested by the exception, 4657, and the model fits successfully. Note that this can take a while, so grab some coffee:

```
# Instantiate and fit random forest classifier
from pyspark.ml.classification import RandomForestClassifier
rfc = RandomForestClassifier(
featuresCol="Features_vec", labelCol="ArrDelayBucket",
  maxBins=4657
)
model = rfc.fit(training_data)
```

Next, we need to evaluate the classifier we've created.

Evaluating a model

We can evaluate the performance of our classifier using the MulticlassClassifica tionEvaluator (*http://bit.ly/2o3nx8e*), which simply wraps the predictions we get from running pyspark.ml.classification.RandomForestClassificationMo del.transform (*http://bit.ly/2oLqg4J*) on the test dataset. Several metrics are available, but we'll start with the raw accuracy:

```
# Evaluate model using test data
predictions = model.transform(test_data)

from pyspark.ml.evaluation import MulticlassClassificationEvaluator
evaluator = MulticlassClassificationEvaluator(
  labelCol="ArrDelayBucket", metricName="accuracy"
)
accuracy = evaluator.evaluate(predictions)
print("Accuracy = {}".format(accuracy))
```

This results in:

```
Accuracy = 0.5971608857699723
```

Not great, but good enough for now. Don't worry, we'll work on making the model more accurate in Chapter 9.

Let's lay eyes on some of the predictions, to see that they're sane. At one point we had a bug where all predictions were 0.0. Seeing a sample with different prediction values takes a bit of cleverness because of the way the transformation sorts the data, so we order the sample by the reservation system departure time before displaying it:

```
# Sanity-check a sample
predictions.sample(False, 0.001, 18).orderBy("CRSDepTime").show(6)
```

Which results in (table has been truncated to fit on the page):

ArrDelay	CRSArrTime	CRSDepTime	...	DepDelay	...	FlightDate	FlightNum	...
-10.0	...09:22:...	...05:59:	...	9.0	...	...12-31	744	...
-18.0	...13:24:...	...10:25:	...	-3.0	...	...12-31	6164	...
25.0	...03:45:...	...02:40:	...	15.0	...	...01-01	4222	...
-6.0	...08:45:...	...06:00:	...	2.0	...	...01-01	4375	...
0.0	...11:35:...	...09:35:	...	1.0	...	...01-01	4123	...
3.0	...14:45:...	...13:20:	...	2.0	...	...01-02	116	...

Now let's see the distribution of the `Prediction` field, to verify we don't have that same bug:

```
predictions.groupBy("Prediction").count().show()
```

This gives us:

Prediction	Count
0.0	3159
1.0	831281
3.0	114768
2.0	191359

This "sanity check" seems okay!

Conclusion

With Spark, we can create, train, and evaluate a classifier or regression in a few lines of code. Surprisingly, it is even more powerful than `scikit-learn`. But to be useful, we've got to deploy our prediction. We'll do that in the next chapter.

Now we have a problem—how do we deploy Spark ML models? Unlike `scikit-learn` models, we can't simply place them inside our web application as an API, because they require the Spark platform to run. This is something we will address in the next chapter.

Conclusion

In this chapter we've taken what we know about the past to predict the future.

In the next chapter, we'll drill down into this prediction to drive a new action that can take advantage of it.

## CHAPTER 8

Deploying Predictive Systems

Building models that can make predictions was hard work. We had to extract the features of our training data from our raw data, vectorize those features, combine those vectors, create an experiment, and then train, test, and evaluate a statistical model. Fun stuff, but a lot of work!

At this point, it is important to understand that *most predictions never make it out of the lab*. This point is as far as they ever get. Nobody ever sees them on a website or even indirectly feels their output in any way. Most predictions die in the laboratory where they were created, and a big reason is that the people who build them don't know how to deploy them. Deploying predictions is our topic in this chapter, and for the aforementioned reason it is an essential one for a practicing data scientist to master.

Code examples for this chapter are available at *Agile_Data_Code_2/ch08* (*http://bit.ly/ 2oTwv4W*). Clone the repository and follow along!

```
git clone https://github.com/rjurney/Agile_Data_Code_2.git
```

Deploying a scikit-learn Application as a Web Service

Deploying a scikit-learn application as a web service is fairly direct. Having created the model, we save it to disk. Then we load the model during the startup of a web application that provides a RESTful (*http://bit.ly/1a1kVX5*) API.

Before we do that, we need to define our API and work backward from it to reach the properties of our model's input. We must map from our API's input to our model's input, and it is rarely the case that the API will receive all the values the model requires as arguments. Many of them must be derived from incomplete input.

We will test our model using `curl`, and then we'll embed it within our application via a web form for entering the values for the regression API. When the form is submitted, a prediction will be returned. This approximates how a prediction is embedded in a real product, albeit with less polish and design.

Saving and Loading scikit-learn Models

In order to access our regression for flight delays inside our web application, we must be able to save it from our script that creates the model and load it in the web application that serves our prediction API. More than just the prediction, we also need to persist those objects that vectorized the model's features.

Check out *ch07/train_sklearn_model.py* (*http://bit.ly/2pfQ5LU*), and you can follow along at the `sklearn` API docs for model persistence (*http://bit.ly/2ov0nCR*).

Saving and loading objects using pickle

The first way to persist an `sklearn` model is with `pickle` (*https://docs.python.org/3/library/pickle.html*). `pickle` isn't specific to `sklearn`; it is a general Python utility for persisting objects to disk. Using it is simple.

We first save the model to disk using `pickle.dumps` (*http://bit.ly/2pjiOzg*) to get the bytes of the object and then write them to disk using a file handle in binary mode (there is also the `pickle.dump` (*http://bit.ly/2pGqqJn*) method to do this directly):

```
import pickle

project_home = os.environ["PROJECT_HOME"]

# Dump the model itself
regressor_path = "{}/data/sklearn_regressor.pkl".format(project_home)

regressor_bytes = pickle.dumps(regressor)
model_f = open(regressor_path, 'wb')
model_f.write(regressor_bytes)

# Dump the DictVectorizer that vectorizes the features
vectorizer_path = "{}/data/sklearn_vectorizer.pkl".format(project_home)

vectorizer_bytes = pickle.dumps(vectorizer)
vectorizer_f = open(vectorizer_path, 'wb')
vectorizer_f.write(vectorizer_bytes)
```

Loading the model is similarly easy with `pickle.loads` (*http://bit.ly/2ouTdi8*) and `pickle.load` (*http://bit.ly/2oO8Uo6*):

```
# Load the model itself
model_f = open(regressor_path, 'rb')
model_bytes = model_f.read()
regressor = pickle.loads(model_bytes)
```

```
# Load the DictVectorizer
vectorizer_f = open(vectorizer_path, 'rb')
vectorizer_bytes = vectorizer_f.read()
vectorizer = pickle.loads(vectorizer_bytes)
```

pickle is a powerful and generic way to store Python objects.

Saving and loading models using sklearn.externals.joblib

Saving a model to disk with sklearn.externals.joblib is a one-liner:

```
from sklearn.externals import joblib

# Dump the model
joblib.dump(regressor, 'data/sklearn_regressor.pkl')
joblib.dump(vectorizer, '../data/sklearn_vectorizer.pkl')
```

So is loading one:

```
# Load the model and vectorizer
regressor = joblib.load('../data/sklearn_regressor.pkl')
vectorizer = joblib.load('../data/sklearn_vectorizer.pkl')
```

We'll use this method later, in this chapter's web application.

Groundwork for Serving Predictions

In starting this section, it became clear that there are a whole host of things we need
to do beyond building a simple API to actually deploy this prediction to the web. To
see what I mean, let's look at an example flight training record:

```
{
  "ArrDelay":5.0,
  "Carrier":"WN",
  "DayOfMonth":31,
  "DayOfWeek":4,
  "DayOfYear":365,
  "DepDelay":14.0,
  "Dest":"SAN",
  "Distance":368.0,
  "FlightNum":"6109",
  "Origin":"TUS"
}
```

With the exception of ArrDelay, which we are predicting, we need to re-create the
values for all these fields, in vectorized form, for our application to reproduce its
behavior inside our API. Straightforward? Not exactly.

For instance, does it really make sense for a user to calculate and supply the day of the
month, week, and year in order to use our API? Surely not. It makes more sense, and

is much more user-friendly, to accept the date as an API argument and calculate these other fields as part of the API's prediction process.

And then there are fields we can't expect a user to know about, such as the distance between the origin and destination. We'll need to create a lookup table from our data and look that value up based on the origin and destination.

This all illustrates an important principle for deploying predictions: *if you can't acquire the data in real time, you can't incorporate it in your model and still be able to deploy it.* This greatly limits what we can do to improve our models.

Our API will now look something like this, in which the name of a field maps to the type of its argument. From these values we can derive the others that make up a flight training record:

```
api_field_type_map = \
{
  "DepDelay": float,
  "Carrier": str,
  "Date": str,
  "Dest": str,
  "FlightNum": str,
  "Origin": str
}
```

Creating Our Flight Delay Regression API

In order to serve our predictions in a web application, we first need to load the model in our application code at startup. Then, in response to requests, we need to accept as arguments those values from which we can derive the features of the model and transform them into the model's vector space. Finally, we feed the vectorized data into our model and return a JSON result.

Let's walk through each part sequentially. Check out *ch08/web/predict_flask.py* (*http:// bit.ly/2o7DJVR*) and *ch08/web/predict_utils.py* (*http://bit.ly/2pG8SNo*).

First, we load the model using `sklearn.externals.joblib.load` (*http://bit.ly/ 2oTnDMA*). Note that we reference the environment variable $PROJECT_HOME so that our loading works from whichever directory in the filesystem we start the Flask app from:

```
# Load our regression model
from sklearn.externals import joblib
project_home = os.environ["PROJECT_HOME"]
vectorizer = joblib.load("{}/data/sklearn_vectorizer.pkl".format(project_home))
regressor = joblib.load("{}/data/sklearn_regressor.pkl".format(project_home))
```

Next we define our API's endpoint and make it a POST so that search engines won't trigger the relatively expensive operation of making the prediction the controller serves:

```
# Make our API a post, so a search engine won't hit it
@app.route("/flights/delays/predict/regress", methods=['POST'])
def regress_flight_delays():
```

We employ the api_field_type_map we defined earlier to fetch the values HTTP POSTed from the frontend's web form for this controller and place them in the record we will feed our regression:

```
api_field_type_map = \
  {
    "DepDelay": float,
    "Carrier": str,
    "Date": str,
    "Dest": str,
    "FlightNum": str,
    "Origin": str
  }
api_form_values = {}
for api_field_name, api_field_type in api_field_type_map.items():
  api_form_values[api_field_name] = request.form.get(
    api_field_name, type=api_field_type
  )

# Set the direct values
prediction_features = {}
prediction_features['Origin'] = api_form_values['Origin']
prediction_features['Dest'] = api_form_values['Dest']
prediction_features['FlightNum'] = api_form_values['FlightNum']
```

We create a reference to an incomplete API called predict_utils.get_flight_ dis tance to determine the Distance field, which is the distance between the Origin and Dest:

```
# Set the derived values
prediction_features['Distance'] = predict_utils.get_flight_distance(
  client, api_form_values['Origin'], api_form_values['Dest']
)
```

We also create an incomplete API, predict_utils.get_regression_date_args, which determines the DayOfYear, DayOfMonth, and DayOfWeek fields from the supplied Date argument:

```
# Turn the date into DayOfYear, DayOfMonth, DayOfWeek
date_features_dict = predict_utils.get_regression_date_args(
  api_form_values['Date']
)
```

```
    for api_field_name, api_field_value in date_features_dict.items():
        prediction_features[api_field_name] = api_field_value
```

Having calculated all the fields of a record in the model's training data, we vectorize this record to map the raw values into the regression's vector space:

```
# Vectorize the features
feature_vectors = vectorizer.transform([prediction_features])
```

Vectorized features in hand, we can now make our prediction:

```
# Make the prediction!
result = regressor.predict(feature_vectors)[0]
```

And finally, we return a JSON object containing our result:

```
# Return a JSON object
result_obj = {"Delay": result}
return json.dumps(result_obj)
```

With that, our regression API controller is complete!

Now, to make it run, we need to fill in the APIs we just defined inline in our controller code: `predict_utils.get_flight_distance` and `predict_utils.get_regres sion_date_args`.

Filling in the predict_utils API

This means we need a function in *predict_utils.py* called `get_flight_distance(ori gin, dest)` that returns the flight distance for each pair of airports. To implement this, let's use PySpark to create a table in MongoDB containing the distance in miles keyed by the origin and destination airport codes. Check out *ch08/origin_dest_distances.py* (*http://bit.ly/2ouGFqM*). We run a simple GROUP BY/AVG query to compute the distances between airports:

```
# Load the on-time Parquet file
on_time_dataframe = spark.read.parquet('data/on_time_performance.parquet')
on_time_dataframe.registerTempTable("on_time_performance")

origin_dest_distances = spark.sql("""
  SELECT Origin, Dest, AVG(Distance) AS Distance
  FROM on_time_performance
  GROUP BY Origin, Dest
  ORDER BY Distance
  """)
origin_dest_distances.repartition(1).write.mode("overwrite") \
  .json("data/origin_dest_distances.json"
  )
os.system(
  "cp data/origin_dest_distances.json/part* data/origin_dest_distances.jsonl"
  )
```

And to load them into MongoDB we run an import of the resulting JSON Lines file. Check out *ch08/import_distances.sh* (*http://bit.ly/2o7C6rt*), which also creates an index on the `Origin/Dest` key:

```
# Import our enriched airline data as the 'airlines' collection
mongoimport -d agile_data_science -c origin_dest_distances --file \
  data/origin_dest_distances.jsonl
mongo agile_data_science --eval \
  'db.origin_dest_distances.ensureIndex({Origin: 1, Dest: 1})'
```

Let's verify our data is in Mongo:

```
> db.origin_dest_distances.find({"Origin": "ATL", "Dest": "JFK"})
{
  "_id" : ObjectId("583bc2e6aeb23e2f187ce737"),
  "Origin" : "ATL",
  "Dest" : "JFK",
  "Distance" : 760
}
```

Finally, in *ch08/web/predict_utils.py*, we turn this into an API, pre dict_utils.get_flight_distance, that uses PyMongo:

```
def get_flight_distance(client, origin, dest):
    """Get the distance between a pair of airport codes"""
    record = client.agile_data_science.origin_dest_distances.find_one({
      "Origin": origin,
      "Dest": dest,
    })
    return record["Distance"]
```

Similarly, we need to create `predict_utils.get_regression_date_args`, although this function is simpler and pure Python thanks to Python's datetime (*https:// docs.python.org/3/library/datetime.html*) built-in library. datetime has methods to get DayOfYear, DayOfYear, and DayOfWeek:

```
def get_regression_date_args(iso_date):
    """Given an ISO date, return the day of year, day of month,
       and day of week, as the API expects them."""
    dt = iso8601.parse_date(iso_date)
    day_of_year = dt.timetuple().tm_yday
    day_of_month = dt.day
    day_of_week = dt.weekday()
    return {
      "DayOfYear": day_of_year,
      "DayOfMonth": day_of_month,
      "DayOfWeek": day_of_week,
    }
```

And that's a wrap! Now we're ready to test it out.

Testing Our API

As we've done before, we can use the handy utility curl (*https://en.wikipedia.org/wiki/CURL*) to test the flight delay regression API. Check out *ch08/test_regression_api.sh* (*http://bit.ly/2pG9VNn*). curl can HTTP POST via the -XPOST option and can supply form values with the -F option:

```
#!/usr/bin/env bash

# Fetch the delay prediction for a hypothetical flight
curl -XPOST 'http://localhost:5000/flights/delays/predict/regress' \
  -F 'DepDelay=5.0' \
  -F 'Carrier=AA' \
  -F 'Date=2016-12-23' \
  -F 'Dest=ATL' \
  -F 'FlightNum=1519' \
  -F 'Origin=SFO' \
| json_pp
```

This results in:

```
  % Total    % Received % Xferd  Average Speed   Time    Time     Time  Current
                                 Dload  Upload   Total   Spent    Left  Speed
100   672  100    29  100    643   3394  75266 --:--:-- --:--:-- --:--:--  104k
{
   "Delay" : -36.4042325748015
}
```

It works! That completes our deployment of an sklearn prediction as a web service.

Pulling Our API into Our Product

The final step for deploying our prediction is to develop a page where our prediction will be served. Let's start by creating a controller for the page. We define a variable, form_config, that we'll use to generate our form in the Jinja template:

```
@app.route("/flights/delays/predict")
def flight_delays_page():
"""Serves flight delay predictions"""

    form_config = [
      {'field': 'DepDelay', 'label': 'Departure Delay'},
      {'field': 'Carrier'},
      {'field': 'Date'},
      {'field': 'Origin'},
      {'field': 'Dest', 'label': 'Destination'},
      {'field': 'FlightNum', 'label': 'Flight Number'},
    ]

    return render_template('flight_delays_predict.html', form_config=form_config)
```

In the template, we create the form's fields in a loop on `form_config`. We create a `div` for the results, and then use jQuery to submit the form and parse and display the results:

```
{% extends "layout.html" %}
{% block body %}
  / <a href="/flights/delays/predict">Flight Delay Prediction</a>

  <p class="lead" style="margin: 10px; margin-left: 0px;">

    Predicting Flight Delays
  </p>

  <!-- Generate form from search_config and request args -->
  <form id="flight_delay_regression"
        action="/flights/delays/predict/regress"
        method="post">
    {% for item in form_config %}
      {% if 'label' in item %}
        <label for="{{item['field']}}">{{item['label']}}</label>
      {% else %}
        <label for="{{item['field']}}">{{item['field']}}</label>
      {% endif %}
        <input name="{{item['field']}}"
               style="width: 36px; margin-right: 10px;"
               value="">
        </input>
    {% endfor %}
      <button type="submit" class="btn btn-xs btn-default" style="height: 25px">
      Submit
      </button>
  </form>

  <div style="margin-top: 10px;">
      <p>Delay: <span id="result" style="display: inline-block;"></span></p>
  </div>

  <script>
    // Attach a submit handler to the form
    $( "#flight_delay_regression" ).submit(function( event ) {

      // Stop form from submitting normally
      event.preventDefault();

      // Get some values from elements on the page
      var $form = $( this ),
        term = $form.find( "input[name='s']" ).val(),
        url = $form.attr( "action" );

      // Send the data using post
      var posting = $.post( url, $( "#flight_delay_regression" ).serialize() );
```

```
        // Put the results in a div
      posting.done(function( data ) {
        result = JSON.parse(data);
        $( "#result" ).empty().append( result.Delay );
      });
    });
  </script>
{% endblock %}
```

The result is simple but suits our purpose for the moment (Figure 8-1). In this case, the flight leaves and arrives early.

Figure 8-1. Flight delay regression page

Deploying Spark ML Applications in Batch with Airflow

Compared to deploying scikit-learn applications, deploying Spark ML applications is more complex. This is because Spark sits between us and our end application. There are two ways to deploy Spark ML predictions: periodically in batch, or in "real time" via Spark Streaming. We will cover both ways, beginning with batch processing.

In order to process data in batch, we need to compose, schedule, and monitor data pipelines. To do so, we need a batch scheduler such as Azkaban (*https://azka ban.github.io/*), Apache Oozie (*http://oozie.apache.org/*), or Apache Airflow (Incubating) (*https://airflow.incubator.apache.org/*). We choose Airflow because it is emerging as the leading choice and it enables high productivity along with the rest of our stack.

We introduced Airflow in Chapter 2. In this section, we'll be using Airflow along with our web application to deploy a data pipeline that will perform the end-to-end operations necessary to make predictions with Spark ML in batch. For simplicity's sake, we've chosen to make predictions on a daily basis. This might work for batches of emails sent out daily, or for building the recommender content of an event feed.

Batch processing with Airflow and Spark can handle tasks scheduled down to a granularity of approximately every five minutes. Below this period of frequency Spark Streaming should be employed.

The required operations to perform predictions in batch, in order, are:

1. Extract features from our data to create a training dataset.
2. Train a classifier from this training data and store it for later use.
3. Collect requests for predictions from a web application and store them in MongoDB.
4. Gather MongoDB requests into files corresponding to daily batches.
5. Load the models and today's requests, make the actual predictions, and store them into a daily bucket.
6. Load the daily batch of predictions into MongoDB.
7. Display today's predictions in our web application.

At one end lies our training data, and at the other end our users. Our task is to connect the two in a production system that is scheduled to operate each and every day. We will begin by describing and constructing the tasks independently and will follow this by using Airflow to tie them together. Let's get started!

Gathering Training Data in Production

We created a script in Chapter 7 to collect training data called *ch07/extract_features.py* (*http://bit.ly/2pRS6dt*). The operations in this script can be used unaltered, once the input and output paths are modified and the script is set up to run from the command line. Therefore, I've copied it to *ch08/extract_features.py* (*http://bit.ly/2oTpIIB*) and edited it from there.

We embed the executable content within a main function so that it can be fed arguments from the command line for the base path in the filesystem. We then call this function using the command-line parameters. Making the content executable from the command line makes it accessible to Airflow. The script startup and PySpark initialization code are written such that they can be run from the PySpark intepreter during development or from the command line in production. We won't use a date parameter in this script, but we will in others that use daily or hourly batches of data as input and output.

To make the script run in development and production environments, we conditionally instantiate the PySpark environment. If the SparkContext (*http://bit.ly/2pVx79N*) and SparkSession (*http://bit.ly/2nRGlqX*) have already been initialized by the PySpark console, no exceptions will be thrown when we reference the variables sc and spark, which means they won't be reinitialized. This is important, because reinitializing the SparkContext will result in an exception that would kill the process if it were run from the command line or via Airflow. At the same time, failing to initialize these variables will also kill the script. Our conditional initialization handles both runtime environments:

```python
#!/usr/bin/env python

import sys, os, re
import json
import datetime, iso8601

# Pass date and base path to main() from Airflow
def main(base_path):

  APP_NAME = "extract_features.py"

  # If there is no SparkSession, create the environment
  try:
    sc and spark
  except NameError as e:
    import findspark
    findspark.init()
    import pyspark
    import pyspark.sql

    sc = pyspark.SparkContext()
    spark = pyspark.sql.SparkSession(sc).builder.appName(APP_NAME).getOrCreate()

  # Load the on-time Parquet file
  input_path = "{}/data/on_time_performance.parquet".format(
    base_path
  )
  on_time_dataframe = spark.read.parquet(input_path)
  on_time_dataframe.registerTempTable("on_time_performance")
```

The work of the script involves converting our ISO date fields to dates, just as we did in the same script in Chapter 7. The end of the script is similarly edited, inserting a base path into the output path. We finish the script with a call to `main` with the command-line arguments for date and base path:

```python
  # Store as a single JSON file
  output_path = "{}/data/simple_flight_delay_features.json".format(
    base_path
  )
  sorted_features.repartition(1).write.mode("overwrite").json(output_path)
  combine_cmd = "cp {}/part* {}/data/simple_flight_delay_features.jsonl".format(
    output_path,
    base_path
  )
  os.system(combine_cmd)

if __name__ == "__main__":
  main(sys.argv[1])
```

We can test our script from the command line—note that the date won't be used, but we provide it anyway to keep this script consistent with the others:

```
python ch08/extract_features.py .
```

Training, Storing, and Loading Spark ML Models

As with `sklearn`, before we can make predictions using the models we've built in Spark ML, we must persist them to disk and load them again. This includes the random forest classifier we trained, as well as the various models that transformed the raw data into vector form. To persist the models, we need to go back to our script from Chapter 7 that created them and add code to persist each and every model in the pipeline to disk. This will enable us to load the models in another script, so we can avoid retraining the model each time we want to apply it. This is important, because training the model takes a lot longer than loading it or using it to make predictions.

Check out *ch08/train_spark_mllib_model.py* (*http://bit.ly/2pVD1Yu*), which we've copied from the last chapter and altered to store each model as a file in the *models/* directory of the project. We have to store and load each model we use to transform the training data so that it can transform the prediction requests as they come in. Note that we've also edited the script to make it executable from the command line, but we'll skip that part this time.

First, let's save the arrival and departure bucketizers. The code to persist the models is emboldened:

```
# Set up the Bucketizer
splits = [-float("inf"), -15.0, 0, 30.0, float("inf")]
arrival_bucketizer = Bucketizer(
  splits=splits,
  inputCol="ArrDelay",
  outputCol="ArrDelayBucket"
)

# Save the model
arrival_bucketizer_path = "{}/models/arrival_bucketizer_2.0.bin".format(
  base_path
)
arrival_bucketizer.write().overwrite().save(arrival_bucketizer_path)

# Apply the model
ml_bucketized_features = arrival_bucketizer.transform(features_with_route)
ml_bucketized_features.select("ArrDelay", "ArrDelayBucket").show()
```

We need to save the string indexer models we create for each string field. Luckily, a `StringIndexerModel` (*http://bit.ly/2opQirO*) can be saved with one call to `StringIndexerModel.save` (*http://bit.ly/2pj3gvD*):

```
#
# Feature extraction tools in with pyspark.ml.feature
#
from pyspark.ml.feature import StringIndexer, VectorAssembler

# Turn category fields into indexes
for column in ["Carrier", "DayOfMonth", "DayOfWeek", "DayOfYear",
               "Origin", "Dest", "Route"]:
  string_indexer = StringIndexer(
    inputCol=column,
    outputCol=column + "_index"
  )

  string_indexer_model = string_indexer.fit(ml_bucketized_features)
  ml_bucketized_features = string_indexer_model.transform(
    ml_bucketized_features
  )

  # Drop the original column
  ml_bucketized_features = ml_bucketized_features.drop(column)

  # Save the pipeline model
  string_indexer_output_path = "{}/models/string_indexer_model_{}.bin".format(
    base_path,
    column
  )
  string_indexer_model.write().overwrite().save(string_indexer_output_path)
```

We also need to save the VectorAssembler (*http://bit.ly/2pj7nI0*), which transforms our several numeric columns and index columns into a single feature vector:

```
# Handle continuous numeric fields by combining them into one feature vector
numeric_columns = ["DepDelay", "Distance"]
index_columns = ["Carrier_index", "DayOfMonth_index",
                 "DayOfWeek_index", "DayOfYear_index", "Origin_index",
                 "Origin_index", "Dest_index", "Route_index"]
vector_assembler = VectorAssembler(
  inputCols=numeric_columns + index_columns,
  outputCol="Features_vec"
)
final_vectorized_features = vector_assembler.transform(ml_bucketized_features)

# Save the numeric vector assembler
vector_assembler_path = "{}/models/numeric_vector_assembler.bin".format(
  base_path
)
vector_assembler.write().overwrite().save(vector_assembler_path)

# Drop the original columns
for column in index_columns:
  final_vectorized_features = final_vectorized_features.drop(column)
```

```
# Inspect the finalized features
final_vectorized_features.show()
```

Finally, we train and store the random forest classification model itself. Note that while during development you create an experiment and split the test and training datasets, in production it is common to use all the data available to tease out a little bit of additional accuracy by learning from the test portion as well:

```
# Instantiate and fit random forest classifier on all the data
from pyspark.ml.classification import RandomForestClassifier
rfc = RandomForestClassifier(
  featuresCol="Features_vec",
  labelCol="ArrDelayBucket",
  predictionCol="Prediction",
  maxBins=4657,
)
model = rfc.fit(final_vectorized_features)

# Save the new model over the old one
model_output_path = \
  "{}/models/spark_random_forest_classifier.flight_delays.5.0.bin".format(
  base_path
)
model.write().overwrite().save(model_output_path)

if __name__ == "__main__":
  main(sys.argv[1])
```

Now we can load the models any time we would like, in batch-mode Spark or Spark Streaming. Let's try running the script from the command line. Note that this may take a few minutes:

```
python ch08/train_spark_mllib_model.py .
```

Now we're ready to move on to creating prediction requests in our web application.

Creating Prediction Requests in Mongo

In order to feed the prediction task and associated data to a Spark ML script operated by a scheduler, we need to generate a table or collection in a database that indicates a prediction is needed. Our web application can easily do so. In the real world, this might correspond to the need to create a prediction or recommendation for a user every day, to place the prediction in the user's content for that day.

In this case, a web application will save a request for a prediction as a record in a MongoDB collection. Then, a daily task scheduled in Airflow will fetch today's prediction tasks and feed them to PySpark ML, which will create the predictions and store the results in another MongoDB collection. The prediction page will then display the latest predictions.

This workflow is crude, but it is hoped that you can imagine how it might work in a more refined manner: generating emails with recommendations, generating daily content, etc. For tasks that don't fit the batch workflow, we'll use Spark Streaming.

Feeding Mongo recommendation tasks from a Flask API

In order to store the desired prediction records in Mongo, we can alter the Flask web application from the previous section to store the request rather than generating a prediction using scikit-learn. Check out *ch08/web/predict_flask.py* (*http://bit.ly/2o7DJVR*) and *ch08/web/predit_utils.py* (*http://bit.ly/2pG8SNo*).

Note that this will be the first time we use pymongo to insert data (*http://bit.ly/2pVDEBk*). Previously all our web controllers have been read-only. This is important to notice, as operating a read/write web application is more time-consuming than one that is read-only.

Most of this API is copied from the code for the sklearn regression API we created in the previous section. In *ch08/web/predict_flask.py* (*http://bit.ly/2o7DJVR*), we fill out the record submitted via a POST request using the same utilities as in the previous API. In addition, we add an ISO-format (*https://en.wikipedia.org/wiki/ISO_8601*) Timestamp to the record, and insert it into the prediction_tasks Mongo collection. Finally, we return the record as JSON as verification that the request was processed correctly:

```
# Make our API a post, so a search engine won't hit it
@app.route("/flights/delays/predict/classify", methods=['POST'])
def classify_flight_delays():
  """POST API for classifying flight delays"""
  api_field_type_map = \
    {
      "DepDelay": int,
      "Carrier": str,
      "FlightDate": str,
      "Dest": str,
      "FlightNum": str,
      "Origin": str
    }

  api_form_values = {}
  for api_field_name, api_field_type in api_field_type_map.items():
    api_form_values[api_field_name] = request.form.get(
      api_field_name, type=api_field_type
    )

  # Set the direct values, which excludes Date
  prediction_features = {}
  for key, value in api_form_values.items():
    prediction_features[key] = value
```

```
# Set the derived values
prediction_features['Distance'] = predict_utils.get_flight_distance(
  client, api_form_values['Origin'],
  api_form_values['Dest']
)

# Turn the date into DayOfYear, DayOfMonth, DayOfWeek
date_features_dict = predict_utils.get_regression_date_args(
  api_form_values['FlightDate']
)
for api_field_name, api_field_value in date_features_dict.items():
  prediction_features[api_field_name] = api_field_value

# Add a timestamp
prediction_features['Timestamp'] = predict_utils.get_current_timestamp()

client.agile_data_science.prediction_tasks.insert_one(
  prediction_features
)
return json_util.dumps(prediction_features)
```

We create a utility to get the current timestamp as a `datetime` (*http://bit.ly/2pjeksL*), `predict_utils.get_current_timestamp`, in *ch08/web/predict_utils.py* (*http://bit.ly/2pG8SNo*). Both pymongo (*https://api.mongodb.com/python/current/*) and `bson.json_util` (*http://bit.ly/2pGjCLE*) will convert the `datetime` into a BSON (*http://bsonspec.org/*) representation. We need `bson.json_util.dumps` (*http://bit.ly/2ouMuVx*) to serialize a `datetime`; `json.dumps` (*http://bit.ly/2oqgzpI*) will not do it.

However, it turns out that we can't feed a `Date` or `ISODate` object to the pymongo_spark package to fetch the data, so we ended up using an ISO string representation for the `Timestamp` field. ISO 8601 strings can function in terms of greater than/less than in queries, so we don't lose any functionality in this case:

```
def get_current_timestamp():
  iso_now = datetime.datetime.now().isoformat()
  return iso_now
```

We can test the API with `curl`, as we did in the last section. Check out *ch08/test_classification_api.sh* (*http://bit.ly/2pVEP3A*):

```
#!/usr/bin/env bash

# Fetch the delay prediction for a hypothetical flight
curl -XPOST 'http://localhost:5000/flights/delays/predict/classify' \
  -F 'DepDelay=5.0' \
  -F 'Carrier=AA' \
  -F 'FlightDate=2016-12-23' \
  -F 'Dest=ATL' \
  -F 'FlightNum=1519' \
  -F 'Origin=SFO' \
| json_pp
```

Which results in:

```
  % Total    % Received % Xferd  Average Speed   Time    Time     Time  Current
                                 Dload  Upload   Total   Spent    Left  Speed
100    925  100    276  100    649  13229   31107 --:--:-- --:--:-- --:--:-- 36055
{
    "FlightDate" : "2016-12-23",
    "DayOfYear" : 358,
    "DayOfMonth" : 23,
    "Origin" : "SFO",
    "FlightNum" : "1519",
    "DepDelay" : null,
    "Dest" : "ATL",
    "Timestamp" : "2016-12-12T15:30:05.272470",
    "Carrier" : "AA",
    "Distance" : 2139,
    "_id" : {
       "$oid" : "584f32fd3bf9e6056dc167ad"
    },
    "DayOfWeek" : 4
}
```

Finally, we check to see the record is in MongoDB:

```
> db.prediction_tasks.find().pretty()

{
        "_id" : ObjectId("584f319c3bf9e6056dc167ac"),
        "Timestamp" : "2016-12-12T15:24:12.439716",
        "DepDelay" : -25,
        "FlightDate" : "2016-12-25",
        "FlightNum" : "1519",
        "DayOfYear" : 360,
        "Carrier" : "DL",
        "DayOfWeek" : 6,
        "Dest" : "SEA",
        "Origin" : "SFO",
        "DayOfMonth" : 25,
        "Distance" : 679
}
```

We can see that our API requests are resulting in prediction requests being stored in MongoDB. Now let's create the web page and form that will call this API to queue predictions for batch and realtime processing with Spark ML.

A frontend for generating prediction requests

Now that we have a POST API for creating prediction requests, we need a web page and form to feed it. This can be nearly identical to the one we created for the sklearn regression in the previous section. Check out this excerpt from *ch08/web/predict_flask.py* (*http://bit.ly/2o7DJVR*):

```
@app.route("/flights/delays/predict_batch")
def flight_delays_batch_page():
    """Serves flight delay predictions"""

    form_config = [
      {'field': 'DepDelay', 'label': 'Departure Delay'},
      {'field': 'Carrier'},
      {'field': 'FlightDate', 'label': 'Date'},
      {'field': 'Origin'},
      {'field': 'Dest', 'label': 'Destination'},
      {'field': 'FlightNum', 'label': 'Flight Number'},
    ]

    return render_template('flight_delays_predict_batch.html',
                           form_config=form_config)
```

The corresponding template is also similar to the original regression template. The changes we made are shown here in bold:

```
{% extends "layout.html" %}
{% block body %}

  / <a href="/flights/delays/predict_batch">
    Flight Delay Prediction via Spark in Batch
      </a>

  <p class="lead" style="margin: 10px; margin-left: 0px;">
    <!-- Airline name and website-->
    Predicting Flight Delays via Spark in Batch
  </p>

  <!-- Generate form from search_config and request args -->
  <form id="flight_delay_classification"
        action="/flights/delays/predict/classify"
        method="post">
    {% for item in form_config %}
      {% if 'label' in item %}
        <label for="{{item['field']}}">{{item['label']}}</label>
      {% else %}
        <label for="{{item['field']}}">{{item['field']}}</label>
      {% endif %}
      <input name="{{item['field']}}"
                style="width: 36px; margin-right: 10px;"
                value="">
      </input>
    {% endfor %}
    <button type="submit" class="btn btn-xs btn-default" style="height: 25px">
      Submit
    </button>
  </form>

  <div style="margin-top: 10px;">
      <p>
```

```
    Prediction Request Successful:
      <span id="result" style="display: inline-block;"></span>
      </p>
 </div>

 <script>
   // Attach a submit handler to the form
   $( "#flight_delay_classification" ).submit(function( event ) {

     // Stop form from submitting normally
     event.preventDefault();

     // Get some values from elements on the page
     var $form = $( this ),
       term = $form.find( "input[name='s']" ).val(),
       url = $form.attr( "action" );

     // Send the data using post
     var posting = $.post(
       url, $( "#flight_delay_classification" ).serialize()
     );

     // Put the results in a div
     posting.done(function( data ) {
       $( "#result" ).empty().append( data );
     });
   });
 </script>
{% endblock %}
```

We test this web page by visiting *http://localhost:5000/flights/delays/predict_batch*,
which should show something like Figure 8-2. Note that we are displaying the raw
JSON for the "fleshed out" prediction request directly on the page. In reality your
application would dictate the correct action to take.

Figure 8-2. Flight delay regression page with prediction

Making a prediction request

Before we move on, we need to create at least one prediction request using the web form, so be sure and enter some reasonable data and hit Submit. If you can't think of any airport codes, simply use those in Figure 8-2.

That completes the plumbing for requests for batch predictions! Requests are being routed from the web application's form through its prediction API and into MongoDB. Now we'll use Spark once again to wrangle our PySpark ML prediction code into making predictions based on the contents of the `prediction_tasks` collection in Mongo.

Fetching Prediction Requests from MongoDB

Now that we have created requests for predictions in MongoDB, it is time to execute the actual predictions using PySpark. To do this we need to fetch the prediction requests from Mongo, load the trained model, and run the predictions on the requests. As before, in order to bring this system into production and get it to end users, we need to set up each script so that it can be executed from the command line by Airflow.

Now that the model is persisted and can be loaded, our next task is to create a script to query MongoDB for one day's prediction requests and store them locally on the filesystem in a directory for that day's requests. As we showed in Chapter 2, we'll need to write our script in such a way that it can be run from the command line so that Airflow can control it.

Check out *ch08/fetch_prediction_requests.py* (*http://bit.ly/2pGe2Jg*), in which we load data from Mongo and write it to the filesystem. This script doesn't do much; most of its length is housekeeping for use from the command line, via `spark-submit` and Airflow. Note that `pymongo-spark` (*http://bit.ly/2oq4P6O*) lets us specify a query to use to fetch records from Mongo for one day alone.

Let's examine the code section by section. As before, the `main` function accepts the date and base path. In this case, the date parameter lets the script act on only those predictions requested today. This could be altered to load prediction requests for this hour, every 10 minutes, etc. (5 to 10 minutes being the approximate lower limit in terms of frequency for batch processing):

```
#!/usr/bin/env python

import sys, os, re
import json
import datetime, iso8601

# Save to Mongo
import pymongo_spark
```

```
pymongo_spark.activate()

# Pass date and base path to main() from Airflow
def main(iso_date, base_path):

  APP_NAME = "fetch_prediction_requests.py"

  # If there is no SparkSession, create the environment
  try:
    sc and spark
  except NameError as e:
    import findspark
    findspark.init()
    import pyspark
    import pyspark.sql

  sc = pyspark.SparkContext()
  spark = pyspark.sql.SparkSession(sc).builder.appName(APP_NAME).getOrCreate()
```

Next up, we use the ISO-formatted date argument to create a Mongo query that
fetches just that day's data. First we compute today's and tomorrow's dates, then we
parameterize a dict defining a Mongo query with these dates. This goes inside a configuration object, which we use as the config argument of our call to load the data
from Mongo:

```
# Get today and tomorrow's dates as ISO strings to scope query
today_dt = iso8601.parse_date(iso_date)
rounded_today = today_dt.date()
iso_today = rounded_today.isoformat()
rounded_tomorrow_dt = rounded_today + datetime.timedelta(days=1)
iso_tomorrow = rounded_tomorrow_dt.isoformat()

# Create Mongo query string for today's data
mongo_query_string = """{{
  "Timestamp": {{
    "$gte": "{iso_today}",
    "$lte": "{iso_tomorrow}"
  }}
}}""".format(
  iso_today=iso_today,
  iso_tomorrow=iso_tomorrow
)
mongo_query_string = mongo_query_string.replace('\n', '')

# Create the config object with the query string
mongo_query_config = dict()
mongo_query_config["mongo.input.query"] = mongo_query_string
```

The actual call uses the pymongo-spark (*http://bit.ly/2oepp9Z*) method mongoRDD
(*http://bit.ly/2o7vWrd*) to load the data:

```
# Load the day's requests using pymongo_spark
prediction_requests = sc.mongoRDD(
    'mongodb://localhost:27017/agile_data_science.prediction_tasks',
    config=mongo_query_config
)
```

As soon as the data is loaded, it is ready to be transformed to JSON and stored. Here we use the date to parameterize the output path inside the directory *data/prediction_tasks_daily.json/*. Each day gets its own directory or folder, which has the effect of creating a primary index on day. In this way, any filesystem supports single indexes on data stored within. This is a pattern we'll see in any script that acts on daily or hourly data and loads from or stores to disk. It is also a pattern for using scripts with Airflow.

Note that we are using the RDD API, so we have to manually `rm` the contents of the directory with a call to `os.system` before saving the data. By contrast, with the Data-Frame API, we often use overwrite mode. Either way, our scripts should always be designed to store output in buckets to replace the content of the previous run's result. Otherwise, the system won't be able to run for a given day more than once, which will prevent the resolution of errors:

```
# Build the day's output path: a date-based primary key directory structure
today_output_path = "{}/data/prediction_tasks_daily.json/{}".format(
    base_path,
    iso_today
)

# Generate JSON records
prediction_requests_json = prediction_requests.map(json_util.dumps)

# Write/replace today's output path
os.system("rm -rf {}".format(today_output_path))
prediction_requests_json.saveAsTextFile(today_output_path)

if __name__ == "__main__":
    main(sys.argv[1], sys.argv[2])
```

Let's test our script from the command line (substitute today's date, whatever that is, for the one listed here):

```
python ch08/fetch_prediction_requests.py 2016-12-12 .
```

and check the output:

```
$ cat data/prediction_tasks.json/2016-12-12/part-00000 | json_pp

{
    "DayOfYear" : 360,
    "Dest" : "SFO",
    "DepDelay" : -35,
    "Origin" : "ATL",
    "DayOfMonth" : 25,
```

```
    "FlightNum" : "1519",
    "FlightDate" : "2016-12-25",
    "DayOfWeek" : 6,
    "Timestamp" : "2016-12-12T16:27:45.463447",
    "Carrier" : "AA",
    "Distance" : 2139,
    "_id" : {
      "$oid" : "584f40813bf9e6080c27d501"
    }
  }
}
```

Okay! We're storing the data in a directory corresponding to the date. This directory structure of dates serves as a primary key for accessing prediction requests. This allows us to process requests one day at a time. Now we need to feed this day's data to Spark ML to make the predictions being requested.

Making Predictions in a Batch with Spark ML

Now that we've collected the prediction requests, it is time to make the actual predictions! Check out *ch08/make_predictions.py* (*http://bit.ly/2oq59Cy*). To make predictions we'll need to load the models we persisted in *ch08/train_spark_mllib_model.py* (*http://bit.ly/2pVD1Yu*) and then route the prediction requests through the same data pipeline that the training data flowed through.

Loading Spark ML models in PySpark

Given that this script must be executable from the command line, we can copy the code from the training script and use it to build the paths to load the models. After accepting the command-line arguments and initializing the Spark environment, we import each and every model in the training data pipeline:

```
#
# Load each and every model in the pipeline
#

# Load the arrival delay bucketizer
from pyspark.ml.feature import Bucketizer
arrival_bucketizer_path = "{}/models/arrival_bucketizer_2.0.bin".format(
  base_path
)
arrival_bucketizer = Bucketizer.load(arrival_bucketizer_path)

# Load all the string indexers into a dict
from pyspark.ml.feature import StringIndexerModel

string_indexer_models = {}
for column in ["Carrier", "DayOfMonth", "DayOfWeek", "DayOfYear",
               "Origin", "Dest", "Route"]:
  string_indexer_model_path = "{}/models/string_indexer_model_{}.bin".format(
    base_path,
```

```
        column
    )
    string_indexer_model = StringIndexerModel.load(string_indexer_model_path)
    string_indexer_models[column] = string_indexer_model

# Load the numeric vector assembler
from pyspark.ml.feature import VectorAssembler
vector_assembler_path = "{}/models/numeric_vector_assembler.bin".format(
 base_path
)
vector_assembler = VectorAssembler.load(vector_assembler_path)

# Load the classifier model
from pyspark.ml.classification import RandomForestClassifier,
from pyspark.ml.classification import RandomForestClassificationModel
random_forest_model_path = \
  "{}/models/spark_random_forest_classifier.flight_delays.5.0.bin".format(
    base_path
  )
rfc = RandomForestClassificationModel.load(
  random_forest_model_path
)
```

Now we're ready to load the prediction requests and flow them through the same prediction data pipeline as the training data.

Making predictions with Spark ML

Taking the date, we build the input path for the day's prediction requests and load the JSON into a DataFrame (*http://bit.ly/2pVyTYo*). To keep the data type consistent with the training data, we need to use the same schema (minus the ArrDelay column that we are predicting and the unused columns CRSDepTime and CRSArrTime) to load the data:

```
# Get today and tomorrow's dates as ISO strings to scope query
today_dt = iso8601.parse_date(iso_date)
rounded_today = today_dt.date()
iso_today = rounded_today.isoformat()

# Build the day's input path: a date-based primary key directory structure
today_input_path = "{}/data/prediction_tasks_daily.json/{}".format(
  base_path,
  iso_today
)

from pyspark.sql.types import StringType, IntegerType, Doubletype
from pyspark.sql.types import DateType, TimestampType
from pyspark.sql.types import StructType, StructField

schema = StructType([
  StructField("Carrier", StringType(), True),
```

```
      StructField("DayOfMonth", IntegerType(), True),
      StructField("DayOfWeek", IntegerType(), True),
      StructField("DayOfYear", IntegerType(), True),
      StructField("DepDelay", DoubleType(), True),
      StructField("Dest", StringType(), True),
      StructField("Distance", DoubleType(), True),
      StructField("FlightDate", DateType(), True),
      StructField("FlightNum", StringType(), True),
      StructField("Origin", StringType(), True),
      StructField("Timestamp", TimestampType(), True),
])

prediction_requests = spark.read.json(today_input_path, schema=schema)
prediction_requests.show()
```

Next, we need to create the Route column:

```
#
# Add a Route variable to replace FlightNum
#

from pyspark.sql.functions import lit, concat
prediction_requests_with_route = prediction_requests.withColumn(
  'Route',
  concat(
    prediction_requests.Origin,
    lit('-'),
    prediction_requests.Dest
  )
)
prediction_requests_with_route.show(6)
```

Now we run the prediction requests through each feature model to vectorize the requests' features. This precisely mirrors the path of the data through the model training script, *ch08/train_spark_mllib_model.py* (*http://bit.ly/2pVD1Yu*), with one exception. We won't be dropping the original raw feature columns because we will need them to uniquely identify the record when we store the prediction output:

```
# Index string fields with the corresponding indexer for that column
for column in ["Carrier", "DayOfMonth", "DayOfWeek", "DayOfYear",
               "Origin", "Dest", "Route"]:
  string_indexer_model = string_indexer_models[column]
  prediction_requests_with_route = string_indexer_model.transform(
    prediction_requests_with_route
  )

# Vectorize numeric columns: DepDelay and Distance
final_vectorized_features = vector_assembler.transform(
  prediction_requests_with_route
)

# Drop the indexes for the nominal fields
index_columns = ["Carrier_index", "DayOfMonth_index","DayOfWeek_index",
```

```
                "DayOfYear_index", "Origin_index", "Origin_index",
                "Dest_index", "Route_index"]
    for column in index_columns:
      final_vectorized_features = final_vectorized_features.drop(column)

    # Inspect the finalized features
    final_vectorized_features.show()
```

Having prepared the prediction requests, we can make the predictions and store the output in its daily bucket. We drop the features vector to return the record to its original columns plus the prediction column:

```
    # Make the prediction
    predictions = rfc.transform(final_vectorized_features)

    # Drop the features vector and prediction metadata to give the original fields
    predictions = predictions.drop("Features_vec")
    final_predictions = predictions.drop("indices").drop("values") \
      .drop("rawPrediction").drop("probability")

    # Inspect the output
    final_predictions.show()

    # Build the day's output path: a date-based primary key directory structure
    today_output_path = "{}/data/prediction_results_daily.json/{}".format(
      base_path,
      iso_today
    )

    # Save the output to its daily bucket
    final_predictions.repartition(1).write.mode("overwrite").json(
      today_output_path
    )

if __name__ == "__main__":
  main(sys.argv[1], sys.argv[2])
```

To test our script from bash, run:

```
    python ch08/make_predictions.py 2016-12-12 .
```

We can see our predictions in the script's output (this table has been truncated to fit on the page):

```
+-------+---------+--------+----+--------+---------+
|Carrier|...|DepDelay|Dest|Distance|...|  Route|Prediction|
+-------+---------+--------+----+--------+---------+----+----+
|     DL|...|    10.0| SFO|   679.0|...|SEA-SFO|     2.0|
+-------+---------+--------+----+--------+---------+----+----+
```

However, let's check the actual file output of our operation with the following command (fill in the current date as you read this):

```
$ cat data/prediction_results_daily.json/2016-12-11/part-* | json_pp
{
   "DayOfWeek" : 6,
   "Prediction" : 2,
   "Carrier" : "DL",
   "Origin" : "SEA",
   "Distance" : 679,
   "Timestamp" : "2016-12-23T00:06:24.489-08:00",
   "FlightNum" : "",
   "DayOfMonth" : 17,
   "FlightDate" : "2016-01-17",
   "DayOfYear" : 17,
   "Dest" : "SFO",
   "DepDelay" : 10,
   "Route" : "SEA-SFO"
}
```

Everything looks great! Now that we've made our predictions for this day, we need to send them to MongoDB to give our application access to them.

Storing Predictions in MongoDB

Our next task is simple housekeeping, mirroring the script that fetched prediction requests from Mongo several steps earlier. Check out *ch08/load_prediction_results.py* (*http://bit.ly/2pVz4D2*), and recall that the PySpark mongo-hadoop documentation (*http://bit.ly/2oepp9Z*) can be a helpful reference when connecting with MongoDB from PySpark.

After we initialize the script so that it will work from the command line, we simply load the day's data and store it in a Mongo collection:

```
# Get today and tomorrow's dates as ISO strings to scope query
today_dt = iso8601.parse_date(iso_date)
rounded_today = today_dt.date()
iso_today = rounded_today.isoformat()

input_path = "{}/data/prediction_results_daily.json/{}".format(
  base_path,
  iso_today
)

# Load and JSONize text
prediction_results_raw = sc.textFile(input_path)
prediction_results = prediction_results_raw.map(json_util.loads)

# Store to MongoDB
prediction_results.saveToMongoDB(
```

```
    "mongodb://localhost:27017/agile_data_science.prediction_results"
)
```

We can inspect our results in the Mongo console:

```
> db.prediction_results.find().pretty()

{
        "_id" : ObjectId("584f418d2eaf0009154e5211"),
        "FlightNum" : "1519",
        "Origin" : "ATL",
        "DayOfWeek" : 6,
        "Dest" : "SFO",
        "DepDelay" : -35,
        "Prediction" : 0,
        "DayOfMonth" : 25,
        "Timestamp" : "2016-12-12T16:27:45.463-08:00",
        "FlightDate" : "2016-12-25",
        "DayOfYear" : 360,
        "Carrier" : "AA",
        "Distance" : 2139
}
```

Now our application can access the results of our batch predictions in MongoDB.

Displaying Batch Prediction Results in Our Web Application

Now that our predictions are available to our web application in Mongo, we need to create a page to display them.

Check out *ch08/web/predict_flask.py* (*http://bit.ly/2o7DJVR*). Before we begin with our controller, we need to import the `datetime` and `iso8601` modules at the top of our module:

```
# Date/time stuff
import iso8601
import datetime
```

Our controller is simple. It accepts an ISO date as a slug argument from a GET request, uses this date to compute today's and tomorrow's ISO dates, and then feeds them to a Mongo date range query to fetch the prediction results for today's ISO date. Finally, it sends the prediction results bound to its template:

```
@app.route("/flights/delays/predict_batch/results/<iso_date>")
def flight_delays_batch_results_page(iso_date):
    """Serves page for batch prediction results"""

    # Get today and tomorrow's dates as ISO strings to scope query
    today_dt = iso8601.parse_date(iso_date)
    rounded_today = today_dt.date()
    iso_today = rounded_today.isoformat()
    rounded_tomorrow_dt = rounded_today + datetime.timedelta(days=1)
    iso_tomorrow = rounded_tomorrow_dt.isoformat()
```

```
# Fetch today's prediction results from Mongo
predictions = client.agile_data_science.prediction_results.find(
  {
    'Timestamp': {
      "$gte": iso_today,
      "$lte": iso_tomorrow,
    }
  }
)

return render_template(
  "flight_delays_predict_batch_results.html",
  predictions=predictions,
  iso_date=iso_date,
)
```

Our template uses the prediction results to generate a table showing the results. Because our prediction was made against buckets ranging from 0.0–2.0, we need to decode these buckets back into minutes in our template. Note that we might have done this earlier in our dataflow logic instead:

```
{% extends "layout.html" %}
{% block body %}

/ <a href="/flights/delays/predict_batch/results/{{ iso_date }}">
    Flight Delay Prediction Results via Spark in Batch
  </a>

<p class="lead" style="margin: 10px; margin-left: 0px;">

  Presenting Flight Delay Predictions via Spark in Batch
</p>

<!-- Generate table from prediction results -->
<table class="table">
    <thead>
      <tr>
          <td>Request Timestamp</td>
          <td>Carrier</td>
          <td>Flight Date</td>
          <td>Origin</td>
          <td>Destination</td>
          <td>Distance</td>
          <td>Departure Delay</td>
          <td><span style="color: red;">Predicted Arrival Delay</span></td>
      </tr>
    </thead>
    <tbody>
      {% for item in predictions %}
          <tr>
              <td>{{ item['Timestamp'] }}</td>
```

```
            <td>{{ item['Carrier'] }}</td>
            <td>{{ item['FlightDate'] }}</td>
            <td>{{ item['Origin'] }}</td>
            <td>{{ item['Dest'] }}</td>
            <td>{{ item['Distance'] }}</td>
            <td>{{ item['DepDelay'] }}</td>
            <td>
                <span style="color: red;">
                    {% if item['Prediction'] == 0.0 %}
                        On Time (0-15 Minute Delay)
                    {% elif item['Prediction'] == 1.0 %}
                        Slightly Late (15-60 Minute Delay)
                    {% elif item['Prediction'] == 2.0 %}
                        Very Late (60+ Minute Delay)
                    {% endif %}
                </span>
            </td>
        </tr>
    {% endfor %}
    </tbody>
</table>

{% endblock %}
```

Now, visit our application at *http://localhost:5000/flights/delays/predict_batch/results/* *2016-12-12* (swap in the current date as you read this). You should see something like Figure 8-3.

Figure 8-3. Flight delay classification results page

In practice, this prediction might find its way into your application in many different ways: via emails you send to users, via a message to the user when he logs in to your system, as part of an event or content feed, or as part of a particular page's content for this day. Perhaps we will employ a designer to help us improve this application for the next edition of this book, but for now this will have to do. :)

Automating Our Workflow with Apache Airflow (Incubating)

We have now completed the application and data pipeline development portion of this section on deploying Spark ML predictions in batch. Recall that we've come full circle: from requesting predictions in our application back to displaying the results of those requests in another page. All the data processing we've done was executable from the command line, which will enable Airflow to work with each portion of the overall data pipeline for our batch predictive system.

Now we will employ Airflow to tie our separate scripts into a single executable system that we can schedule to run each and every day to do its job in production. Note that Airflow is controlled by using the `airflow` Python module. To get started, we need to create yet another Python script that can employ Airflow to combine our scripts into a single dataflow.

Setting up Airflow

In this section we will set up Airflow. We introduced Airflow in Chapter 2 but haven't used it since. If your memory is hazy, you should review the introduction before proceeding (see "Scheduling with Apache Airflow (Incubating)" on page 59).

Note that it might feel natural to name your script *airflow.py*, but this will occlude the *airflow* Python module and will cause problems. For this reason, we create an airflow directory and use the script name *setup.py*.

Check out *ch08/airflow/setup.py* (*http://bit.ly/2pj1H0A*). Let's go through it section by section.

We begin with our imports, and by importing the `PROJECT_HOME` environment variable:

```
import sys, os, re

from airflow import DAG
from airflow.operators.bash_operator import BashOperator

from datetime import datetime, timedelta
import iso8601

PROJECT_HOME = os.environ["PROJECT_HOME"]
```

Then we establish the default arguments with which we will create our directed acyclic graph (DAG) and individual operators:

```
default_args = {
  'owner': 'airflow',
  'depends_on_past': False,
  'start_date': iso8601.parse_date("2016-12-01"),
  'email': ['russell.jurney@gmail.com'],
  'email_on_failure': True,
```

```
    'email_on_retry': True,
    'retries': 3,
    'retry_delay': timedelta(minutes=5),
}
```

Creating a DAG for creating our model

Next, we instantiate an Airflow DAG (*http://bit.ly/2oCwW5f*) for our feature extraction and model training:

```
# Timedelta 1 is 'run daily'
training_dag = DAG(
    'agile_data_science_batch_prediction_model_training',
    default_args=default_args
)
```

Before defining any operators, we first define a `bash_command` (which is what it sounds like) that will be shared by all PySpark tasks in this workflow. In this command, we employ `spark-submit` to run a PySpark script. This command will be parameterized by the `params` supplied to the `BashOperator` (*http://bit.ly/2pj8SWD*).

We use a mix of user-specified and Airflow system variables to parameterize `spark-submit`. We create one command for our scripts that use a date, and one for those that only need a base path. User-specified variables include the hostname of the Spark master `{{ params.master }}`, as well as the full path to the script to execute `{{ params.base_path }}/{{ params.filename }}` and the script's base path argument `{{ params.base_path }}`. Airflow supplies the `{{ ds }}` variable, which contains the date/time given via the `airflow` command or specified by the Airflow scheduler. The documentation could make this clearer, but using the `ds` variable ties our PySpark scripts into the date capabilities of Airflow such as the `scheduler` and `back fill` commands:

```
# We use the same two commands for all our PySpark tasks
pyspark_bash_command = """
spark-submit --master {{ params.master }} \
  {{ params.base_path }}/{{ params.filename }} \
  {{ params.base_path }}
"""
pyspark_date_bash_command = """
spark-submit --master {{ params.master }} \
  {{ params.base_path }}/{{ params.filename }} \
  {{ ds }} {{ params.base_path }}
"""
```

Note that during development we specify the Spark master as `local` but during production we would simply switch this to the hostname of our Spark master.

Next, we create our first `BashOperator` (*http://bit.ly/2pj8SWD*), which runs the first script in our data pipeline: *ch08/extract_features.py* (*http://bit.ly/2oTpIIB*). Note that because our scripts are all executable from the command line, running them with spark-submit via BashOperators is easy. We supply the parameters to go along with our PySpark bash command—the Spark master, filename, and base path—leaving the date/time to Airflow:

```
# Gather the training data for our classifier
extract_features_operator = BashOperator(
  task_id = "pyspark_extract_features",
  bash_command = pyspark_bash_command,
  params = {
    "master": "local[8]",
    "filename": "ch08/extract_features.py",
    "base_path": "{}/".format(PROJECT_HOME)
  },
  dag=training_dag
)
```

Then we create a BashOperator for our model training script, *ch08/train_spark_mllib_model.py* (*http://bit.ly/2pVD1Yu*), which we assign a task_id of pyspark_train_classifier_model:

```
# Train and persist the classifier model
train_classifier_model_operator = BashOperator(
  task_id = "pyspark_train_classifier_model",
  bash_command = pyspark_bash_command,
  params = {
    "master": "local[8]",
    "filename": "ch08/train_spark_mllib_model.py",
    "base_path": "{}/".format(PROJECT_HOME)
  },
  dag=training_dag
)
```

The first two tasks we've created are tied together: the second is dependent on the first. One line of code creates this relationship so they can operate together:

```
# The model training depends on the feature extraction
train_classifier_model_operator.set_upstream(extract_features_operator)
```

Creating a DAG for operating our model

Now that we've created a training_dag for creating our model, we need another DAG that will employ the model every day to make predictions. This one will have a schedule_interval set to a datetime.timedelta (*http://bit.ly/2oTzlXT*) of 1, indicating it should execute daily:

```
daily_prediction_dag = DAG(
  'agile_data_science_batch_predictions_daily',
  default_args=default_args,
  schedule_interval=timedelta(1)
)
```

The first script that gets a task in this DAG is *ch08/fetch_prediction_requests.py* (*http://bit.ly/2pGe2Jg*). We name the task something logical, pyspark_fetch_predic tion_requests:

```
# Fetch prediction requests from MongoDB
fetch_prediction_requests_operator = BashOperator(
  task_id = "pyspark_fetch_prediction_requests",
  bash_command = pyspark_date_bash_command,
  params = {
    "master": "local[8]",
    "filename": "ch08/fetch_prediction_requests.py",
    "base_path": "{}/".format(PROJECT_HOME)
  },
  dag=daily_prediction_dag
)
```

The second script in this pipeline is *ch08/make_predictions.py* (*http://bit.ly/2oq59Cy*), whose operator we name make_predictions_operator:

```
# Run another simple PySpark script that depends on the previous one
make_predictions_operator = BashOperator(
  task_id = "pyspark_make_predictions",
  bash_command = pyspark_date_bash_command,
  params = {
    "master": "local[8]",
    "filename": "ch08/make_predictions.py",
    "base_path": "{}/".format(PROJECT_HOME)
  },
  dag=daily_prediction_dag
)
```

Our final script in this DAG is *ch08/load_prediction_results.py* (*http://bit.ly/2pVz4D2*), whose operator we name load_prediction_results_operator:

```
# Load today's predictions to Mongo
load_prediction_results_operator = BashOperator(
  task_id = "pyspark_load_prediction_results",
  bash_command = pyspark_date_bash_command,
  params = {
    "master": "local[8]",
    "filename": "ch08/load_prediction_results.py",
    "base_path": "{}/".format(PROJECT_HOME)
  },
  dag=daily_prediction_dag
)
```

Now that we've created the operators for the daily_prediction_dag, we need to tie them together in formal dependencies. The three scripts get two dependencies, this time flowing downstream instead of upstream. The end result is the same either way, approaching it from upstream or downstream:

```
# Set downstream dependencies
fetch_prediction_requests_operator.set_downstream(make_predictions_operator)
make_predictions_operator.set_downstream(load_prediction_results_operator)
```

That concludes our Airflow setup script. Next we'll run the script and get to know the `airflow` command.

Using Airflow to manage and execute DAGs and tasks

First we need to set up our script with the Airflow system and verify everything has parsed, before moving on to testing each task and then each DAG in its entirety.

Linking our Airflow script to the Airflow DAGs directory. In order to run our script and add our DAGs to Airflow, we need to link it to our Airflow *dags/* directory, which should be *~/airflow/dags/*:

```
ln -s $PROJECT_HOME/ch08/airflow/setup.py ~/airflow/dags/setup.py
```

Verify the link before executing it. Note that the actual path will vary according to the value of the environment variable $PROJECT_HOME:

```
$ ls -lah ~/airflow/dags/

total 16
drwxr-xr-x    5 rjurney  staff    170B Dec 12 18:07 .
drwxr-xr-x   13 rjurney  staff    442B Dec 12 18:07 ..
drwxr-xr-x    4 rjurney  staff    136B Dec 12 18:07 __pycache__
lrwxr-xr-x    1 rjurney  staff     62B Dec  3 23:02 airflow_test.py -> \
   /Users/rjurney/Software/Agile_Data_Code_2/ch02/airflow_test.py
lrwxr-xr-x    1 rjurney  staff     63B Dec 12 18:07 setup.py -> \
   /Users/rjurney/Software/Agile_Data_Code_2/ch08/airflow/setup.py
```

Executing our Airflow setup script. Now we can execute the script in place in *~/airflow/dags/* to add it to the Airflow system. Its output is brief and doesn't tell us much, but the absence of errors indicates everything is all right:

```
$ python ~/airflow/dags/setup.py

[2016-12-12 18:10:53,413] {__init__.py:36} INFO - Using executor
                SequentialExecutor
```

Querying Airflow from the command line. We can use the `airflow list_dags` command to see that our DAGs are set up within Airflow. This shows the test DAG we set up in Chapter 2, as well as the two DAGs we defined in our script:

```
$ airflow list_dags

agile_data_science_airflow_test
agile_data_science_batch_prediction_model_training
agile_data_science_batch_predictions_daily
```

Now we can use the `list_tasks` command on each of these DAGs to see the tasks they are composed of. First let's check out `agile_data_science_batch_predic` `tion_model_training`:

```
$ airflow list_tasks agile_data_science_batch_prediction_model_training
```

```
pyspark_extract_features
pyspark_train_classifier_model
```

And next let's `list_tasks` on `agile_data_science_batch_predictions_daily`:

```
$ airflow list_tasks agile_data_science_batch_predictions_daily
```

```
pyspark_fetch_prediction_requests
pyspark_load_prediction_results
pyspark_make_predictions
```

Testing tasks in Airflow. Now we can use the `airflow` command to test the execution of each task we've just created. Check out *ch08/test_airflow.sh* (*http://bit.ly/2oTiYKT*). Replace the date with today's date as you read this, or export the date via `export` `ISO_DATE=`date "+%Y-%m-%d"`` and plug `$ISO_DATE` into each command in place of the date, as we do in *ch08/test_airflow.sh*:

```
airflow test agile_data_science_batch_prediction_model_training \
    pyspark_extract_features 2016-12-12
```

You will see the voluminous output of `spark-submit`, but before that several elements are of interest. Airflow will display the task attempt number (1 of 4 in this case) as well as the actual `spark-submit` command it is executing. You can use this command to debug any problems that come up. If successful, the system will indicate that the command executed with return code 0:

```
--------------------------------------------------------------------
Starting attempt 1 of 4
--------------------------------------------------------------------

[2016-12-12 19:36:13,491] {models.py:1219} INFO - Executing <Task(BashOperator):
    pyspark_extract_features> on 2016-12-12 00:00:00
[2016-12-12 19:36:13,502] {bash_operator.py:55} INFO - tmp dir root location:
/var/folders/0b/74l_65015_5fcbmbdz1w2xl40000gn/T
[2016-12-12 19:36:13,503] {bash_operator.py:64} INFO - Temporary script location:
/var/folders/0b/74l_65015_5fcbmbdz1w2xl40000gn/T/airflowtmpymttr3lj//var/ \
    folders/0b/74l_65015_5fcbmbdz1w2xl40000gn/T/airflowtmpymttr3lj/ \
        pyspark_extract_featurestk4dvpse
[2016-12-12 19:36:13,503] {bash_operator.py:65} INFO - Running command:
spark-submit --master local[8]    /Users/rjurney/Software/Agile_Data_Code_2//ch08/
extract_features.py    2016-12-12
/Users/rjurney/Software/Agile_Data_Code_2/

...
```

```
[2016-12-12 20:06:22,971] {bash_operator.py:80} INFO - Command exited with return
    code 0
```

Now try the same thing for the `pyspark_train_classifier_model` task in the same `agile_data_science_batch_prediction_model_training` DAG. Then repeat this step for each task in the `agile_data_science_batch_predictions_daily` DAG, starting with:

```
airflow test agile_data_science_batch_predictions_daily \
    pyspark_fetch_prediction_requests
```

Run the rest of the test commands in *ch08/test_airflow.sh* (*http://bit.ly/2oTiYKT*) before proceeding. That verifies that all our tasks work! But will the tasks work together?

Testing DAGs in Airflow. Now that we've tested our tasks, we need to test our DAGs in their entirety. We can do this with the `airflow backfill` command configured for a single day. Run `airflow backfill` alone to see the command's options. Note that backfill can also do what its name implies—"backfill" any holes in your data, such as when creating a new data pipeline that needs to fill in historical data:

```
[2016-12-12 19:46:22,679] {__init__.py:36} INFO - Using executor
            SequentialExecutor
usage: airflow backfill [-h] [-t TASK_REGEX] [-s START_DATE] [-e END_DATE]
                        [-m] [-l] [-x] [-a] [-i] [-I] [-sd SUBDIR]
                        [--pool POOL] [-dr]
                        dag_id
airflow backfill: error: the following arguments are required: dag_id
```

The command to test our `agile_data_science_batch_prediction_model_training` DAG is as follows. Note that this may take a few minutes:

```
airflow backfill -s 2016-12-12 -e 2016-12-12
    agile_data_science_batch_prediction_model_training
```

And the command to test our `agile_data_science_batch_predictions_daily` DAG is:

```
airflow backfill -s 2016-12-12 -e 2016-12-12
    agile_data_science_batch_predictions_daily
```

`backfill` has limited debug output, but it does print the path to a logfile for each execution. You can `cat` or `tail -f` that logfile for more information. Assuming both tasks run without any problems, we're ready to check out the Airflow web interface to see how things are going.

Monitoring tasks in the Airflow web interface. If you haven't already, run the Airflow scheduler and Airflow web interface via the following commands:

```
airflow scheduler -D
airflow webserver -D
```

Now visit the Airflow interface at *http://localhost:8080/admin/#/* (Figure 8-4). If you see the Zeppelin interface instead, stop the Zeppelin daemon:

```
zeppelin/bin/zeppelin-daemon.sh stop
```

If our DAGs are marked inactive, click the refresh button beside them and they should Refresh as active.

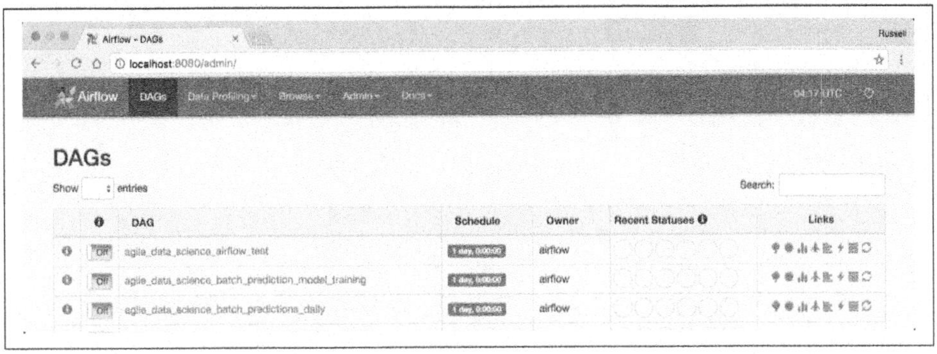

Figure 8-4. Airflow admin home page listing DAGs

Clicking the DAG named `agile_data_science_batch_predictions_daily` will show you a graph view of this DAG (Figure 8-5). Note how the graph shows the dependencies we set up in *ch08/airflow/setup.py* (*http://bit.ly/2pj1H0A*) for the DAG `agile_data_science_batch_predictions_daily`.

Figure 8-5. Airflow DAG page

Click the Task Duration link (*http://localhost:8080/admin/airflow/duration?root=&days=30&dag_id=agile_data_science_batch_predictions_daily*), which should display a chart showing the runtime of our backfill operations (Figure 8-6).

Figure 8-6. Task Duration chart

Play around with the Airflow web interface. There is a lot there to discover.

Conclusion

This concludes our deployment of a predictive system in batch using Airflow. It is hoped that this example will extend to real tasks you need to accomplish.

Deploying Spark ML via Spark Streaming

With the rise of Apache Kafka, Spark Streaming has become an increasingly popular way of processing data in "near real time." Our Spark Streaming workflow will reuse the code we created in the last section for training, storing, and loading the classifier model. But from there it will diverge, starting with how we create prediction requests.

In this case, our web application will emit a Kafka event when a prediction is needed, and after streaming through a Kafka cluster, it will arrive at a Spark Streaming process that will vectorize the features and make the prediction using the model it loads from disk. It will then write the result to a database, where the original web application will read and deliver the result.

Note that an important limitation to this method of deployment is that you can only use one model at a time. This can be a bottleneck for some applications, like making content-based recommendations in a recommender system, where one model is needed for each user, because you can't loop through many models in one Spark Streaming process.

Gathering Training Data in Production

We will reuse the code and Airflow configuration for gathering training data from the previous section on deploying a predictive system in batch. You can follow along with *ch08/extract_features.py* (*http://bit.ly/2oTpIIB*) and refer back to "Gathering Training Data in Production" on page 235. Even in a Spark Streaming deployment, we still gather training data in production using PySpark in batch and Airflow.

Training, Storing, and Loading Spark ML Models

Again, we will reuse the code and Airflow configuration for training and persisting our model from the previous section on deploying a predictive system in batch. You can follow along with *ch08/train_spark_mllib_model.py* (*http://bit.ly/2pVD1Yu*) and "Training, Storing, and Loading Spark ML Models" on page 237. Even in a Spark Streaming deployment, we still need Airflow to productionize the training and persistence of the model, which we will then deploy in Spark Streaming. Figure 8-7 illustrates our backend architecture.

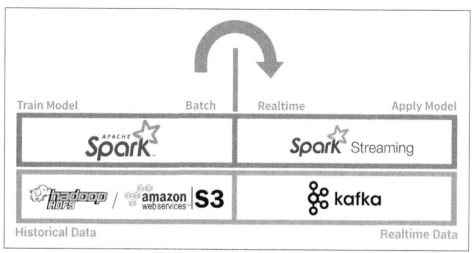

Figure 8-7. Backend architecture

Sending Prediction Requests to Kafka

In order to feed the prediction task and associated data to a Spark ML script deployed in batch, we need to generate Kafka events that indicate a prediction is needed. Our web application can easily do so using a form and an associated form controller that generates a prediction request as a Kafka message.

This is in contrast to the scikit-learn deployment via a web API, where the result was directly computed inside the web application. In the real world, this might correspond to a wide variety of circumstances, because any computation that takes longer than a fraction of a second is best deployed via Kafka. Kafka workers are precisely the place you want to handle a spike in load that would produce latency—Kafka is designed to handle such variable loads, and web applications are not.

In this case, a web application will emit a request for a prediction as a message in a Kafka topic. Then, a Spark Streaming minibatch will fetch today's prediction requests and feed them to PySpark ML, which will create the predictions and store the results in a MongoDB collection. The prediction request page will then display the result of that prediction request's prediction.

Setting up Kafka

Before proceeding, we'll need to set up Kafka as we did in Chapter 2. You may want to refer to "Distributed Streams with Apache Kafka" on page 54 to refresh yourself on Kafka, as this section is largely a rehash of that section. If you've already completed some of these steps and haven't restarted your computer, you may be able to skip those steps you have already completed.

We'll need to start up Zookeeper and the Kafka server, and we'll need to create a Kafka topic for our prediction requests.

Start Zookeeper. Zookeeper helps to orchestrate Kafka, so we need to start it first. Start up a new console for Zookeeper, and run:

```
kafka/bin/zookeeper-server-start.sh kafka/config/zookeeper.properties
```

Start the Kafka server. Now, in another new console, run the Kafka server:

```
kafka/bin/kafka-server-start.sh kafka/config/server.properties
```

Create a topic. Open another new console. We'll use this one to run different Kafka commands, and then will leave it open as a console consumer for our prediction request topic.

Kafka messages are grouped into topics, so we need to create one before we can send messages through Kafka:

```
kafka/bin/kafka-topics.sh \
    --create \
    --zookeeper localhost:2181 \
    --replication-factor 1 \
    --partitions 1 \
    --topic flight_delay_classification_request
```

We should see the following message:

```
Created topic "flight_delay_classification_request".
```

Verify our new prediction request topic. We can see the topic we created with the list topics command:

```
$ kafka/bin/kafka-topics.sh --list --zookeeper localhost:2181

flight_delay_classification_request
test
```

We need to monitor this topic, so let's run the console consumer on flight_delay_classification_request:

```
kafka/bin/kafka-console-consumer.sh \
    --bootstrap-server localhost:9092 \
    --topic flight_delay_classification_request \
    --from-beginning
```

That's it. Now Kafka is ready to send and receive prediction requests, and we will see them as they occur! Now let's set up our web application to emit requests.

Feeding Kafka recommendation tasks from a Flask API

We will turn to `kafka-python` (*https://github.com/dpkp/kafka-python*) to act as Producer and emit Kafka events from our web application in *ch08/web/flask_predict.py* (*http://bit.ly/2o7DJVR*).

First we need to import `kafka-python` and set up our `KafkaProducer` (*http://bit.ly/2oOorUH*) object, which will emit our events. We do so up top in our script, in case another controller needs Kafka. We also import the Python package `uuid` (*https://docs.python.org/3.1/library/uuid.html*), which will create a unique ID for our prediction requests:

```
# Set up Kafka
from kafka import KafkaProducer, TopicPartition
producer = KafkaProducer(bootstrap_servers=['localhost:9092'],api_version=(0,10))
PREDICTION_TOPIC = 'flight_delay_classification_request'

import uuid
```

Next, we create a new API for prediction requests, based on the one we created for our batch requests, with a couple of changes. Instead of inserting requests into Mongo, we will emit JSON requests to our Kafka topic. These requests will each feature a Universally Unique Identifier (*http://bit.ly/2pj7QtS*) (UUID) to identify them—a UUID is a random string long enough that it is very unlikely any other such string will overlap this one:

```
# Make our API a post, so a search engine won't hit it
@app.route("/flights/delays/predict/classify_realtime", methods=['POST'])
def classify_flight_delays_realtime():

  # Define the form fields to process
  """POST API for classifying flight delays"""
  api_field_type_map = \
    {
      "DepDelay": float,
      "Carrier": str,
      "FlightDate": str,
      "Dest": str,
      "FlightNum": str,
      "Origin": str
    }

  # Fetch the values for each field from the form object
  api_form_values = {}
  for api_field_name, api_field_type in api_field_type_map.items():
    api_form_values[api_field_name] = request.form.get(
      api_field_name, type=api_field_type
    )

  # Set the direct values, which excludes Date
  prediction_features = {}
```

```
    for key, value in api_form_values.items():
        prediction_features[key] = value

    # Set the derived values
    prediction_features['Distance'] = predict_utils.get_flight_distance(
        client, api_form_values['Origin'],
        api_form_values['Dest']
    )

    # Turn the date into DayOfYear, DayOfMonth, DayOfWeek
    date_features_dict = predict_utils.get_regression_date_args(
        api_form_values['FlightDate']
    )
    for api_field_name, api_field_value in date_features_dict.items():
        prediction_features[api_field_name] = api_field_value

    # Add a timestamp
    prediction_features['Timestamp'] = predict_utils.get_current_timestamp()

    # Create a unique ID for this message
    unique_id = str(uuid.uuid4())
    prediction_features['UUID'] = unique_id

    message_bytes = json.dumps(prediction_features).encode()
    producer.send(PREDICTION_TOPIC, message_bytes)

    response = {"status": "OK", "id": unique_id}
    return json_util.dumps(response)
```

We can test this API with curl and then by monitoring the console consumer we set up in the last section:

```
curl -XPOST 'http://localhost:5000/flights/delays/predict/classify_realtime' \
    -F 'DepDelay=5.0' \
    -F 'Carrier=AA' \
    -F 'FlightDate=2016-12-23' \
    -F 'Dest=ATL' \
    -F 'FlightNum=1519' \
    -F 'Origin=SFO' | json_pp
```

The response features a status code and a UUID:

```
  % Total    % Received % Xferd  Average Speed   Time    Time     Time  Current
                                 Dload  Upload   Total   Spent    Left  Speed
100   711  100    62  100   649   7322  76650 --:--:-- --:--:-- --:--:--  126k
{
    "status" : "OK",
    "id" : "fbb5b61c-2c7b-4db6-a22f-dae270c59797"
}
```

The request should show up in the console consumer, now with a UUID:

```
{
  "Distance": 2139.0,
  "Carrier": "AA",
  "DayOfYear": 358,
  "UUID": "fbb5b61c-2c7b-4db6-a22f-dae270c59797",
  "DayOfMonth": 23,
  "Origin": "SFO",
  "FlightNum": "1519",
  "Dest": "ATL",
  "DepDelay": 5.0,
  "DayOfWeek": 4,
  "FlightDate": "2016-12-23",
  "Timestamp": "2016-12-13T20:21:29.233822"
}
```

That's it! We're producing prediction request events in Kafka.

A frontend for generating prediction requests

Now we need a frontend for creating and displaying prediction requests and responses. This will look similar to the one we created for our scikit-learn regression web service earlier in this chapter, but with a new twist: a polling form.

Polling requests and LinkedIn InMaps. This feature is different from those we've created before that used simple AJAX (*https://mzl.la/2oYXz57*)-style requests to POST a form and then display the content of the response. This form fits in between the two forms we created earlier in this chapter (the realtime form we created in "Pulling Our API into Our Product" on page 232 that queried the scikit-learn model directly in our web application and immediately displayed its output on the page, and the form we created in "A frontend for generating prediction requests" on page 242 that submitted a request for a prediction and didn't expect an answer, because the output was displayed on another page after a batch process).

This time our form will expect a response from its submission request, but not an immediate response. It will first receive a response that indicates the prediction request has been received. This signals the client to send another request to a different endpoint to receive an answer. If the prediction isn't ready, a response will indicate that the client should wait a suitable period before repeating its request. In the meantime, the client will display a "processing" message on the page. When a response is finally ready, it will be displayed on the page.

Figure 8-8 illustrates the frontend architecture of our application.

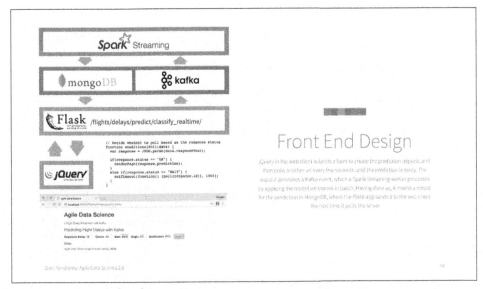

Figure 8-8. Frontend architecture

Many real products use this pattern for data processing and predictions. For instance, LinkedIn InMaps (*http://oreil.ly/2o7Gwyi*) used this pattern. After user authentication via the LinkedIn API, the client would submit an asynchronous request for a network visualization for that user's network to be produced. This would generate a request for a network image to be prepared. A "render farm" of servers would perform a force-directed layout for each network and would render the background image for each user's map. When the map was prepared, the render worker created a record in a database. Meanwhile, the client would repeatedly poll a second endpoint, with a delay between each request, awaiting its map. A message on screen indicated the map was being created, until the map was finally transmitted and displayed (Figure 8-9). A social feature enabled users to share their maps, creating a viral loop that distributed the product.

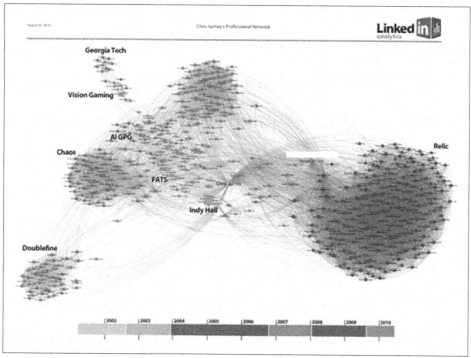

Figure 8-9. LinkedIn InMaps prototype

We'll be using a polling form to display flight delay predictions. This will require two endpoints and their corresponding controllers, and some simple JavaScript.

A controller for the page. Check out *ch08/web/predict_flask.py* (*http://bit.ly/2o7DJVR*), where we define a simple controller to serve the template for our prediction page:

```
@app.route("/flights/delays/predict_kafka")
def flight_delays_page_kafka():
    """Serves flight delay prediction page with polling form"""

    form_config = [
      {'field': 'DepDelay', 'label': 'Departure Delay'},
      {'field': 'Carrier'},
      {'field': 'FlightDate', 'label': 'Date'},
      {'field': 'Origin'},
      {'field': 'Dest', 'label': 'Destination'},
    ]

    return render_template(
      'flight_delays_predict_kafka.html', form_config=form_config
    )
```

An API controller for serving prediction responses. We also need a simple controller for serving the predictions when they are ready, signaled by their presence in MongoDB for any given UUID. This is simple CRUD work, which makes up the bulk of most consumer web applications:

```
@app.route("/flights/delays/predict/classify_realtime/response/<unique_id>")
def classify_flight_delays_realtime_response(unique_id):
  """Serves predictions to polling requestors"""

  prediction = \
    client.agile_data_science.flight_delay_classification_response.find_one(
      {
        "id": unique_id
      }
    )

  response = {"status": "WAIT", "id": unique_id}
  if prediction:
    response["status"] = "OK"
    response["prediction"] = prediction

  return json_util.dumps(response)
```

We can verify that it works with `curl`:

```
curl \
 'http://localhost:5000/flights/delays/predict/classify_realtime \
  /response/EXAMPLE_UUID_g3t03qtq3t' | json_pp
```

Which results in:

```
% Total    % Received % Xferd  Average Speed   Time    Time     Time  Current
                                Dload  Upload   Total   Spent    Left  Speed
100    51  100    51    0      0   7834       0 --:--:-- --:--:-- --:--:-- 25500
{
   "id" : "EXAMPLE_UUID_g3t03qtq3t",
   "status" : "WAIT"
}
```

Now let's insert a record for this UUID in Mongo:

```
db.flight_delay_classification_response.insert(
  {
    id: "EXAMPLE_UUID_g3t03qtq3t",
    prediction: {"test": "data"}
  }
)
```

and try again:

```
curl 'http://localhost:5000/flights/delays/predict/classify_realtime/ \
  response/EXAMPLE_UUID_g3t03qtq3t' | json_pp
```

This simply returns our record as the prediction portion of our response:

```
  % Total    % Received % Xferd  Average Speed   Time    Time    Time  Current
                                  Dload  Upload   Total   Spent   Left  Speed
100   175 100   175    0     0  31605       0 --:--:-- --:--:-- --:--:-- 87500
{
   "id" : "EXAMPLE_UUID_g3t03qtq3t",
   "status" : "OK",
   "prediction" : {
      "_id" : {
         "$oid" : "5850dc50ebc402b548a0234c"
      },
      "id" : "EXAMPLE_UUID_g3t03qtq3t",
      "prediction" : {
         "test" : "data"
      }
   }
}
```

Creating a template with a polling form. The template for this controller is *ch08/web/ templates/flight_delays_predict_kafka.html* (*http://bit.ly/2ouOQU9*), which we copied from *ch08/web/templates/flight_delays_predict.html* (*http://bit.ly/2pGtR2z*) and then edited in place. Open it up and follow along:

```
{% extends "layout.html" %}
{% block body %}
   <!-- Navigation guide -->
   / <a href="/flights/delays/predict_kafka">
      Flight Delay Prediction with Kafka
   </a>

   <p class="lead" style="margin: 10px; margin-left: 0px;">

      Predicting Flight Delays with Kafka
   </p>

   <!-- Generate form from search_config and request args -->
   <form id="flight_delay_classification"
         action="/flights/delays/predict/classify_realtime"
         method="post">
   {% for item in form_config %}
      {% if 'label' in item %}
         <label for="{{item['field']}}">{{item['label']}}</label>
      {% else %}
         <label for="{{item['field']}}">{{item['field']}}</label>
      {% endif %}
         <input name="{{item['field']}}"
                style="width: 36px; margin-right: 10px;"
                value="">
         </input>
   {% endfor %}
   <button type="submit" class="btn btn-xs btn-default" style="height: 25px">
      Submit
   </button>
```

```
    </form>

    <div style="margin-top: 10px;">
        <p>Delay: <span id="result" style="display: inline-block;"></span></p>
    </div>


    <script src="/static/js/flight_delay_predict_polling.js"></script>
{% endblock %}
```

The template itself is simple; the real work happens in the JavaScript file, *ch08/web/ static/flight_delay_predict_polling.js* (*http://bit.ly/2oTzTwR*). Let's go through it part by part. We've broken the task up into functions to keep things clean and simple.

As we've done before, we use jQuery.submit (*https://api.jquery.com/submit/*) to attach a function to the submission of our HTML form. Within this function we process the form's input and post it to the form's endpoint at */flights/delays/predict/classify_realtime*. Once a response is received indicating a successful prediction request has been submitted, we begin to poll a separate endpoint using a unique ID for the prediction request returned in the response:

```
// Attach a submit handler to the form
$( "#flight_delay_classification" ).submit(function( event ) {

  // Stop form from submitting normally
  event.preventDefault();

  // Get some values from elements on the page
  var $form = $( this ),
    term = $form.find( "input[name='s']" ).val(),
    url = $form.attr( "action" );

  // Send the data using post
  var posting = $.post(
    url,
    $( "#flight_delay_classification" ).serialize()
  );

  // Submit the form and parse the response
  posting.done(function( data ) {
    response = JSON.parse(data);

    // If the response is OK, print a message to wait and start polling
    if(response.status == "OK") {
      $( "#result" ).empty().append( "Processing..." );

      // Every 1 second, poll the response URL until we get a response
      poll(response.id);
    }
  });
});
```

This polling is handled by the `poll` function. `poll` accepts the ID of the request and generates a URL for the response endpoint at */flights/delays/predict/classify_realtime/ response/*, which takes a slug at the end as a parameter. It submits an initial asynchronous GET request to this URL, and refers the response to the function `conditional Poll`:

```
// Poll the prediction URL
function poll(id) {
  var responseUrlBase = "/flights/delays/predict/classify_realtime/response/";
  console.log("Polling for request id " + id + "...");

  // Append the UUID to the URL as a slug argument
  var predictionUrl = responseUrlBase + id;

  $.ajax(
  {
    url: predictionUrl,
    type: "GET",
    complete: conditionalPoll
  });
}
```

`conditionalPoll` does what it sounds like—it either polls the endpoint again if the status of the response is `WAIT`, or it renders the response on the page via the function `renderPage` if the status is `OK`:

```
// Decide whether to poll based on the response status
function conditionalPoll(data) {
  var response = JSON.parse(data.responseText);

  if(response.status == "OK") {
    renderPage(data);
  }
  else if(response.status == "WAIT") {
    setTimeout(function() {poll(response.id)}, 1000);
  }
}
```

`renderPage` is very simple. It draws the prediction response on the page, in the same place as the realtime, `scikit-learn` prediction frontend did:

```
// Render the response on the page for splits:
// [-float("inf"), -15.0, 0, 30.0, float("inf")]
function renderPage(response) {

  var displayMessage;

  if(response.Prediction == 0) {
    displayMessage = "Early (15+ Minutes Early)";
  }
  else if(response.Prediction == 1) {
    displayMessage = "Slightly Early (0-15 Minute Early)";
```

```
  }
  else if(response.Prediction == 2) {
    displayMessage = "Slightly Late (0-30 Minute Delay)";
  }
  else if(response.Prediction == 3) {
    displayMessage = "Very Late (30+ Minutes Late)";
  }

  $( "#result" ).empty().append( displayMessage );
}
```

That wraps up the frontend for our Kafka-based prediction! Now let's try things out.

Making a prediction request

To test our page, visit *http://localhost:5000/flights/delays/predict_kafka* and open a JavaScript console. Now, enter some test data and submit the form. Be sure to fill out all the fields. You should see a waiting message and a request each second to the prediction response URL, as in Figure 8-10.

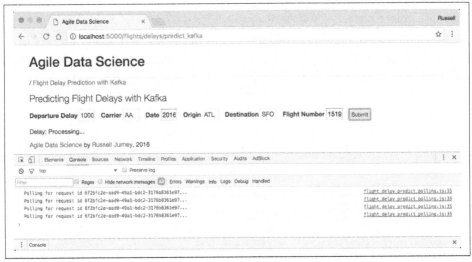

Figure 8-10. Kafka-based flight delay prediction page

Now that our model is prepared, we're creating Kafka events for each prediction request, and our frontend is ready to display the results, we're ready to start making predictions using Spark Streaming!

Making Predictions in Spark Streaming

Now that we've created a frontend for making prediction requests via Kafka, as well as for displaying the result on the web, we need to finish up the middle where PySpark Streaming processes Kafka events and inserts the result in Mongo for the frontend to render. Note that you can learn more about deploying PySpark Streaming in the Spark Streaming Programming Guide (*http://bit.ly/2ouM818*).

Check out *ch08/make_predictions_streaming.py* (*http://bit.ly/2o7trFf*). We initialize the system in a similar way as we do in batch, albeit with a StreamingContext (*http://bit.ly/2oOkAqO*) as well as a SparkSession (*http://bit.ly/2nRGlqX*). So long as they both come from the same SparkContext (*http://bit.ly/2oTAQoV*), they will play well together (although, as we will see, Spark Streaming is primarily RDD-based).

Note that our main function only takes one argument this time, the base_path. The date isn't needed, as our script will process any Kafka event that it sees.

In order to run a Spark Streaming script, we have to include the Spark Streaming package, which currently goes by the name org.apache.spark:spark-streaming-kafka-0-8_2.11:2.1.0 (the version may have changed by the time you're reading this). We can achieve this at the command line during development using the PySpark console:

```
PYSPARK_DRIVER_PYTHON=ipython pyspark --packages \
    org.apache.spark:spark-streaming-kafka-0-8_2.11:2.1.0
```

However, to make our script command-line executable, we must use findspark to do the import, via findspark.add_packages (*http://bit.ly/2opWT5y*). We also need to initialize pymongo-spark (*http://bit.ly/2oepp9Z*), as we'll be storing results directly in Mongo. In contrast with batch, with Spark Streaming it is necessary to do both things at once (make the prediction and store the result in Mongo):

```
#!/usr/bin/env python

import sys, os, re
import json
import datetime, iso8601

from pyspark import SparkContext, SparkConf
from pyspark.sql import SparkSession, Row
from pyspark.streaming import StreamingContext
from pyspark.streaming.kafka import KafkaUtils, OffsetRange, TopicAndPartition

# Save to Mongo
from bson import json_util
import pymongo_spark
pymongo_spark.activate()

def main(base_path):

  APP_NAME = "make_predictions_streaming.py"

  # Process data every 10 seconds
  PERIOD = 10
  BROKERS = 'localhost:9092'
```

```
PREDICTION_TOPIC = 'flight_delay_classification_request'

try:
  sc and ssc
except NameError as e:
  import findspark

  # Add the streaming package and initialize
  findspark.add_packages(
    ["org.apache.spark:spark-streaming-kafka-0-8_2.11:2.1.0"]
  )
  findspark.init()

  import pyspark
  import pyspark.sql
  import pyspark.streaming

  conf = SparkConf().set("spark.default.parallelism", 1)
  sc = SparkContext(
    appName="Agile Data Science: PySpark Streaming 'Hello, World!'", conf=conf
  )
  ssc = StreamingContext(sc, PERIOD)
  spark = pyspark.sql.SparkSession(sc).builder.appName(APP_NAME).getOrCreate()
```

The code for loading the models comes directly from *ch08/make_predictions.py* (*http://bit.ly/2oq59Cy*), and I will not repeat it here. We load the models in main before doing anything else. The beauty of Spark Streaming is that you can reuse code from Spark in batch mode, enabling you to prototype there or create common libraries of code between batch and realtime systems.

Once we load our models, we need to fetch messages from Kafka using KafkaU tils.createDirectStream (*http://bit.ly/2oTwluh*):

```
#
# Process Prediction Requests in Streaming
#

stream = KafkaUtils.createDirectStream(
  ssc,
  [PREDICTION_TOPIC],
  {
    "metadata.broker.list": BROKERS,
    "group.id": "0",
  }
)
```

Since our messages are JSON, we'll need to parse them. The pprint (*http://bit.ly/2pGpwfB*) method lets us take a peek at our data as it flows through Spark Streaming:

```
object_stream = stream.map(lambda x: json.loads(x[1]))
object_stream.pprint()
```

At this point our prediction requests are RDDs (*http://bit.ly/2p5IM9z*) of Python dicts. The models we've created work with DataFrames, so we need to convert them. In order to do this, we first need to create `spark.sql.Rows` (*http://bit.ly/2ouR2ee*) out of the dicts. In doing so, we'll need to convert our ISO 8601 date strings to `datetime` objects using `iso8601.parse_date` (*https://pypi.python.org/pypi/iso8601*). As before, we pprint the result:

```
row_stream = object_stream.map(
    lambda x: Row(
        FlightDate=iso8601.parse_date(x['FlightDate']),
        Origin=x['Origin'],
        Distance=x['Distance'],
        DayOfMonth=x['DayOfMonth'],
        DayOfYear=x['DayOfYear'],
        UUID=x['UUID'],
        DepDelay=x['DepDelay'],
        DayOfWeek=x['DayOfWeek'],
        FlightNum=x['FlightNum'],
        Dest=x['Dest'],
        Timestamp=iso8601.parse_date(x['Timestamp']),
        Carrier=x['Carrier']
    )
)
row_stream.pprint()
```

Our next step is not intuitive, because it is a single step where all the work happens. This doesn't seem to jive with the dataflow orientation of Spark. However, in Spark Streaming you often employ `DStream.foreachRDD` (*http://bit.ly/2ouIxzW*) to perform a long series of operations on the `RDD` within the `DStream`. In this sense, Streaming really sits on top of other Spark abstractions, enabling you to use normal Spark techniques on streaming data.

Let's start with the call itself, a one-liner:

```
# Do the classification and store to Mongo
row_stream.foreachRDD(classify_prediction_requests)
```

Note that we define this function within our `main` function, so that it will have access to the models we've loaded there. We might have passed them in as arguments, but that's ungainly. The downside of defining the function inside `main` is that it isn't importable from outside by another script.

`classify_prediction_requests` (*http://bit.ly/2o7r2KK*) takes an RDD as its argument, and then employs `SparkSession.createDataFrame` (*http://bit.ly/2pGlt2U*) to convert the `Row` we prepared into a full-blown DataFrame. As with the batch version of this script, we need to set up the schema first, this time with a UUID field. Once the DataFrame is created, we can employ `DataFrame.show` (*http://bit.ly/2pjhT20*) to see what is going on:

```
def classify_prediction_requests(rdd):

  from pyspark.sql.types import StringType, IntegerType, DoubleType, DateType,
    TimestampType
  from pyspark.sql.types import StructType, StructField

  prediction_request_schema = StructType([
    StructField("Carrier", StringType(), True),
    StructField("DayOfMonth", IntegerType(), True),
    StructField("DayOfWeek", IntegerType(), True),
    StructField("DayOfYear", IntegerType(), True),
    StructField("DepDelay", DoubleType(), True),
    StructField("Dest", StringType(), True),
    StructField("Distance", DoubleType(), True),
    StructField("FlightDate", DateType(), True),
    StructField("FlightNum", StringType(), True),
    StructField("Origin", StringType(), True),
    StructField("Timestamp", TimestampType(), True),
    StructField("UUID", StringType(), True),
  ])

  prediction_requests_df = spark.createDataFrame(
    rdd, schema=prediction_request_schema
  )
  prediction_requests_df.show()
```

As we did in batch, we need to derive the Route field from the Origin and Dest fields:

```
#
# Add a Route variable to replace FlightNum
#

from pyspark.sql.functions import lit, concat
prediction_requests_with_route = prediction_requests_df.withColumn(
  'Route',
  concat(
    prediction_requests_df.Origin,
    lit('-'),
    prediction_requests_df.Dest
  )
)
prediction_requests_with_route.show(6)
```

Now that we have a DataFrame, we simply repeat the prediction code from *ch08/ make_preditions.py* (*http://bit.ly/2oq59Cy*), which results in a prediction within a DataFrame. Again we take a peek at the output with show, just as we would in batch:

```
# Vectorize string fields with the corresponding pipeline for that column
# Turn category fields into categoric feature vectors, then drop
# intermediate fields
for column in ["Carrier", "DayOfMonth", "DayOfWeek", "DayOfYear",
               "Origin", "Dest", "Route"]:
  string_indexer_model = string_indexer_models[column]
```

```
prediction_requests_with_route = string_indexer_model.transform(
  prediction_requests_with_route
)

# Vectorize numeric columns: DepDelay, Distance, and index columns
final_vectorized_features = vector_assembler.transform(
  prediction_requests_with_route
)

# Inspect the vectors
final_vectorized_features.show()

# Drop the individual index columns
index_columns = ["Carrier_index", "DayOfMonth_index", "DayOfWeek_index",
                 "DayOfYear_index", "Origin_index", "Dest_index",
                 "Route_index"]
for column in index_columns:
  final_vectorized_features = final_vectorized_features.drop(column)

# Inspect the finalized features
final_vectorized_features.show()

# Make the prediction
predictions = rfc.transform(final_vectorized_features)

# Drop the features vector and prediction metadata to give the original
# fields
predictions = predictions.drop("Features_vec")
final_predictions = predictions.drop("indices").drop("values") \
  .drop("rawPrediction").drop("probability")

# Inspect the output
final_predictions.show()
```

Finally, we need to convert the predictions DataFrame into RDDs, because pymongo-spark doesn't work with DataFrames, it works with RDDs composed of dicts (and not even pyspark.sql.Rows). Also, the call to saveToMongoDB (*http://bit.ly/2o7CjKU*) will fail if the RDD is empty, so we need to only saveToMongoDB if there are results:

```
# Store to Mongo
if final_predictions.count() > 0:
  final_predictions.rdd.map(lambda x: x.asDict()).saveToMongoDB(
    "mongodb://localhost:27017/agile_data_science.flight_ \
      delay_classification_response"
  )
```

Whew! That's it. If everything is working as expected, our predictions will be routed from Kafka through Spark ML and back into MongoDB.

Testing the Entire System

Now we're about to have what I hope is a great deal of fun! We get to test the system from end to end. But before doing so, I want to take a moment and review what we've done.

Overall system summary

We collected public data from the web describing 5.4 million flights of commercial airlines. We got to know that data through exploratory data analysis, interactive visualization, and search. This prepared us for the process by which we turned the flights into training data for a statistical model to predict flight delays using Spark, a tool that can process data at any scale. Then we set up a web frontend that generated prediction requests and sent them to a distributed queue in the form of Kafka, which again can handle data of any scale. Spark Streaming let us use the models we prepared in batch to turn Kafka messages into predictions in real time, the results of which we stored in MongoDB, where our web frontend could access them. Finally, the predictions were displayed to the user.

Rubber meets road

Okay, let's go! To try things out, run our script from `bash`:

```
python ch08/make_predictions_streaming.py .
```

The output is voluminous, but the key parts correspond to our `pprints` and `shows`. At this point you should see the empty output that follows (truncated to fit the page):

```
-------------------------------------------
Time: 2016-12-20 18:06:40
-------------------------------------------

+-------+---------+---------+---------+--------+
|Carrier|...|Timestamp|UUID|
+-------+---------+---------+---------+--------+

+-------+---------+---------+---------+--------+
|Carrier|...|NumericFeatures_vec|Features_vec|
+-------+---------+---------+---------+--------+

+-------+---------+---------+---------+--------+
|Carrier|...|UUID|Features_vec|
+-------+---------+---------+---------+--------+

+-------+---------+---------+---------+--------+
|Carrier|...|UUID|Prediction|
+-------+---------+---------+---------+--------+
```

Now, visit *http://localhost:5000/flights/delays/predict_kafka* and, for fun, open the JavaScript console. Enter a nonzero departure delay, an ISO-formatted date (I used

2016-12-25, which was in the future at the time I was writing this), a valid carrier code (use AA or DL if you don't know one), an origin and destination (my favorite is ATL → SFO), and a valid flight number (e.g., 1519), and hit Submit. Watch the debug output in the JavaScript console as the client polls for data from the response endpoint at */flights/delays/predict/classify_realtime/response/*.

Quickly switch windows to your Spark console. Within 10 seconds, the length we've configured of a minibatch, you should see something like the following:

```
-------------------------------------------
Time: 2016-12-20 18:06:50
-------------------------------------------
{
'Dest': 'ORD',
'DayOfYear': 360,
'FlightDate': '2016-12-25',
'Distance': 606.0,
'DayOfMonth': 25,
'UUID': 'a01b5ccb-49f1-4c4d-af34-188c6ae0bbf0',
'FlightNum': '2010',
'Carrier': 'AA',
'DepDelay': -100.0,
'DayOfWeek': 6,
'Timestamp': '2016-12-20T18:06:45.307114',
'Origin': 'ATL'
}


-------------------------------------------
Time: 2016-12-20 18:06:50
-------------------------------------------
Row(Carrier='AA', DayOfMonth=25, DayOfWeek=6, DayOfYear=360, DepDelay=-100.0,
Dest='ORD', Distance=606.0, FlightDate=datetime.datetime(2016,
12, 25, 0, 0, tzinfo=<iso8601.Utc>), FlightNum='2010',
Origin='ATL', Timestamp=datetime.datetime(2016, 12, 20, 18,
6, 45, 307114, tzinfo=<iso8601.Utc>),
UUID='a01b5ccb-49f1-4c4d-af34-188c6ae0bbf0')

+-------+----------+---------+---------+
|Carrier|...|                      UUID|
+-------+----------+---------+---------+
|     AA|...|a01b5ccb-49f1-4c4...|
+-------+----------+---------+---------+


+-------+----------+---------+---------+
|Carrier|...|              Features_vec|
+-------+----------+---------+---------+
|     AA|...|(8009,[2,38,51,34...|
+-------+----------+---------+---------+


+-------+----------+---------+---------+
|Carrier|...|              Features_vec|
+-------+----------+---------+---------+
```

```
|     AA|...|(8009,[2,38,51,34...|
+-------+----------+---------+---------+

+-------+----------+---------+---------+
|Carrier|...|Prediction|
+-------+----------+---------+---------+
|     AA|...|       0.0|
+-------+----------+---------+---------+
```

Paydirt!

Switching back to your browser, you should see the prediction result proudly displayed, as in Figure 8-11. Pretty amazing to watch, yeah!? As I write this I am submitting requests over and over, and I am amazed at how it all fits together, and how this same code might work with a petabyte of data on a large Spark cluster with hundreds of web servers to match. The point of all the trouble we've gone through in this book is to build applications that will scale all the way up to that level. I hope this application and the book describing it serve as an example you can learn from and extend.

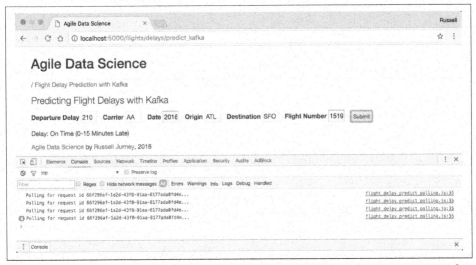

Figure 8-11. Flight delay polling for results as Kafka and Spark Streaming process prediction request

Conclusion

In this chapter we've taken the predictive model we built in the last chapter and integrated it into a real product facing the web. We did so in three different ways: in real time using scikit-learn as a web service, in batch using Spark and Airflow, and in "sub-real time" using Kafka and Spark Streaming. I hope you can use what we've covered in this chapter to deploy your own models as full-blown predictive systems in new data products!

I would very much like to hear how you've used Agile Data Science and the example in this chapter to build your own products, and I'd like to help you do so. Don't hesitate to reach out. You can email me personally at *russell.jurney@gmail.com*, or sign up (*http://bit.ly/2oVPPyB*) for the Agile Data Science email list, *agile-data-science@googlegroups.com*.

Now we turn to improving the model we've created. Once a model meets reality in the form of a product and catches on, product development often turns into a relentless drive to improve that model in as much as it impacts the bottom line. I hope your products have this "problem," and so this is what we focus on next.

## CHAPTER 9

Improving Predictions

Now that we have deployed working models predicting flight delays, it is time to "make believe" that our prediction has proven useful based on user feedback, and further that the prediction is valuable enough that prediction quality is important. In this case, it is time to iteratively improve the quality of our prediction. If a prediction is valuable enough, this becomes a full-time job for one or more people.

In this chapter we will tune our Spark ML classifier and also do additional feature engineering to improve prediction quality. In doing so, we will show you how to iteratively improve predictions.

Code examples for this chapter are available at *Agile_Data_Code_2/ch09* (*http://bit.ly/ 2oRjXwB*). Clone the repository and follow along!

```
git clone https://github.com/rjurney/Agile_Data_Code_2.git
```

Fixing Our Prediction Problem

At this point we realized that our model was always predicting one class, no matter the input. We began by investigating that in a Jupyter notebook (*http://bit.ly/2ocIVXt*) at *ch09/Debugging Prediction Problems.ipynb* (*http://bit.ly/2pRnjO1*).

The notebook itself is very long, and we tried many things to fix our model. It turned out we had made a mistake. We were using OneHotEncoder (*http://bit.ly/2p2VV28*) on top of the output of StringIndexerModel (*http://bit.ly/2opQirO*) when we were encoding our nominal/categorical string features. This is how you should encode features for models other than decision trees, but it turns out that for decision tree models, you are supposed to take the string indexes from StringIndexerModel and directly compose them with your continuous/numeric features in a VectorAssembler (*http://bit.ly/2pj7nI0*). Decision trees are able to infer the fact that indexes represent categories. One benefit of directly adding `StringIndexes` to your feature vectors is that you then get easily interpretable feature importances.

When we discovered this, we had to go back and edit the book so that we didn't teach something that was wrong, and so this is now what you see. We thought it worthwhile to link to the notebook, though, to show how this really works in the wild: you build broken shit and then fix it.

When to Improve Predictions

Not all predictions should be improved. Often something fast and crude will work well enough as an MVP (minimum viable product). Only predictions that prove useful should be improved. It is possible to sink large volumes of time into improving the quality of a prediction, so it is essential that you connect with users before getting sucked into this task. This is why we've included the discussion of improving predictions in its own chapter.

Improving Prediction Performance

There are a few ways to improve an existing predictive model. The first is by tuning the parameters of the statistical model making your prediction. The second is feature engineering.

Tuning model hyperparameters to improve predictive model quality can be done by intuition, or by brute force through something called a grid or random search. We're going to focus on feature engineering, as hyperparameter tuning is covered elsewhere. A good guide to hyperparameter tuning is available in the Spark documentation on model selection and tuning (*https://spark.apache.org/docs/latest/ml-tuning.html*).

As we move through this chapter, we'll be using the work we've done so far to perform feature engineering. Feature engineering is the most important part of making good predictions. It involves using what you've discovered about the data through exploratory data analysis in order to feed your machine learning algorithm better, more consequential data as input.

Experimental Adhesion Method: See What Sticks

There are several ways to decide which features to use, and Saurav Kaushik has written a post on Analytics Vidhya (*http://bit.ly/2mqwJyK*) that introduces them well. The method we employ primarily, which we jokingly entitle the *Experimental Adhesion Method*, is to quickly select all the features that we can simply compute, and try them all using a random forest or gradient boosted decision tree model (note that even if our application requires another type of model, we still use decision trees to guide feature selection). Then we train the model and inspect the model's feature importances to "see what sticks." The most important variables are retained, and this forms the basic model we begin with.

Feature engineering is an iterative process. Based on the feature importances, we ponder what new things we might try using the data we have available. We start with the simplest idea, or the one that is easiest to implement. If the feature importances indicate one type of feature is important, and we can't easily compute new features similar to this one, we think about how we might acquire new data to join to our training data to use as features.

The key is to be logical and systematic in our exploration of the feature space. You should think about how easy a potential feature is to compute, as well as what it would teach you if it turned out to be important. Are there other, similar features that you could try if this candidate worked? Develop hypotheses and test them in the form of new features. Evaluate each new feature in an experiment and reflect on what you've learned before engineering the next feature.

Establishing Rigorous Metrics for Experiments

In order to improve our classification model, we need to reliably determine its prediction quality in the first place. To do so, we need to beef up our cross-validation code, and then establish a baseline of quality for the original model. Check out *ch09/ baseline_spark_mllib_model.py* (*http://bit.ly/2pKV8ko*), which we copied from *ch09/ train_spark_mllib_model.py* (*http://bit.ly/2owYwO6*) and altered to improve its cross-validation code.

In order to evaluate the prediction quality of our classifier, we need to use more than one metric. Spark ML's `MulticlassClassificationEvaluator` (*http://bit.ly/ 2plCH8Y*) offers four metrics: accuracy, weighted precision, weighted recall, and f1.

Defining our classification metrics

The raw *accuracy* is just what it sounds like: the number of correct predictions divided by the number of predictions. This is something to check first, but it isn't adequate alone. *Precision* is a measure of how useful the result is. *Recall* describes how complete the results are. The *f1* score incorporates both precision and recall to determine overall quality. Taken together, the changes to these metrics between consecutive runs of training our model can give us a clear picture of what is happening with our model in terms of prediction quality. We will use these metrics along with feature importance to guide our feature engineering efforts.

Feature importance

Model quality metrics aren't enough to guide the iterative improvements of our model. To understand what is going on with each new run, we need to employ a type of model called a decision tree (*https://en.wikipedia.org/wiki/Decision_tree*).

In Spark ML, the best general-purpose multiclass classification model is an implementation of a random forest (*http://bit.ly/2hqdHsW*), the `RandomForestClassifica tionModel` (*http://bit.ly/2pM3yuC*), fit by the `RandomForestClassifier`. Random forests can classify or regress, and they have an important feature that helps us interrogate predictive models through a feature called *feature importance*.

The importance of a feature is what it sounds like: a measure of how important that feature was in contributing to the accuracy of the model. This information is incredibly useful, as it can serve as a guiding hand to feature engineering (*http://bit.ly/2oReF4o*). In other words, if you know how important a feature is, you can use this clue to make changes that increase the accuracy of the model, such as removing unimportant features and trying to engineer features similar to those that are most important. Feature engineering is a major theme of Agile Data Science, and it is a big part of why we've been doing iterative visualization and exploration (the purpose of which is to shed light on and drive feature engineering).

Note that the state of the art for many classification and regression tasks is a gradient boosted decision tree (*http://bit.ly/2obFMbA*), but as of version 2.1.0 Spark ML's implementation—the `GBTClassificationModel` (*http://bit.ly/2oYpX57*), which is fit by the `GBTClassifier`—can only do binary classification.

Implementing a more rigorous experiment

In order to be confident in our experiment for each measure, we need to repeat it at least twice to see how it varies. This is the degree to which we cross-validate. In addition, we need to loop and run the measurement code once for each score. Once we've collected several scores for each metric, we look at both the average and standard deviation for each score. Taken together, these scores give us a picture of the quality of our classifier.

To begin, we need to iterate and repeat our experiment *N* times. For each experiment we need to compute a test/train split, then we need to train the model on the training data and apply it to the test data. Then we use `MulticlassClassificationEvaluator` (*http://bit.ly/2pICH8Y*) to get a score, once for each metric. We gather the scores in a list for each metric, which we will evaluate at the end of the experiment:

```
#
# Cross-validate, train, and evaluate classifier: loop 5 times for 4 metrics
#

from collections import defaultdict
```

```python
scores = defaultdict(list)
metric_names = ["accuracy", "weightedPrecision", "weightedRecall", "f1"]
split_count = 3

for i in range(1, split_count + 1):
  print("\nRun {} out of {} of test/train splits in cross validation...". \
    format(
      i,
      split_count,
    )
    )

  # Test/train split
  training_data, test_data = final_vectorized_features.limit(1000000).\
    randomSplit([0.8, 0.2])

  # Instantiate and fit random forest classifier on all the data
  from pyspark.ml.classification import RandomForestClassifier
  rfc = RandomForestClassifier(
    featuresCol="Features_vec",
    labelCol="ArrDelayBucket",
    predictionCol="Prediction",
    maxBins=4657,
  )
  model = rfc.fit(training_data)

  # Save the new model over the old one
  model_output_path = " \
    {}/models/spark_random_forest_classifier.flight_delays.baseline.\
      bin".format(
    base_path
  )
  model.write().overwrite().save(model_output_path)

  # Evaluate model using test data
  predictions = model.transform(test_data)

  # Evaluate this split's results for each metric
  from pyspark.ml.evaluation import MulticlassClassificationEvaluator
  for metric_name in metric_names:
    evaluator = MulticlassClassificationEvaluator(
      labelCol="ArrDelayBucket",
      predictionCol="Prediction",
      metricName=metric_name
    )
    score = evaluator.evaluate(predictions)

    scores[metric_name].append(score)
    print("{} = {}".format(metric_name, score))
```

This leaves us with a defaultdict of scores, with one list for each metric. Now we need to compute the average and standard deviation of each list to give us the overall average and standard deviation of each metric:

```
#
# Evaluate average and STD of each metric and print a table
#
import numpy as np
score_averages = defaultdict(float)

# Compute the table data
average_stds = [] # ha
for metric_name in metric_names:
  metric_scores = scores[metric_name]

  average_accuracy = sum(metric_scores) / len(metric_scores)
  score_averages[metric_name] = average_accuracy

  std_accuracy = np.std(metric_scores)

  average_stds.append((metric_name, average_accuracy, std_accuracy))

# Print the table
print("\nExperiment Log")
print("--------------")
print(tabulate(average_stds, headers=["Metric", "Average", "STD"]))
```

This results in:

```
Experiment Log
--------------

Metric                Average      STD
-----------------    ---------  -----------
accuracy             0.594443   0.000382382
weightedPrecision    0.642419   0.00352101
weightedRecall       0.594443   0.000382382
f1                   0.522397   0.000438121
```

The standard deviations indicate that we might not even need to perform k-fold cross-validation, but an inspection of the underlying scores says otherwise:

```
$ scores

defaultdict(list,
            {'accuracy': [
              0.5960317877085193,
              0.5962539640360968,
              0.5962346664334288
              ],
             'f1': [0.5251883509444727,
                    0.5266212073123311,
                    0.5258877000496558],
              'weightedPrecision': [0.6495952645815938,
```

```
                        0.6498757953978488,
                        0.6549703272382899],
      'weightedRecall': [0.5960317877085194,
                        0.5962539640360968,
                        0.5962346664334288]]})
```

There is actually significant variation between runs, and this could obscure a small improvement (or degradation) in prediction quality.

The iterations take time, and this discourages experimentation. A middle ground should be found.

Comparing experiments to determine improvements

Now that we have our baseline metrics, we can repeat this code as we improve the model and see what the effect is in terms of the four metrics available to us. So it seems we are done, that we can start playing with our model and features. However, we will quickly run into a problem. We will lose track of the score from the previous run, printed on the screen above many logs for each run, unless we write it down each time. And this is tedious. So, we need to automate this process.

What we need to do is load a score log from disk, evaluate the current score in terms of the previous one, and store a new entry to the log back to disk for the next run to access. The following code achieves this aim.

First we use `pickle` to load any existing score log. If this is not present, we initialize a new log, which is simply an empty Python `list`. Next we prepare the new log entry— a simple Python `dict` containing the average score for each of four metrics. Then we subtract the previous run's score to determine the change in this run. This is the information we use to evaluate whether our change worked or not (along with any changes in feature importances, which we will address as well). Finally, we append the new score entry to the log and store it back to disk:

```
#
# Persist the score to a score log that exists between runs
#
import pickle

# Load the score log or initialize an empty one
try:
  score_log_filename = "{}/models/score_log.pickle".format(base_path)
  score_log = pickle.load(open(score_log_filename, "rb"))
  if not isinstance(score_log, list):
    score_log = []
except IOError:
  score_log = []

# Compute the existing score log entry
score_log_entry = {
  metric_name: score_averages[metric_name] for metric_name in metric_names
```

```
    }

    # Compute and display the change in score for each metric
    try:
      last_log = score_log[-1]
    except (IndexError, TypeError, AttributeError):
      last_log = score_log_entry

    experiment_report = []
    for metric_name in metric_names:
      run_delta = score_log_entry[metric_name] - last_log[metric_name]
      experiment_report.append((metric_name, run_delta))

    print("\nExperiment Report")
    print("-----------------")
    print(tabulate(experiment_report, headers=["Metric", "Score"]))

    # Append the existing average scores to the log
    score_log.append(score_log_entry)

    # Persist the log for next run
    pickle.dump(score_log, open(score_log_filename, "wb"))
```

Now when we run our script, we will get a report that shows the change between this run and the last run. We can use this, along with our feature importances, to direct our efforts at improving the model. For instance, an example test run shows the model accuracy increase by .003:

```
Experiment Report
-----------------
Metric                  Score
-----------------    -----------
accuracy              0.00300548
weightedPrecision   -0.00592227
weightedRecall        0.00300548
f1                   -0.0105553
```

Inspecting changes in feature importance

We can use the list of columns given to our final VectorAssembler (*http://bit.ly/ 2pj7nI0*) along with RandomForestClassificationModel.featureImportances (*http://bit.ly/2otFXLk*) to derive the importance of each named feature. This is extremely valuable, because like with our prediction quality scores, we can look at changes in feature importances for all features between runs. If a newly introduced feature turns out to be important, it is usually worth adding to the model, so long as it doesn't hurt quality.

We begin by altering our experiment loop to record feature importances for each run. Check out the abbreviated content from *ch09/improved_spark_mllib_model.py* (*http:// bit.ly/2oxdrHZ*):

```
feature_importances = defaultdict(list)

...

for i in range(1, split_count + 1):
print("\nRun {} out of {} of test/train splits in cross validation...".format(
    i,
    split_count,
  )
 )

...

#
# Collect feature importances
#
feature_names = vector_assembler.getInputCols()
feature_importance_list = model.featureImportances
for feature_name, feature_importance in \
    zip(feature_names, feature_importance_list):
  feature_importances[feature_name].append(feature_importance)
```

Next, we need to compute the average of the importance for each feature. Note that we use a `defaultdict(float)` to ensure that accessing empty keys returns zero. This will be important when comparing entries in the log with different sets of features:

```
# Compute averages for each feature
feature_importance_entry = defaultdict(float)
for feature_name, value_list in feature_importances.items():
  average_importance = sum(value_list) / len(value_list)
  feature_importance_entry[feature_name] = average_importance
```

In order to print the feature importances, we need to sort them first, by descending order of importance:

```
# Sort the feature importances in descending order and print
import operator
sorted_feature_importances = sorted(
  feature_importance_entry.items(),
  key=operator.itemgetter(1),
  reverse=True
)

print("\nFeature Importances")
print("-------------------")
print(tabulate(sorted_feature_importances, headers=['Name', 'Importance']))
```

Next we need to perform the same housekeeping as we did for the model score log: load the model, create an entry for this experiment, load the last experiment and compute the change for each feature between that experiment and the current one, and then print a report on these deltas.

First we load the last feature log. If it isn't available because it doesn't exist, we initialize the `last_feature_log` with zeros for each feature, so that new features will have a positive score equal to their amount:

```
# Load the feature importance log or initialize an empty one
try:
    feature_log_filename = "{}/models/feature_log.pickle".format(base_path)
    feature_log = pickle.load(open(feature_log_filename, "rb"))
    if not isinstance(feature_log, list):
        feature_log = []
except IOError:
    feature_log = []

# Compute and display the change in score for each feature
try:
    last_feature_log = feature_log[-1]
except (IndexError, TypeError, AttributeError):
    last_feature_log = defaultdict(float)
    for feature_name, importance in feature_importance_entry.items():
        last_feature_log[feature_name] = importance
```

Next we compute the change between the last run and the current one:

```
# Compute the deltas
feature_deltas = {}
for feature_name in feature_importances.keys():
    run_delta = \
        feature_importance_entry[feature_name] - last_feature_log[feature_name]
    feature_deltas[feature_name] = run_delta
```

In order to display them, we need to sort the feature importance changes in descending order, to show the biggest change first:

```
# Sort feature deltas, biggest change first
import operator
sorted_feature_deltas = sorted(
    feature_deltas.items(),
    key=operator.itemgetter(1),
    reversed=True
)
```

Then we display the sorted feature deltas:

```
# Display sorted feature deltas
print("\nFeature Importance Delta Report")
print("-------------------------------")
print(tabulate(sorted_feature_deltas, headers=["Feature", "Delta"]))
```

Finally, as with the score log, we append our entry to the log and save it for the next run:

```
# Append the existing average deltas to the log
feature_log.append(feature_importance_entry)
```

```
# Persist the log for next run
pickle.dump(feature_log, open(feature_log_filename, "wb"))
```

Testing our model for the first time results in the following output. We'll use the raw feature importances as well as the changes in feature importance to guide our creation or alteration of features as we improve the model:

```
Experiment Log
--------------
Metric               Average        STD
-------------------  ---------  -----------
accuracy             0.594014   0.000270987
weightedPrecision    0.570674   0.0821537
weightedRecall       0.594014   0.000270987
f1                   0.521789   3.70999e-05


Experiment Report
-----------------
Metric                     Score
-------------------  ------------
accuracy             -0.000429286
weightedPrecision    -0.0717445
weightedRecall       -0.000429286
f1                   -0.000608931


Feature Importances
-------------------
Name                Importance
----------------  ------------
DepDelay          0.882216
Route_index       0.0571401
Origin_index      0.0142741
Distance          0.0134583
Dest_index        0.00745796
DayOfYear         0.00544761
Carrier_index     0.00454088
DayOfMonth        9.31109e-05
DayOfWeek         5.2597e-05


Feature Importance Delta Report
-------------------------------
Feature             Delta
----------------  -------
Distance                0
Dest_index              0
DayOfWeek               0
Origin_index            0
DayOfYear               0
Carrier_index           0
Route_index             0
DayOfMonth              0
DepDelay                0
```

Conclusion

Now that we have the ability to understand the effect of changes between experimental runs, we can detect changes that improve our model. We can start adding features to test their effect on the model's prediction quality, and pursue related features that help improve quality! Without this setup, we would be hard put to make positive changes. With it, we are only bounded by our creativity in our efforts to improve the model.

Time of Day as a Feature

In examining our feature importances, it looks like the date/time fields have some impact. What if we extracted the hour/minute as an integer from the datetime for departure/arrival fields? This would inform the model about morning versus afternoon versus red-eye flights, which surely affects on-time performance, as there is more traffic in the morning than overnight.

Check out *ch09/explore_delays.py* (*http://bit.ly/2pLSldJ*). Let's start by exploring the premise of this feature, that lateness varies by the time of day of the flight:

```
spark.sql("""
  SELECT
    HOUR(CRSDepTime) + 1 AS Hour,
    AVG(ArrDelay),
    STD(ArrDelay)
  FROM features
  GROUP BY HOUR(CRSDepTime)
  ORDER BY HOUR(CRSDepTime)
""").show(24)
```

Here's the result:

```
+----+-------------------+---------------------+
|Hour|      avg(ArrDelay)|stddev_samp(ArrDelay)|
+----+-------------------+---------------------+
|   1|-0.9888343067527446|     35.96846550716142|
|   2|0.21487576223466862|    35.744333727508334|
|   3| 1.5671059921857282|     35.00946190001324|
|   4| 2.3711289989006086|    36.182339627895345|
|   5| 3.0942288270090894|    37.547244850760876|
|   6|  4.239319300385845|    38.400571868893834|
|   7|  5.234954994309625|     39.28255300783613|
|   8|  6.453546045667625|     39.99971120960918|
|   9|  7.186654216429772|     41.40488311224806|
|  10|  8.365290552625943|    42.940647757026625|
|  11|  9.268328745619563|    43.626137917652855|
|  12|  9.841703616195401|    43.52976518121594|
|  13| 10.066688650580275|    41.92576203774942|
|  14|  9.283710900023337|     40.6576680093127|
|  15|  7.423578894503908|     37.93024949987321|
|  16|  6.026947232249046|      36.2827909463706|
```

```
|   17|   2.878606342393896|    34.521580465809635|
|   18|   1.202488132263873|    35.281643789718856|
|   19|   3.921360847741216|     51.57255339085103|
|   20|   1.416023166023166|     35.07002923779163|
|   21|    1.01067615658363|    33.710428616724336|
|   22| -1.6537734227264913|    44.14071722078961|
|   23| -2.4204632317424886|    38.33508514261801|
|   24| -2.3249719752460805|     35.6965483893959|
+----+-------------------+--------------------+
```

The scheduled hour of the flight does matter! Flights scheduled to leave at 1 P.M. are 10 minutes late on average, compared with about 2.5 minutes early for flights scheduled for departure at 11 P.M. The standard deviation doesn't vary a lot, but is highest around midday as well. This looks like a feature worth adding!

While we're here, what about scheduled arrival time? Let's run the same calculation for CRSArrTime:

```
spark.sql("""
  SELECT
    HOUR(CRSArrTime) + 1 AS Hour,
    AVG(ArrDelay),
    STD(ArrDelay)
  FROM features
  GROUP BY HOUR(CRSArrTime)
  ORDER BY HOUR(CRSArrTime)
""").show(24)
```

This results in:

```
+----+--------------------+--------------------+
|Hour|       avg(ArrDelay)|stddev_samp(ArrDelay)|
+----+--------------------+--------------------+
|   1| -1.7116259174208655|    36.33240606655376|
|   2| -1.2394161336909428|    34.65716885698246|
|   3|  -0.560109126391461|    35.93678468759135|
|   4| -0.03119026777898...|    34.18894939261768|
|   5|  1.0004041388403222|    34.89927883531852|
|   6|  1.8046307093420586|   35.983884598879854|
|   7|  2.7098903974183797|   36.828717160294616|
|   8|  3.2653490352035015|    37.94922697845916|
|   9|   4.460970473403804|    38.75981742307256|
|  10|   5.733407037370677|   39.332218073928395|
|  11|   7.415162373324524|     41.6390996526558|
|  12|   8.394327378488986|   42.304599584222764|
|  13|   9.13641026800476|    44.15236003931785|
|  14|   9.263586544185449|    43.95699577126197|
|  15|   9.463244251854364|   42.694962099183385|
|  16|   9.158153249212814|   40.631824365179185|
|  17|   8.851837125560714|    39.32989266521008|
|  18|   8.374134395914735|    40.76013328408966|
|  19|   6.383113511268045|   40.175828363537185|
|  20|   4.743589743589744|   33.043381854132626|
```

```
|  21|    6.129032258064516|    43.144599976836396|
|  22|   1.6219806017174276|     41.76914003060987|
|  23|   0.9266386975097186|    41.750524061849795|
|  24|  -1.0140736298134196|     40.40944633965604|
+----+--------------------+---------------------+
```

This looks similar and just as significant. We'll add it as well.

Let's start a new file for our new and improved model, based on *ch09/train_spark_mllib_model.py* (*http://bit.ly/2owYwO6*). Check out *ch09/improved_spark_mllib_model.py* (*http://bit.ly/2oxdrHZ*). The code to add the CRSDepHourOfDay column is simple:

```python
from pyspark.sql.functions import hour
features_with_hour = features_with_route.withColumn(
  "CRSDepHourOfDay",
  hour(features.CRSDepTime)
)
features_with_hour = features_with_hour.withColumn(
  "CRSArrHourOfDay",
  hour(features.CRSArrTime)
)
features_with_hour.select(
  "CRSDepTime",
  "CRSDepHourOfDay",
  "CRSArrTime",
  "CRSArrHourOfDay").show()
```

This results in:

```
+--------------------+---------------+--------------------+---------------+
|          CRSDepTime|CRSDepHourOfDay|          CRSArrTime|CRSArrHourOfDay|
+--------------------+---------------+--------------------+---------------+
|2015-01-01 07:30:...|              7|2015-01-01 10:10:...|             10|
|2014-12-31 23:25:...|             23|2015-01-01 02:15:...|              2|
|2015-01-01 01:00:...|              1|2015-01-01 03:45:...|              3|
|2015-01-01 09:55:...|              9|2015-01-01 11:30:...|             11|
|2015-01-01 00:55:...|              0|2015-01-01 02:25:...|              2|
|2015-01-01 05:45:...|              5|2015-01-01 07:15:...|              7|
|2015-01-01 02:45:...|              2|2015-01-01 04:15:...|              4|
|2015-01-01 07:25:...|              7|2015-01-01 08:50:...|              8|
|2015-01-01 11:00:...|             11|2015-01-01 12:30:...|             12|
|2015-01-01 12:15:...|             12|2015-01-01 13:40:...|             13|
|2015-01-01 03:55:...|              3|2015-01-01 05:25:...|              5|
|2015-01-01 08:40:...|              8|2015-01-01 10:05:...|             10|
|2015-01-01 00:15:...|              0|2015-01-01 02:12:...|              2|
|2014-12-31 23:00:...|             23|2015-01-01 00:52:...|              0|
|2015-01-01 13:10:...|             13|2015-01-01 15:02:...|             15|
|2015-01-01 05:30:...|              5|2015-01-01 06:35:...|              6|
|2014-12-31 21:50:...|             21|2014-12-31 22:50:...|             22|
|2015-01-01 00:30:...|              0|2015-01-01 01:40:...|              1|
|2015-01-01 01:05:...|              1|2015-01-01 02:15:...|              2|
```

```
|2015-01-01 07:55:...|                    7|2015-01-01 08:55:...|                    8|
+-------------------+---------------+-------------------+---------------+
```

This is followed by code that adds the column to be indexed and then the index to be included in the final Features_vec, which we omit but you can see in *ch09/ improved_spark_mllib_model.py (http://bit.ly/2pYQ63a)*. Since we set up our experiment code to test and compare prediction quality between runs, we can test this script from bash:

```
python ch09/improved_spark_mllib_model.py .
```

This results in the following output:

```
Experiment Log
--------------
Metric              Average           STD
-----------------   ---------   -----------
accuracy            0.594656    0.000509343
weightedPrecision   0.641538    0.00372632
weightedRecall      0.594656    0.000509343
f1                  0.5233      0.000700844


Experiment Report
-----------------
Metric                  Score
-----------------   ----------
accuracy            0.00108926
weightedPrecision   0.0154773
weightedRecall      0.00108926
f1                  0.00210414


Feature Importances
-------------------
Name                Importance
-----------------   ------------
DepDelay            0.886486
Route_index         0.0598883
Distance            0.0129897
Origin_index        0.0120841
CRSArrHourOfDay     0.00982592
Dest_index          0.00877569
Carrier_index       0.00448823
DayOfYear           0.00412094
CRSDepHourOfDay     0.0012717
DayOfWeek           6.92304e-05
DayOfMonth          2.07392e-07


Feature Importance Delta Report
-------------------------------
Feature             Delta
-----------------   ------------
CRSArrHourOfDay     0.00982592
```

```
DepDelay           0.00671702
CRSDepHourOfDay    0.0012717
DayOfWeek          -2.72792e-05
DayOfMonth         -8.81635e-05
Origin_index       -0.00152788
Distance           -0.00188322
Route_index        -0.00214609
Dest_index         -0.0032327
DayOfYear          -0.00377184
Carrier_index      -0.00513747
```

Interpreting the output, it looks like the combined effect of these fields is to impact feature importance by about 1%, but the effect on accuracy is insignificant. We'll leave the fields in, although they don't help much. Without resorting to advanced time series analysis, it seems we've milked all we can from date/time-based features.

Incorporating Airplane Data

Recall from "Investigating Airplanes (Entities)" on page 162 that we incorporated data on airplane manufacturers into our data model. For instance, we analyzed the distribution of manufacturers in the American commercial fleet. In this section, we're going to join in airline data and see what impact this has on the model's accuracy.

I wonder whether properties of the aircraft (called the "metal" of the flight) influence delays? For instance, bigger aircraft fly higher and can go over weather, while smaller aircraft may be less able to do so. I can't honestly think of a reason why the engine manufacturer, airplane manufacturer, or manufacture year would have an impact on the model, but since we're importing one field, we may as well try them all! Note that we can simply drop any features that don't rank as very significant. The beauty of our experimental model with decision trees is that it doesn't cost extra to try extra fields. Sometimes you can simply let the model decide what matters.

Note that when dealing with team members and with other teams who need an accounting of your time in order to coordinate with you, a description of the experiments you are running will help keep the teams in sync. For instance, "We are attempting to incorporate a new dataset which we scraped from the FAA website into our flight delay predictive model" would make a good experimental description during an agile sprint.

Extracting Airplane Features

To add airplane features to our model, we need to create a new feature extraction script, *ch09/extract_features_with_airplanes.py* (*http://bit.ly/2otEGUz*). We can do this by copying and altering *ch09/extract_features.py* (*http://bit.ly/2plzdmM*). We'll skip the code that's duplicated from the original file (first described in Chapter 7), and just show the changes.

First we add `TailNum` to the fields we select from our training data. Because this column also appears in our airplane dataset, we need to name it differently or we won't easily be able to access the column after the join. We'll name it `FeatureTailNum`:

```
# Select a few features of interest
simple_on_time_features = spark.sql("""
SELECT
  FlightNum,
  FlightDate,
  DayOfWeek,
  DayofMonth AS DayOfMonth,
  CONCAT(Month, '-', DayofMonth) AS DayOfYear,
  Carrier,
  Origin,
  Dest,
  Distance,
  DepDelay,
  ArrDelay,
  CRSDepTime,
  CRSArrTime,
  CONCAT(Origin, '-', Dest) AS Route,
  TailNum AS FeatureTailNum
FROM on_time_performance
""")

simple_on_time_features.select(
  "FlightNum",
  "FlightDate",
  "FeatureTailNum"
).show(10)

...

def alter_feature_datetimes(row):

  flight_date = iso8601.parse_date(row['FlightDate'])
  scheduled_dep_time = convert_datetime(row['FlightDate'], row['CRSDepTime'])
  scheduled_arr_time = convert_datetime(row['FlightDate'], row['CRSArrTime'])

  # Handle overnight flights
  if scheduled_arr_time < scheduled_dep_time:
    scheduled_arr_time += datetime.timedelta(days=1)

  doy = day_of_year(row['FlightDate'])

  return {
    'FlightNum': row['FlightNum'],
    'FlightDate': flight_date,
    'DayOfWeek': int(row['DayOfWeek']),
    'DayOfMonth': int(row['DayOfMonth']),
    'DayOfYear': doy,
    'Carrier': row['Carrier'],
```

```
        'Origin': row['Origin'],
        'Dest': row['Dest'],
        'Distance': row['Distance'],
        'DepDelay': row['DepDelay'],
        'ArrDelay': row['ArrDelay'],
        'CRSDepTime': scheduled_dep_time,
        'CRSArrTime': scheduled_arr_time,
        'Route': row['Route'],
        'FeatureTailNum': row['FeatureTailNum'],
    }

timestamp_features = filled_on_time_features.rdd.map(alter_feature_datetimes)
timestamp_df = timestamp_features.toDF()
```

Next, we load the airplane data and left join it to our features dataset. Note that null is a problematic value for our StringIndexer. But we don't want to discard empty values or rows either, because whether a variable is present or not is something our decision tree model can use to learn. We use DataFrame.selectExpr (*http://bit.ly/2oYBpxy*) to COALESCE (*http://bit.ly/2p30w4B*) our null values to the string 'Empty'. This will get its own index from StringIndexer and things will work out well. Also note that we rename FeatureTailNum back to TailNum for the final output:

```
# Load airplanes and left join on tail numbers
airplanes_path = "{}/data/airplanes.json".format(
  base_path
)
airplanes = spark.read.json(airplanes_path)

features_with_airplanes = timestamp_df.join(
  airplanes,
  on=timestamp_df.FeatureTailNum == airplanes.TailNum,
  how="left_outer"
)

features_with_airplanes = features_with_airplanes.selectExpr(
  "FlightNum",
  "FlightDate",
  "DayOfWeek",
  "DayOfMonth",
  "DayOfYear",
  "Carrier",
  "Origin",
  "Dest",
  "Distance",
  "DepDelay",
  "ArrDelay",
  "CRSDepTime",
  "CRSArrTime",
  "Route",
  "FeatureTailNum AS TailNum",
  "COALESCE(EngineManufacturer, 'Empty') AS EngineManufacturer",
```

```
    "COALESCE(EngineModel, 'Empty') AS EngineModel",
    "COALESCE(Manufacturer, 'Empty') AS Manufacturer",
    "COALESCE(ManufacturerYear, 'Empty') AS ManufacturerYear",
    "COALESCE(Model, 'Empty') AS Model",
    "COALESCE(OwnerState, 'Empty') AS OwnerState"
)
```

Finally, we store the final output to a new path. We'll have to remember to alter our model training script to point at this new path:

```
# Store as a single JSON file
output_path = "{}/data/simple_flight_delay_features_airplanes.json".format(
    base_path
)
sorted_features.repartition(1).write.mode("overwrite").json(output_path)

# Copy the partial file to a JSON Lines file
combine_cmd = \
    "cp {}/part* {}/data/simple_flight_delay_features_airplanes.jsonl".format(
    output_path,
    base_path
)
os.system(combine_cmd)
```

Now we're ready to incorporate the features into our model.

Incorporating Airplane Features into Our Classifier Model

Now we need to create a new script that incorporates our new airplane features into our classifier model. Check out *ch09/spark_model_with_airplanes.py* (*http://bit.ly/2pYVBie*), which we copied from *ch09/improved_spark_mllib_model.py* (*http://bit.ly/2oxdrHZ*) and altered.

First we need to load the training data with the additional fields, including Route (which is now calculated in *ch09/extract_features_with_airplanes.py* (*http://bit.ly/2otEGUz*)):

```
schema = StructType([
    StructField("ArrDelay", DoubleType(), True),
    StructField("CRSArrTime", TimestampType(), True),
    StructField("CRSDepTime", TimestampType(), True),
    StructField("Carrier", StringType(), True),
    StructField("DayOfMonth", IntegerType(), True),
    StructField("DayOfWeek", IntegerType(), True),
    StructField("DayOfYear", IntegerType(), True),
    StructField("DepDelay", DoubleType(), True),
    StructField("Dest", StringType(), True),
    StructField("Distance", DoubleType(), True),
    StructField("FlightDate", DateType(), True),
    StructField("FlightNum", StringType(), True),
    StructField("Origin", StringType(), True),
    StructField("Route", StringType(), True),
```

```
  StructField("TailNum", StringType(), True),
  StructField("EngineManufacturer", StringType(), True),
  StructField("EngineModel", StringType(), True),
  StructField("Manufacturer", StringType(), True),
  StructField("ManufacturerYear", StringType(), True),
  StructField("OwnerState", StringType(), True),
])

input_path = "{}/data/simple_flight_delay_features_airplanes.json".format(
  base_path
)
features = spark.read.json(input_path, schema=schema)
features.first()
```

Because we left joined our new features in, we need to know how many of the resulting training records have null values for their fields. Null values will crash the String
Indexer for a field, so we've explicitly altered our feature extraction code to remove
them. There should be no nulls, so we'll print a table with a warning if they are
present:

```
#
# Check for nulls in features before using Spark ML
#
null_counts = [( \
  column, features_with_hour.where(
    features_with_hour[column].isNull()).count()) \
      for column in features_with_hour.columns]
cols_with_nulls = filter(lambda x: x[1] > 0, null_counts)
print("\nNull Value Report")
print("-----------------")
print(tabulate(cols_with_nulls, headers=["Column", "Nulls"]))
```

Next we add the hour of day fields as normal, and we bucketize the ArrDelay field to
get the ArrDelayBucket. Then we need to index all our string columns, including our
new airplane features:

```
#
# Feature extraction tools in pyspark.ml.feature
#
from pyspark.ml.feature import StringIndexer, VectorAssembler

# Turn category fields into indexes
string_columns = ["Carrier", "Origin", "Dest", "Route",
                  "TailNum", "EngineManufacturer",
                  "EngineModel", "Manufacturer",
                  "ManufacturerYear", "Owner",
                  "OwnerState"]
for column in string_columns:
  string_indexer = StringIndexer(
    inputCol=column,
    outputCol=column + "_index"
  )
```

```
string_indexer_model = string_indexer.fit(ml_bucketized_features)
ml_bucketized_features = string_indexer_model.transform(
  ml_bucketized_features
)

# Save the pipeline model
string_indexer_output_path = \
  "{}/models/string_indexer_model_3.0.{}.bin".format(
  base_path,
  column
)
string_indexer_model.write().overwrite().save(string_indexer_output_path)
```

Next, we need to create a new `VectorAssembler` to combine our features into one feature vector, the column `Features_vec`. As before, an index field name is the field name with `_index` appended. This time around, we use a list comprehension to compute the index columns:

```
# Combine continuous numeric fields with indexes of nominal ones
# into one feature vector
numeric_columns = [
  "DepDelay", "Distance",
  "DayOfMonth", "DayOfWeek",
  "DayOfYear", "CRSDepHourOfDay",
  "CRSArrHourOfDay"]
index_columns = [column + "_index" for column in string_columns]

vector_assembler = VectorAssembler(
  inputCols=numeric_columns + index_columns,
  outputCol="Features_vec"
)
final_vectorized_features = vector_assembler.transform(ml_bucketized_features)

# Save the numeric vector assembler
vector_assembler_path = "{}/models/numeric_vector_assembler_4.0.bin".format(
  base_path
)
vector_assembler.write().overwrite().save(vector_assembler_path)
```

The rest of the code is identical to *ch09/improved_spark_mllib_model.py* (*http://bit.ly/2oxdrHZ*). To test our new features out in a new experiment, we run:

```
python ch09/spark_model_with_airplanes.py .
```

Note that on the first go around, our model failed because we needed to increase the `maxBins` parameter to 4896 to accommodate our new fields. After that, the script ran without incident. Let's check out our results:

```
Experiment Log
--------------
Metric               Average          STD
----------------     ---------    -----------
accuracy             0.594262     0.000256266
weightedPrecision    0.513819     9.43221e-05
weightedRecall       0.594262     0.000256266
f1                   0.522066     0.000348499


Experiment Report
-----------------
Metric                  Score
----------------     -----------
accuracy             -0.000394734
weightedPrecision    -0.127719
weightedRecall       -0.000394734
f1                   -0.00123417


Feature Importances
-------------------
Name                         Importance
-----------------------      -----------
DepDelay                     0.859874
Route_index                  0.0628756
CRSArrHourOfDay              0.0166273
Distance                     0.013517
TailNum_index                0.012384
Origin_index                 0.011521
Dest_index                   0.00709832
Carrier_index                0.00695651
DayOfYear                    0.00416167
CRSDepHourOfDay              0.00218328
OwnerState_index             0.00144406
Manufacturer_index           0.00061876
EngineManufacturer_index     0.000421311
EngineModel_index            0.000311177
ManufacturerYear_index       4.56816e-06
DayOfWeek                    1.26539e-06
DayOfMonth                   0


Feature Importance Delta Report
-------------------------------
Feature                      Delta
-----------------------      -----------
TailNum_index                0.012384
CRSArrHourOfDay              0.00680138
Route_index                  0.00298732
Carrier_index                0.00246828
OwnerState_index             0.00144406
CRSDepHourOfDay              0.000911583
Manufacturer_index           0.00061876
Distance                     0.000527296
```

```
EngineManufacturer_index    0.000421311
EngineModel_index           0.000311177
DayOfYear                   4.07316e-05
ManufacturerYear_index      4.56816e-06
DayOfMonth                 -2.07392e-07
DayOfWeek                  -6.7965e-05
Origin_index               -0.000563111
Dest_index                 -0.00167737
DepDelay                   -0.0266118
```

It looks like our efforts were mostly for naught—they actually hurt the quality of the model! The single exception is that adding the `TailNum` helps in terms of feature importance by 0.012. Apparently some airplanes are more prone to delay than others, but this isn't down to the properties of the airplane we tried.

Let's try pulling all the fields but `TailNum` and see how that impacts the score. While we're at it, let's pull `DayOfMonth` and `DayOfWeek`, since they have nearly no impact at all. We simply remove these columns from our `StringIndexer` mappings:

```python
# Turn category fields into indexes
string_columns = ["Carrier", "Origin", "Dest", "Route",
                  "TailNum"]
for column in string_columns:
  string_indexer = StringIndexer(
    inputCol=column,
    outputCol=column + "_index"
  )

  string_indexer_model = string_indexer.fit(ml_bucketized_features)
  ml_bucketized_features = string_indexer_model.transform(
    ml_bucketized_features)

  # Save the pipeline model
  string_indexer_output_path = \
    "{}/models/string_indexer_model_4.0.{}.bin".format(
      base_path,
      column
    )
  string_indexer_model.write().overwrite().save(string_indexer_output_path)

# Combine continuous numeric fields with indexes of nominal ones
# into one feature vector
numeric_columns = [
  "DepDelay", "Distance",
  "DayOfYear",
  "CRSDepHourOfDay",
  "CRSArrHourOfDay"]
index_columns = [column + "_index" for column in string_columns]

vector_assembler = VectorAssembler(
  inputCols=numeric_columns + index_columns,
  outputCol="Features_vec"
```

```
)
final_vectorized_features = vector_assembler.transform(ml_bucketized_features)

# Save the numeric vector assembler
vector_assembler_path = \
  "{}/models/numeric_vector_assembler_5.0.bin".format(base_path)
vector_assembler.write().overwrite().save(vector_assembler_path)
```

This impacts the score in a positive way, but not in a significant way: an improvement of 0.00031884 in accuracy. However, at this point all our features are contributing significantly to the model's prediction quality, which is where we want to be:

```
Feature Importances
-------------------
Name                 Importance
---------------      -----------
DepDelay             0.879979
Route_index          0.0575757
Distance             0.0174215
TailNum_index        0.0120175
CRSArrHourOfDay      0.0117084
Origin_index         0.00789092
Carrier_index        0.00457943
DayOfYear            0.00408886
Dest_index           0.00311852
CRSDepHourOfDay      0.00161978
```

Remember: *when it comes to predictive models, simpler is better*. If a feature doesn't sizably influence prediction accuracy, remove it. The model's quality will increase, it will perform faster in production, and you will have an easier time understanding the impact of additional features on the model. A simpler model will be less susceptible to bias.

Incorporating Flight Time

One thing we haven't considered yet is the flight time. We should be able to subtract the takeoff time from the landing time and get the duration of the flight. Since distance is a top-3 feature, and the hour of day matters, it seems like flight time might eke out a bit more prediction quality. Let's try!

In order to compute the difference between arrival and departure, we need to cast these fields to Unix timestamps, which is defined as the number of seconds since January 1, 1970. Fortunately, the Spark SQL function unix_timestamp (*http://bit.ly/2oxjZWY*) does what we need.

Check out *ch09/extract_features_with_flight_time.py* (*http://bit.ly/2pKQRgY*), which we copied from *ch09/extract_features_with_airplanes.py* (*http://bit.ly/2otEGUz*). We only need to change one line, our selectExpr, to add the date math for our Flight Time field:

```
features_with_airplanes = features_with_airplanes.selectExpr(
  "FlightNum",
  "FlightDate",
  "DayOfWeek",
  "DayOfMonth",
  "DayOfYear",
  "Carrier",
  "Origin",
  "Dest",
  "Distance",
  "DepDelay",
  "ArrDelay",
  "CRSDepTime",
  "CRSArrTime",
  "Route",
  "FeatureTailNum AS TailNum",
  "COALESCE(EngineManufacturer, 'Empty') AS EngineManufacturer",
  "COALESCE(EngineModel, 'Empty') AS EngineModel",
  "COALESCE(Manufacturer, 'Empty') AS Manufacturer",
  "COALESCE(ManufacturerYear, 'Empty') AS ManufacturerYear",
  "COALESCE(Model, 'Empty') AS Model",
  "COALESCE(OwnerState, 'Empty') AS OwnerState",
  "unix_timestamp(CRSArrTime) - unix_timestamp(CRSDepTime) AS FlightTime",
)
```

I am constantly thankful for the power of SQL, which is baked into Spark. Combined with dataflow programming, it is the best programming model available. Let's incorporate the FlightTime field into our model.

Check out *ch09/spark_model_with_flight_time.py* (*http://bit.ly/2pYQDlx*), which we copied from *ch09/spark_model_with_airplanes.py* (*http://bit.ly/2pYVBie*) and edited. We need to add the field to our StructTypes and update the input path. Then we need to include the field in our VectorAssembler, as it is numeric it can be directly incorporated into the features vector:

```
schema = StructType([
  StructField("ArrDelay", DoubleType(), True),
  StructField("CRSArrTime", TimestampType(), True),
  StructField("CRSDepTime", TimestampType(), True),
  StructField("Carrier", StringType(), True),
  StructField("DayOfMonth", IntegerType(), True),
  StructField("DayOfWeek", IntegerType(), True),
  StructField("DayOfYear", IntegerType(), True),
  StructField("DepDelay", DoubleType(), True),
  StructField("Dest", StringType(), True),
  StructField("Distance", DoubleType(), True),
  StructField("FlightDate", DateType(), True),
  StructField("FlightNum", StringType(), True),
  StructField("Origin", StringType(), True),
  StructField("Route", StringType(), True),
  StructField("TailNum", StringType(), True),
  StructField("EngineManufacturer", StringType(), True),
```

```
    StructField("EngineModel", StringType(), True),
    StructField("Manufacturer", StringType(), True),
    StructField("ManufacturerYear", StringType(), True),
    StructField("OwnerState", StringType(), True),
    StructField("FlightTime", IntegerType(), True),
])

input_path = "{}/data/simple_flight_delay_features_flight_times.json".format(
    base_path
)
features = spark.read.json(input_path, schema=schema)
features.first()

...

# Combine continuous numeric fields with indexes of nominal ones
# into one feature vector
numeric_columns = [
    "DepDelay", "Distance",
    "DayOfYear",
    "CRSDepHourOfDay",
    "CRSArrHourOfDay",
    "FlightTime"]
index_columns = [column + "_index" for column in string_columns]

vector_assembler = VectorAssembler(
    inputCols=numeric_columns + index_columns,
    outputCol="Features_vec"
)
final_vectorized_features = vector_assembler.transform(ml_bucketized_features)
```

Now we're ready to test the new model:

```
python ch09/spark_model_with_flight_time.py .
```

This output suggests a significant improvement in performance! weightedPrecision is up by 0.12, and the FlightTime contributes about half a percent to the feature importance. Also note that the feature importance of FlightTime comes at the expense of Distance and DepDelay, which seems expected: Distance is conceptually similar to FlightTime, and DepDelay is the most important feature. Taken together, the performance and feature importance metrics indicate that FlightTime is a worthwhile improvement to our model:

```
Experiment Report
-----------------

Metric                   Score
-----------------    ----------
accuracy             0.00124616
weightedPrecision    0.117773
weightedRecall       0.00124616
f1                   0.00453277
```

```
Feature Importances
--------------------
Name              Importance
---------------   ------------
DepDelay          0.860049
Route_index       0.0742784
CRSArrHourOfDay   0.0135059
Origin_index      0.0123399
TailNum_index     0.0120064
Distance          0.00649571
Carrier_index     0.00563587
DayOfYear         0.00479174
FlightTime        0.00452475
CRSDepHourOfDay   0.00378075
Dest_index        0.00259198


Feature Importance Delta Report
-------------------------------
Feature            Delta
---------------   ------------
Route_index        0.0167027
FlightTime         0.00452475
Origin_index       0.00444897
CRSDepHourOfDay    0.00216097
CRSArrHourOfDay    0.00179746
Carrier_index      0.00105644
DayOfYear          0.00070288
TailNum_index      -1.10573e-05
Dest_index         -0.00052654
Distance           -0.0109258
DepDelay           -0.0199308
```

At this point, once again it seems that we've exhausted the possibilities of the date/
time features (at least, without resorting to more sophisticated time series analysis
techniques than I know).

Conclusion

In this chapter we covered how to improve on our model using the data we've already
collected. We can use this approach in combination with our ability to deploy applications to continuously improve our predictive systems.

Manual Installation

In this appendix, we cover the details of installing the tools for the stack used in this book.

Installing Hadoop

You can download the latest version of Hadoop from the Apache Hadoop downloads page (*http://hadoop.apache.org/releases.html*). At the time of writing, the latest Hadoop was 2.7.3, but this will probably have changed by the time you're reading this.

A recipe for a headless install of Hadoop is available in *manual_install.sh* (*http://bit.ly/2otYl6R*). In addition to downloading and unpackaging Hadoop, we also need to set up our Hadoop environment variables (HADOOP_HOME, HADOOP_CLASSPATH, and HADOOP_CONF_DIR), and we need to put Hadoop's executables in our PATH. First, set up a PROJECT_HOME variable to help find the right paths. You will need to set this yourself by editing your *.bash_profile* file:

```
export PROJECT_HOME=/Users/rjurney/Software/Agile_Data_Code_2
```

Now we can set up our environment directly. Here is the relevant section of *manual_install.sh*:

```
# May need to update this link... see http://hadoop.apache.org/releases.html
curl -Lko /tmp/hadoop-2.7.3.tar.gz \
   http://apache.osuosl.org/hadoop/common/hadoop-2.7.3/hadoop-2.7.3.tar.gz

mkdir hadoop
tar -xvf /tmp/hadoop-2.7.3.tar.gz -C hadoop --strip-components=1
echo '# Hadoop environment setup' >> ~/.bash_profile
export HADOOP_HOME=$PROJECT_HOME/hadoop
echo 'export HADOOP_HOME=$PROJECT_HOME/hadoop' >> ~/.bash_profile
```

```
export PATH=$PATH:$HADOOP_HOME/bin
echo 'export PATH=$PATH:$HADOOP_HOME/bin' >> ~/.bash_profile
export HADOOP_CLASSPATH=$(hadoop classpath)
echo 'export HADOOP_CLASSPATH=$(hadoop classpath)' >> ~/.bash_profile
export HADOOP_CONF_DIR=$HADOOP_HOME/etc/hadoop
echo 'export HADOOP_CONF_DIR=$HADOOP_HOME/etc/hadoop' >> ~/.bash_profile
```

Installing Spark

At the time of writing, the current version of Spark is 2.1.0. To install Spark on your local machine, follow the directions in the docs (*http://spark.apache.org/docs/latest/*). Or, we perform a headless Spark install in *manual_install.sh* (*http://bit.ly/2otYl6R*):

```
# May need to update this link... see http://spark.apache.org/downloads.html
curl -Lko /tmp/spark-2.1.0-bin-without-hadoop.tgz \
  http://d3kbcqa49mib13.cloudfront.net/spark-2.1.0-bin-without-hadoop.tgz

mkdir spark
tar -xvf /tmp/spark-2.1.0-bin-without-hadoop.tgz -C spark --strip-components=1
echo "" >> ~/.bash_profile
echo "# Spark environment setup" >> ~/.bash_profile
export SPARK_HOME=$PROJECT_HOME/spark
echo 'export SPARK_HOME=$PROJECT_HOME/spark' >> ~/.bash_profile
export HADOOP_CONF_DIR=$PROJECT_HOME/hadoop/etc/hadoop/
echo 'export HADOOP_CONF_DIR=$PROJECT_HOME/hadoop/etc/hadoop/' >> ~/.bash_profile
export SPARK_DIST_CLASSPATH=`$HADOOP_HOME/bin/hadoop classpath`
echo 'export SPARK_DIST_CLASSPATH=`$HADOOP_HOME/bin/hadoop classpath`' >> \
  ~/.bash_profile
export PATH=$PATH:$SPARK_HOME/bin
echo 'export PATH=$PATH:$SPARK_HOME/bin' >> ~/.bash_profile

# Have to set spark.io.compression.codec in Spark local mode
cp spark/conf/spark-defaults.conf.template spark/conf/spark-defaults.conf
echo 'spark.io.compression.codec org.apache.spark.io.SnappyCompressionCodec' >>
  spark/conf/spark-defaults.conf

# Give Spark 8 GB of RAM
echo "spark.driver.memory 8g" >> $SPARK_HOME/conf/spark-defaults.conf

echo "PYSPARK_PYTHON=python3" >> $SPARK_HOME/conf/spark-env.sh
echo "PYSPARK_DRIVER_PYTHON=python3" >> $SPARK_HOME/conf/spark-env.sh

# Set up log4j config to reduce logging output
cp $SPARK_HOME/conf/log4j.properties.template $SPARK_HOME/conf/log4j.properties
sed -i .bak 's/INFO/ERROR/g' $SPARK_HOME/conf/log4j.properties
```

Note that this download URL may change; you can get the current URL for a console install from the Spark downloads page (*http://spark.apache.org/downloads.html*).

Installing MongoDB

Instructions for installing MongoDB are available on the website (*http://bit.ly/2p3Em2a*), as is an excellent tutorial (*http://bit.ly/2pLIfqq*). I recommend consulting each of these before moving on.

Download the latest version of MongoDB for your operating system from the download center (*http://www.mongodb.org/downloads*), then install it using the following commands:

```
curl -Lko /tmp/$MONGO_FILENAME $MONGO_DOWNLOAD_URL
mkdir mongodb
tar -xvf /tmp/$MONGO_FILENAME -C mongodb --strip-components=1
export PATH=$PATH:$PROJECT_HOME/mongodb/bin
echo 'export PATH=$PATH:$PROJECT_HOME/mongodb/bin' >> ~/.bash_profile
mkdir -p mongodb/data/db
```

Now start the MongoDB server:

```
mongodb/bin/mongod --dbpath mongodb/data/db &
```

You'll need to rerun this command if you shut down your computer. Now open the Mongo shell, and get help:

```
mongob/bin/mongo --eval help
```

Finally, create a collection by inserting a record, and then retrieve it:

```
> db.test_collection.insert(
  {'name': 'Russell Jurney', 'email': 'russell.jurney@gmail.com'})

WriteResult({ "nInserted" : 1 })

> db.test_collection.findOne({'name': 'Russell Jurney'})
{
        "_id" : ObjectId("56f20fa811a5b44cf943313c"),
        "name" : "Russell Jurney",
        "email" : "russell.jurney@gmail.com"
}
>
```

We're cooking with Mongo!

Installing the MongoDB Java Driver

You'll also need to install the MongoDB Java Driver (*http://bit.ly/2ou374t*). At the time of writing, the 3.4.2 version is the latest stable build. You can install it with `curl` as follows:

```
curl -Lko lib/mongo-java-driver-3.4.2.jar \
    http://central.maven.org/maven2/org/mongodb/mongo-java-driver/3.4.0/ \
        mongo-java-driver-3.4.0.jar
```

Installing mongo-hadoop

The `mongo-hadoop` (*https://github.com/mongodb/mongo-hadoop*) project connects Hadoop and Spark with MongoDB. You can download it from the releases page (*https://github.com/mongodb/mongo-hadoop/releases*).

Building mongo-hadoop

You will need to build the project, using the included `gradlew` command, and then copy the JARs into *lib/*:

```
# Install the mongo-hadoop project in the mongo-hadoop directory
# in the root of our project
curl -Lko /tmp/r1.5.2.tar.gz \
  https://github.com/mongodb/mongo-hadoop/archive/r1.5.2.tar.gz
mkdir mongo-hadoop
tar -xvzf /tmp/r1.5.2.tar.gz -C mongo-hadoop --strip-components=1


# Now build the mongo-hadoop-spark jars
cd mongo-hadoop
./gradlew jar
cd ..
cp mongo-hadoop/spark/build/libs/mongo-hadoop-spark-*.jar lib/
cp mongo-hadoop/build/libs/mongo-hadoop-*.jar lib/
```

Installing pymongo_spark

Next, we need to install the pymongo_spark package (*http://bit.ly/2o2mX9w*), which makes storing to Mongo a one-liner from PySpark. pymongo_spark is contained within the `mongo-hadoop` project:

```
# Now build the pymongo_spark package
cd mongo-hadoop/spark/src/main/python
python setup.py install
cd $PROJECT_HOME
cp mongo-hadoop/spark/src/main/python/pymongo_spark.py lib/
export PYTHONPATH=$PYTHONPATH:$PROJECT_HOME/lib
echo 'export PYTHONPATH=$PYTHONPATH:$PROJECT_HOME/lib' >> ~/.bash_profile
```

Installing Elasticsearch

Excellent tutorials on Elasticsearch are available on the website (*http://bit.ly/2pZDrwR*). Grab it from the downloads page (*http://www.elastic.co/downloads*), then install it with the following commands:

```
curl -Lko /tmp/elasticsearch-2.3.5.tar.gz \
  https://download.elastic.co/elasticsearch/release/org/elasticsearch/ \
    distribution/tar/elasticsearch/2.3.5/elasticsearch-2.3.5.tar.gz
```

```
mkdir elasticsearch
tar -xvzf /tmp/elasticsearch-2.3.5.tar.gz -C elasticsearch --strip-components=1
```

Run Elasticsearch via:

```
elasticsearch/bin/elasticsearch 2>1 > /dev/null &
```

That's it. Our local search engine is up and running! Note that you'll need to rerun this command if you shut down your computer. Inserting a record and querying Elasticsearch is easy with `curl`:

```
curl -XPUT 'localhost:9200/customer/external/1?pretty' -d '
{
  "name": "Russell Jurney"
}'
```

```
curl 'localhost:9200/customer/_search?q=*&pretty'
```

Here's the output of our search query:

```
{
  "took" : 81,
  "timed_out" : false,
  "_shards" : {
    "total" : 5,
    "successful" : 5,
    "failed" : 0
  },
  "hits" : {
    "total" : 1,
    "max_score" : 1.0,
    "hits" : [ {
      "_index" : "customer",
      "_type" : "external",
      "_id" : "1",
      "_score" : 1.0,
      "_source" : {
        "name" : "Russell Jurney"
      }
    } ]
  }
}
```

Installing Elasticsearch for Hadoop

You can download Elasticsearch for Hadoop from the ES-Hadoop download page (*https://www.elastic.co/downloads/hadoop*) and install it with the following commands:

```
# Install Elasticsearch for Hadoop
curl -Lko /tmp/elasticsearch-hadoop-5.0.0-alpha5.zip \
  http://download.elastic.co/hadoop/elasticsearch-hadoop-5.0.0-alpha5.zip
unzip /tmp/elasticsearch-hadoop-5.0.0-alpha5.zip
```

```
mv elasticsearch-hadoop-5.0.0-alpha5 elasticsearch-hadoop
cp elasticsearch-hadoop/dist/elasticsearch-hadoop-5.0.0-alpha5.jar lib/
cp elasticsearch-hadoop/dist/elasticsearch-spark-20_2.10-5.0.0-alpha5.jar lib/
echo "spark.speculation false" >> $PROJECT_HOME/spark/conf/spark-defaults.conf
```

Setting Up Our Spark Environment

Having to set up the Mongo and Elasticsearch JAR each time we call pyspark from the command line is a drag. Fortunately, we can use Spark's configuration file, *spark/conf/spark-defaults.conf*, to load the JARs automatically. Specifically, the spark.jars (*http://bit.ly/1yClm8O*) environment variable can handle the loading.

In *manual_install.sh* (*http://bit.ly/2otYl6R*), we run:

```
# Set up Mongo and Elasticsearch jars for Spark
echo "spark.jars $PROJECT_HOME/lib/mongo-hadoop-spark-2.0.0-rc0.jar,\
$PROJECT_HOME/lib/mongo-java-driver-3.2.2.jar,\
$PROJECT_HOME/lib/mongo-hadoop-2.0.0-rc0.jar,\
$PROJECT_HOME/lib/elasticsearch-spark-20_2.10-5.0.0-alpha5.jar,\
$PROJECT_HOME/lib/snappy-java-1.1.2.6.jar,\
$PROJECT_HOME/lib/lzo-hadoop-1.0.0.jar" \
>> spark/conf/spark-defaults.conf
```

Once we have done this, we need only run PYSPARK_DRIVER_PYTHON=ipython pyspark to run PySpark.

Installing Kafka

At the time of writing, the latest stable version of Kafka is 0.10.2.0. You can get the current stable version from the downloads page (*https://kafka.apache.org/downloads*), then install it as follows (replacing the version number as needed):

```
# Install Apache Kafka
curl -Lko /tmp/kafka_2.11-0.10.2.0.tgz \
   http://www-us.apache.org/dist/kafka/0.10.2.0/kafka_2.11-0.10.2.0.tgz
mkdir kafka
tar -xvzf /tmp/kafka_2.11-0.10.2.0.tgz -C kafka --strip-components=1
```

That's it! Kafka is ready to go. Note that this is local mode, and of course, the purpose of Kafka is that it can operate at nearly any scale in distributed mode. It is very convenient to develop in local mode, however, and only later deploy in distributed mode.

Installing scikit-learn

Anaconda (*https://docs.continuum.io/anaconda/*) comes with scikit-learn, so you don't need to do anything if you installed Anaconda. If not, you will need to install sklearn.

You can do this with `pip`:

```
pip install sklearn
```

or `easy_install`:

```
easy_install sklearn
```

The `sklearn` install may require you to first install `numpy` and `scipy` (*https://www.scipy.org/scipylib/download.html*), two scientific computing libraries.

You can get acquainted with `sklearn` through its excellent tutorial (*http://bit.ly/2oZy816*).

Installing Zeppelin

At the time of writing, the latest version of Apache Zeppelin was 0.6.2. You can get the current release from the downloads page (*https://zeppelin.apache.org/download.html*), and update the version numbers in the following commands as needed. Installing Zeppelin is easy. Again, referring to *manual_install.sh* (*http://bit.ly/2otYl6R*):

```
# Install Apache Zeppelin
curl -Lko /tmp/zeppelin-0.6.2-bin-all.tgz \
  http://www-us.apache.org/dist/zeppelin/zeppelin-0.6.2/ \
    zeppelin-0.6.2-bin-all.tgz
mkdir zeppelin
tar -xvzf /tmp/zeppelin-0.6.2-bin-all.tgz -C zeppelin --strip-components=1

# Configure Zeppelin
cp zeppelin/conf/zeppelin-env.sh.template zeppelin/conf/zeppelin-env.sh
echo "export SPARK_HOME=$PROJECT_HOME/spark" >> zeppelin/conf/zeppelin-env.sh
echo "export SPARK_MASTER=local" >> zeppelin/conf/zeppelin-env.sh
echo "export SPARK_CLASSPATH=" >> zeppelin/conf/zeppelin-env.sh
```

To start Zeppelin, run `zeppelin/bin/zeppelin-daemon.sh start` and then visit *http://localhost:8080* to check out the user interface. It is a good idea to work through the Zeppelin tutorial (*http://bit.ly/2pMNoRD*) after installation.

Index

Symbols

A

power of, 70
querying from the commend line, 260
running DAGs in, 69
setting up, 256
testing DAGs in, 262
testing tasks in, 68, 261
using scripts with, 61-63, 65-68
airflow command, 60, 68, 257, 261
algorithms (code), 168
Amazon EC2 Management Console, 34
Amazon Elastic MapReduce, 208
Anaconda Python distribution, 40
Apache Airflow (see Airflow (Apache))
Apache Hadoop, 46, 81, 315
Apache HBase, 122
Apache Kafka, 45, 54-57, 266-277, 320
Apache Oozie, 60
Apache Parquet, 31, 42-45
Apache Phoenix, 122
Apache Zeppelin, 263, 321
Apache Zookeeper, 55, 267
application development (see agile software
    development)
application servers, 31, 48
applied researchers (team role), 18
atomic records, 90
automating form submission, 143
automating workflows with Airflow, 256-264
Avro serialization system, 43, 85
AWS (Amazon Web Services), 32-34
aws command, 34

B

B-tree indexes, 123, 137
backfill command (Airflow), 70, 262
bar charts
    creating, 172-174
    iterating on, 174-183
    updating, 181
batch processing
    deploying Spark MLlib applications,
        234-264
    making predictions in, 248-252
    prototyping and, 56, 132, 279
    publishing/database layer, 120
    real-time versus, 56, 132
big data, 4
Blank, Steve, 102
Bootstrap, booting, 73

Bostock, Mike, 74, 128, 173
browsers
    about, 32
    paginating flight data, 106
    presenting flight records in, 96-101
BTS website, 78
Bucketizer class, 219
bucketizing continuous variables for classifica-
    tion, 211-219
bulk storage, 31
Bureau of Transportation Statistics, 78, 92
business development (team role), 18, 21

C

Career Explorer project (LinkedIn), 9
categorical variables
    classification and, 187
    vectorizing, 201, 203, 220
cd command, 33
charts
    about, 8-8
    creating bar chart, 172-183
    database normalization, 121
    entity extraction, 132-140
    quality considerations, 120
    time series, 121
    visualizing data with, 119-148
classification
    about, 187, 189
    addressing nulls, 210
    bucketizing continuous variables for,
        211-219
    building a classifier with Spark MLlib,
        208-223
    defining metrics, 289
    incorporating airplane features, 305-310
    loading training data with specified schema,
        208
    replacing data, 210
clear command (Airflow), 69
Clements-Croome, Derek, 26
code review, 25
Coleman, Alex, 104
collaboration space, 26
collecting data
    flight data, 91-94
    training data, 235-237, 265
    with Kafka, 45
collectors (events), 31

PySpark
  about, 47
  bucketizing data with, 219
  building a classifier, 208-221
  Elasticsearch and, 52-54
  entity resolution in, 177-181
  extracting features with, 193-198
  extracting flight data, 133
  feature vectorization and, 219-221
  grouping data in, 150
  indexing airplane documents, 167
  processing streams, 57-58
  pushing data to MongoDB, 49
pyspark command, 47
Python
  creating Airflow DAGs in, 63-65
  Flask framework, 71
  json module, 43-45
  machine learning capabilities, 31, 58
  MediaWiki API, 158
  pickle utility, 226
  pip command, 34
  pyelasticsearch API, 54
  pymongo API, 71, 240
  usage considerations, 39-42

Q

quality assurance engineers (team role), 19
quality of charts, 120
querying data
  building queries programmatically, 169-172
  flight volume, 124-132
  from command line, 260
  in MongoDB, 151
  indexes and, 136
  subqueries versus dataflow programming, 164

R

r3.xlarge instance type, 34
random forests, 290
RandomForestClassificationModel class, 294
RDD API, 48, 212
real-time versus batch processing, 56, 132
records
  about, 7-8
  atomic, 90
  collecting and displaying, 89-117
  database normalization, 121

regression analysis
  about, 187
  building with scikit-learn, 198-207
  linear regression, 188
  loading data, 198
  preparing experiments, 204
  preparing training data, 201
  sampling data, 199
  testing the model, 205-207
  training the model, 204
  vectorizing features, 201-203
  vectorizing results, 200
reports
  about, 8-8
  exploring data with, 149-183
research versus application development, 11-14
researchers (team role), 18, 21
reverse engineering web forms, 140
run command (Airflow), 69

S

scalability
  agile platforms and, 22
  publish/decorate model, 120-124
  simplicity and, 30
scheduling with Apache Airflow, 59-70
schemas
  extracting and exposing features in, 85
  loading training data with, 208
  NoSQL and, 84
scientific method, 11
scikit-learn library
  about, 198
  building regressions with, 198-207
  deploying applications as web services, 225-234
  installing, 320
  machine learning and, 198
  machine learning with, 58
scripts
  executing for Airflow setup, 260
  linking to DAGs directory, 260
  spark-submit, 61
  using with Airflow, 61-63, 65-68
Scrum methodology, 3
search engines, connecting to Web, 114-117
searching data
  code versus configuration considerations, 168

test command (Airflow), 68
testing
    DAGs in Airflow, 262
    entire predictive systems, 283-285
    flight delay regression API, 232
    regression model, 205-207
    tasks in Airflow, 68, 261
third order form (normalization), 123
Thrift serialization system, 85
time of day of flights, 298-302
time series charts, 121
timestamps, 195-196, 240-241
training data
    collecting, 235-237, 265
    features and, 188
    loading with specified schema, 208
    predictive analytics and, 187
    preparing, 201
training the regression model, 204
Tunkelang, Daniel, 4

U

UDFs (user-defined functions), 217
Unicode standard, 43
user experience designers (team role), 18, 21
UTF-8 character encoding, 43
UUID (Univesally Unique Identifer), 268

V

Vagrant
    Elasticsearch and, 50
    Jupyter Notebooks and, 40
    Python 3 and, 39
    setting up, 33
    system requirements, 33
variables
    categorical, 187, 201, 203, 220
    continuous, 187, 201, 211-219, 220
    nominal, 187, 201, 203, 220
VectorAssembler class, 220, 238, 287
vectorizing
    features, 201-203, 219-221
    regression results, 200
VirtualBox
    installing, 33
    system requirements, 33
visualizing data
    histograms and, 212

with charts and tables, 119-148
with D3.js, 74
VM (virtual machine)
    setting up Vagrant, 33
    system requirements, 33

W

Warden, Pete, 85
waterfall method
    about, 5
    problems with, 10-11
    pull of the, 4, 15
    research versus application development,
        11-14
WBAN Master List, 80
weather data, 80, 185-223
web applications, lightweight, 70-73
web developers (team role), 18, 21
web forms
    automating submission, 143
    reverse engineering, 140
web pages
    building in Flask, 135, 151
    creating home page, 153, 166
    improving with multimedia content,
        155-161
    linking back to, 138, 152
    publishing enriched data to, 159-161
    semi-structured data in, 154
web services, deploying scikit-learn applica-
    tions as, 225-234
Wickham, Hadley, 198
Wikipedia content, incorporating into flight
    data, 158
wikipedia package, 158
Williams, Hugh E., 82
workflows
    automating with Airflow, 256-264
    lightweight web applications, 70
    software stack, 70

X

xgboost library, 198

Z

Zeppelin (Apache), 263, 321
Zookeeper (Apache), 55, 267

About the Author

Russell Jurney cut his data teeth in casino gaming, building web apps to analyze the performance of slot machines in the US and Mexico. After dabbling in entrepreneurship, interactive media, and journalism, he moved to Silicon Valley to build analytics applications at scale at Ning and LinkedIn. Russell is now principal consultant at Data Syndrome, where he helps companies apply the principles and methods in this book to build analytics products.

Colophon

The animal on the cover of *Agile Data Science* is a silvery marmoset (*Mico argentatus*). These small New World monkeys live in the eastern parts of the Amazon rainforest and Brazil. Despite their name, silvery marmosets can range in color from near-white to dark brown. Brown marmosets have hairless ears and faces and are sometimes referred to as bare-ear marmosets. Reaching an average size of 22 cm, marmosets are about the size of squirrels, which makes their travel through tree canopies and dense vegetation very easy. Silvery marmosets live in extended families of around 12, where all the members help care for the young. Marmoset fathers carry their infants around during the day and return them to the mother every two to three hours to be fed. Babies wean from their mother's milk at around six months and full maturity is reached at one to two years old. The marmoset's diet consists mainly of sap and tree gum. They use their sharp teeth to gouge holes in trees to reach the sap, and will occasionally eat fruit, leaves, and insects as well. As the deforestation of the rainforest continues, however, marmosets have begun to eat food crops grown by people; as a result, many farmers view them as pests. Large-scale extermination programs are underway in agricultural areas, and it is still unclear what impact this will have on the overall silvery marmoset population. Because of their small size and mild disposition, marmosets are regularly used as subjects of medical research. Studies on the fertilization, placental development, and embryonic stem cells of marmosets may reveal the causes of developmental problems and genetic disorders in humans. Outside of the lab, marmosets are popular at zoos because they are diurnal (active during daytime) and full of energy; their long claws mean they can quickly move around in trees, and both males and females communicate with loud vocalizations.

Many of the animals on O'Reilly covers are endangered; all of them are important to the world. To learn more about how you can help, go to *animals.oreilly.com*.

The cover image is from Lydekker's *Royal Natural History*. The cover fonts are URW Typewriter and Guardian Sans. The text font is Adobe Minion Pro; the heading font is Adobe Myriad Condensed; and the code font is Dalton Maag's Ubuntu Mono.

Learn from experts.
Find the answers you need.

Sign up for a **10-day free trial** to get **unlimited access** to all of the content on Safari, including Learning Paths, interactive tutorials, and curated playlists that draw from thousands of ebooks and training videos on a wide range of topics, including data, design, DevOps, management, business—and much more.

Start your free trial at:
oreilly.com/safari

(No credit card required.)

©2016 O'Reilly Media, Inc. O'Reilly is a registered trademark of O'Reilly Media, Inc. D2565

CPSIA information can be obtained
at www.ICGtesting.com
Printed in the USA
BVOW09s0258060617

486075BV00003B/4/P

9 781491 960110